Predication and Expression in Functional Grammar

A. MACHTELT BOLKESTEIN
HENK A. COMBÉ
SIMON C. DIK
CASPER DE GROOT
JADRANKA GVOZDANOVIĆ
ALBERT RIJKSBARON
CO VET

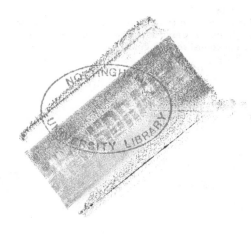

ACADEMIC PRESS · 1981
A Subsidiary of Harcourt Brace Jovanovich, Publishers
London   New York   Toronto   Sydney   San Francisco

344245

ACADEMIC PRESS INC. (LONDON) LTD.
24/28 Oval Road,
London NW1

United States Edition published by
ACADEMIC PRESS INC.
111 Fifth Avenue
New York, New York 10003

British Library Cataloguing in Publication Data

Bolkestein, A. M.
    Predication and expression in functional grammar.
    1. Grammar, Comparative and general—Syntax
    2. Functionalism (Linguistics)
    I. Title
    415   P291

    ISBN 0–12–111350–7
    LCCCN 810729

Typeset by Gloucester Typesetting Services
and printed in Great Britain by
T. J. Press (Padstow) Ltd., Padstow, Cornwall

Contributing Authors

A. MACHTELT BOLKESTEIN
Department of Latin
University of Amsterdam
Oude Turfmarkt 129
1012 GC Amsterdam
The Netherlands

HENK A. COMBÉ
Department of Spanish
University of Amsterdam
Spuistraat 210
Amsterdam
The Netherlands

SIMON C. DIK
Institute for General Linguistics
University of Amsterdam
Spuistraat 210
Amsterdam
The Netherlands

CASPER DE GROOT
Department of Language and Literature
Tilburg University
POB 90153
5000LE Tilburg
The Netherlands

JADRANKA GVOZDANOVIĆ
Department of Slavic Studies
University of Amsterdam
Spuistraat 210
Amsterdam
The Netherlands

ALBERT RIJKSBARON
Department of Greek
University of Amsterdam
Oude Turfmarkt 129
1012 GC Amsterdam
The Netherlands

CO VET
Department of French
State University at Groningen
Broerstraat 5
9700 AB Groningen
The Netherlands

Preface

This collection of studies discusses a number of vexed problems in different languages, within the general framework of the theory of Functional Grammar. The general unifying theme of these studies is the question how one could deal with construction types in which there seems to be a discrepancy between the syntactic form in which they themselves present and the underlying network of semantic relations which must be postulated in order to be able to understand their semantic content. Such construction types present special problems for a theory such as Functional Grammar, in which the use of structure-changing transformations is avoided. We do not aim at presenting definitive solutions to these problems in this monograph. Rather, we demonstrate what sorts of solutions are in principle available within the framework of Functional Grammar and what advantages and disadvantages these solutions have. In this way we hope to shed some light on both the phenomenology of discongruous relations between predication and expression as they occur in different languages and the capacities and limitations of the theory of Functional Grammar as developed so far.

This monograph grew out of a work group in which the authors intensively discussed their individual contributions. Although this has made for a high degree of unity in the perspective from which the different problems are approached, each author is individually responsible for the content of his or her specific contribution.

Amsterdam   *The Authors*
September 1981

Contents

Preface   vii
List of abbreviations and symbols   xiii

**1   Predication and Expression: the Problem and the
      Theoretical Framework   1**
      SIMON C. DIK

1.0   Introduction   1
1.1   Statement of the problem   1
1.2   Some elements of Functional Grammar   3
      Notes   16
      References   17

**2   Discrepancies between Predication and Expression
      in Natural Languages   19**
      SIMON C. DIK

2.0   Introduction   19
2.1   Complex predications   19
2.2   Complex terms   22
2.3   Types of differences between underlying structure and
      expression form   23
      2.3.1   Displacement   23
      2.3.2   Morphological adjustment   27
      2.3.3   Non-finite expression of the embedded predicate   28
2.4   Possible solutions   31
2.5   A final illustration   35
2.6   Conclusion   39
      Notes   38
      References   39

3   Sentence-Intertwining in Hungarian   41
      CASPER DE GROOT

3.0   Introduction   41
3.1   Function assignment in Hungarian   42
      3.1.1   Syntactic function assignment   42
      3.1.2   Pragmatic function assignment   44
3.2   Displacement   47
3.3   Pseudo-arguments   51
3.4   Conclusion   60
      Notes   60
      References   62

4   Embedded Predications, Displacement and Pseudo-argument Formation in Latin   63
A. MACHTELT BOLKESTEIN

4.0 Introduction   63
4.1 Theme,Predication organization v. Displacement   65
   4.1.1 Main clauses   65
   4.1.2 Embedded predications   70
   4.1.3 Displacement without morphological adjustment   72
4.2 Pseudo-argument formation   74
   4.2.1 "Prolepsis": displacement and finite expression of the embedded predicate   74
      4.2.1.1 The empirical data   77
      4.2.1.2 Solutions (1), (2) and (3) reconsidered   83
      4.2.1.3 Pragmatic conditions on pseudo-argument formation   86
   4.2.2 The "personal passive" or "Nominativus cum Infinitivo" (NcI) construction   90
      4.2.2.1 Empirical observations   91
      4.2.2.2 Topic and Focus patterns within complex sentences   96
      4.2.2.3 Reconsideration of the empirical data: an explanation   100
4.3 Conclusion   106
   Notes   108
   References   112

5   Embedded Themes in Spoken Dutch: two ways out   113
SIMON C. DIK

5.0 Introduction   113
5.1 Theme,Predication constructions in main clauses   114
5.2 Theme,Predication constructions in subordinate clauses   118
   5.2.1 Main clause ordering in subordinate clauses   120
   5.2.2 Reduplication of the subordinator   121
5.3 Conclusion   123
   Notes   124
   Reference   124

6   Word Order and Displacement in Serbo-Croatian   125
JADRANKA GVOZDANOVIĆ

6.0 Introduction   125
6.1 Word order and contrastive accent   125
   6.1.1 Word order in Serbo-Croatian   125
   6.1.2 Contrastive accent   126
   6.1.3 Pragmatic functions   128
6.2 Constituent placement and pragmatic functions   129
   6.2.1 Simple sentences   129

6.2.2 Complex sentences 132
6.3 Displacement 133
    6.3.1 Real displacement 133
    6.3.2 Seeming displacement 137
6.4 Summary and conclusions 138
    Notes 139
    References 139

7 Subject Assignment in the Impersonal Constructions of French **143**
CO VET

7.0 Introduction 143
7.1 Some traditional and transformational approaches 144
7.2 Two hypotheses about Subject assignment 147
7.3 The genuinely impersonal verbs 150
7.4 Impersonal constructions with intransitive, pronominal and passive verbs 151
7.5 The constructions with *sembler* 153
7.6 The verb category of *menacer, pouvoir, devoir* etc. 157
7.7 Conclusion 160
    Notes 161
    References 163

8 The Interaction of Subject and Topic in Portuguese **165**
SIMON C. DIK

8.0 Introduction 165
8.1 Status and position of the Subject 166
    8.1.1 Preverbal and postverbal Subjects 166
    8.1.2 Subject downgrading 167
    8.1.3 Subject postposing 169
    8.1.4 A postverbal pattern position for the Subject 171
8.2 Some displacement and Raising phenomena 175
8.3 Conclusion 182
    Notes 183
    References 184

9 Some Discrepancy Phenomena in Spanish **185**
HENK A. COMBÉ

9.0 Introduction 185
9.1 Impersonal constructions: *parecer, resultar* and *poder* 186
    9.1.1 Possible constructions 186
    9.1.2 Discrepancy 189
    9.1.3 Two more candidates for the same predication 190
    9.1.4 *Fácil + de +* infinitive 193
9.2 "Degraded" antecedents in relative clauses 195
9.3 Intertwining 199

9.4   Concluding remarks   201
       Notes   202
       References   203

**10   Factivity as a Condition for an Optional Expression
       Rule in Latin: the "Ab Urbe Condita" Construction
       and its Underlying Representation   205**
       A. MACHTELT BOLKESTEIN

10.0   Introduction   205
10.1   The main properties of the AUC   206
10.2   The formation of the complex term   209
10.3   The nature of the rule of AUC-formation   211
       10.3.1   Function assignment   211
       10.3.2   The rule of AUC-formation: a peculiar type of
                nominalization   212
10.4   Conditions triggering the rule of AUC-formation   214
       10.4.1   Semantic conditions for AUC-formation: factivity   215
       10.4.2   Pragmatic function arrangement and AUC-
                formation   218
10.5   The representation of factivity in underlying predications 224
10.6   Summary and conclusions   228
       Notes   230
       References   232

11   Relative Clause Formation in Ancient Greek   235
       ALBERT RIJKSBARON

11.0   Introduction   235
11.1   Relative clauses in Ancient Greek   237
       11.1.1   The data   237
       11.1.2   Conditions of attraction   238
11.2   An analysis in FG terms   241
11.3   Parallels with noun–adjective/participle constructions   243
11.4   Conclusion of Sections 11.1–3   246
11.5   Semantic, pragmatic and stylistic (dis)similarities   248
       11.5.1   Noun–adjective constructions   248
       11.5.2   Noun–relative clause constructions   251
       Appendix: the feasibility of a promotion analysis   253
       Notes   253
       References   257

Author Index   261
Subject Index   263
Selective Index of Predicates   266

Abbreviations and symbols

FG = Functional Grammar
TG = Transformational Grammar

Semantic functions
Ag = Agent
Go = Goal
Rec = Recipient
Ben = Beneficiary
Instr = Instrument
Loc = Location
Temp = Time
Dir = Direction
Proc = Processed
Fo = Force
Po = Positioner
So = Source
Comp = Company
Exp = Experiencer
Phen = Phenomenon
Compl = Complement
Poss = Possessor
$\emptyset$ = Zero function
Mann = Manner

Syntactic functions
Subj = Subject
Obj = Object

Pragmatic functions
Top = Topic
Foc = Focus

Categories
A = Adjectival
N = Nominal
V = Verbal

Vf = Finite verb
Vi = Infinite verb
CL = Clitic
ENCL = Enclitic
PRO = Pronoun
Refl = Reflexive
NP = Noun phrase
PP = Prepositional phrase
SUB = Subordinate clause
sub = Subordinator

Term operators
d = definite
i = indefinite
1 = singular
m = plural
Q = interrogative

Positions
S = Subject position
O = Object position
V = Verb position
P1 = Clause-initial position
X = Other position

Cases
nom = nominative
gen = genitive
dat = dative
acc = accusative
subl = sublative
sup-es = super essive

General
X, Y = arbitrary category or function
$x_1, \ldots, x_n$ = term variables

φ = arbitrary predicate
ω = arbitrary term operator
π = arbitrary predicate operator
x₁, xⱼ etc. = variables symbolizing distinct referents
LIPOC = Language-Independent Preferred Order of Constituents
1sg, 2sg, 3sg = fiirst, second, third person singular
1pl, 2pl, 3pl = first, second, third person plural

part = participle
inf = infinitive
masc = masculine
fem = feminine
neu = neutral
– – –→ = "is realized as"
$\{\ \}$ = unordered set

1 Predication and Expression: the Problem and the Theoretical Framework

SIMON C. DIK

Institute for General Linguistics
University of Amsterdam

1.0 Introduction

This chapter first explicates the problem which forms the central theme of discussion in this volume: the status of possible discrepancies between underlying predications and their surface realizations (Section 1.1). An outline is then given of the basic elements of the theory of Functional Grammar (FG), with special reference to those points which are essential to an understanding of the theoretical implications of the central problem (Section 1.2). Chapter 2 will provide a more detailed discussion of these theoretical implications.

The sketch of FG given in Section 1.2 is necessarily global and incomplete. For further background information on the theory of FG the reader is referred to Dik (1978, 1980a, 1980b) and to Hoekstra *et al.* (1981).

1.1 Statement of the problem

Most languages have certain construction types whose syntactic surface form seems to be at variance with the network of semantic relations which must be postulated in order to understand their semantic content. Let us illustrate these construction types with some examples.

The following pair constitutes a notorious case from the history of Transformational Grammar:

(1) John is eager to please

(2) John is easy to please

The syntactic form of these two sentences is at first sight identical, but the semantic relations expressed are quite different. In (1), *eager* indicates a relationship between "John" and the activity of his pleasing someone; in (2), it is expressed that "John" is such that it is not difficult to please him. These differences come out in different possible paraphrases of (1) and (2):

(3) a *Pleasing John is eager
     b *It is eager to please John

(4) a   Pleasing John is easy
     b   It is easy to please John

As is well known, Transformational Grammar has used such pairs as (1)–(2) in arguing for the distinction between two levels of syntactic representation: deep structure and surface structure. According to this view, (1) and (2) would be assigned different deep structures, which are then mapped on to the same surface structure by means of transformational rules.

As a second example, consider the construction:

(5) I believe John to be a fool

In this case, *John* seems to behave as if it were an Object to the verb *believe*, whereas semantically it is rather an argument of "to be a fool". On the other hand, *believe* can be semantically interpreted as indicating some attitudinal relation between "I" on the one hand and the content of "John is a fool" on the other. Again, there seems to be a discrepancy between syntactic form and semantic relationships. This discrepancy is not present in the alternative construction:

(6) I believe that John is a fool

Any descriptively adequate grammar of English will have to account, in a principled way, for the relationship between (5) and (6), and for the fact that in (5), but not in (6), there is a discrepancy between syntactic form and semantic structure.

As a third example, consider the following Latin construction:

(7) Orator occisus facinus pessimum videbatur
     orator killed   crime   terrible   was considered

Translated literally, this construction would come out as: "The killed orator was considered to be a terrible crime", but this, of course, is nonsense. What (7) in fact means is "The killing of the orator was considered a terrible crime". Thus, the expression *orator occisus*, which would normally refer to a person having a certain property, must here be interpreted as referring to an act, perpetrated with respect to a person.

Again, there is a discrepancy between syntactic form and semantic content; and again, there are alternative expression forms available in Latin in which no such discrepancy exists:

(8) Oratorem occisum esse facinus pessimum videbatur
     orator-acc killed-acc be crime terrible was considered
     "The orator to have been killed was considered a terrible crime"

(9) Quod orator occisus esset facinus pessimum videbatur
     that orator killed was crime terrible was considered
     "That the orator was killed was considered a terrible crime".

An adequate grammar of Latin will have to account for the relations between (7), (8), and (9), as well as for the fact that in (7), but not in (8) and (9), there is a discrepancy between the syntactic form of the construction and the semantic content contained in the construction.

The studies in this volume discuss different sorts of constructions of the general type exemplified by (2), (5), and (7), as they occur in Ancient Greek, Dutch, French, Hungarian, Latin, Portuguese, Serbo-Croatian, and Spanish. The problems involved in these construction types are among the most difficult ones for any theory of the syntax and semantics of natural languages. They have special relevance for the theory of FG, in which structure-changing, transformational operations are avoided wherever possible.

The next section sketches the basic principles incorporated in this theory.

1.2 Some elements of Functional Grammar

The following elements of FG are of special importance for a proper appreciation of the discussions contained in this volume.

Functional notions play an important part in the descriptive apparatus of FG. Three types of function are distinguished:

Semantic functions (such as Agent, Goal, Recipient), which define the roles of participants in the states of affairs designated by predications;

Syntactic functions (Subject and Object), which define different perspectives on the states of affairs designated by predications;

Pragmatic functions (such as Topic and Focus), which mark the informational status of constituents within the wider communicative settings in which they are used.

The power of the descriptive apparatus (i.e. the types of rules and structures allowed by the theory) is rather heavily constrained by the following principles:

Structure-changing operations, which delete, permute, substitute, or otherwise destroy elements of pre-established structures, are not allowed;

Filtering devices by means of which structures which have been produced at one stage in the descriptive process can later be rejected as ill-formed, are avoided;

Lexical items are not decomposed into more abstract elements: all along the descriptive production line, the structures used in generating linguistic expressions contain integral lexemes of the object language.

The general structure of a grammar as defined by FG can be read off from Fig. 1. Although not all details of this diagram will be discussed in the present context, it can be used for general reference with respect to the notions and terms to be introduced below.

Linguistic expressions are described in terms of a general schema of the form:

(10) Theme, Predication, Tail

which is exemplified in a construction such as:

(11) As for John,   he didn't read it,   that book of yours
        Theme   Predication   Tail

Theme and Tail are treated as constituents standing outside the Predication proper, with the following pragmatic functions. *Theme* defines a "universe of discourse" for the Predication to bear upon. *Tail* gives afterthought information specifying or modifying given elements contained in the Predication.

The Predication proper has the following general structure:

(12) $\pi \, \phi \, (x_1) \, (x_2) \ldots (x_n)$ $n \geqslant 1$

in which π indicates one or more predicate operators (such as operators for Tense, Aspect, Negation, etc.), ϕ indicates some predicate, and $(x_1) \ldots (x_n)$ indicate positions for a number of argument terms associated with the predicate. Predicates are expressions designating properties or relations; terms are expressions which can be used to refer to entities in some world. A predication is thus basically the application of some predicate to an

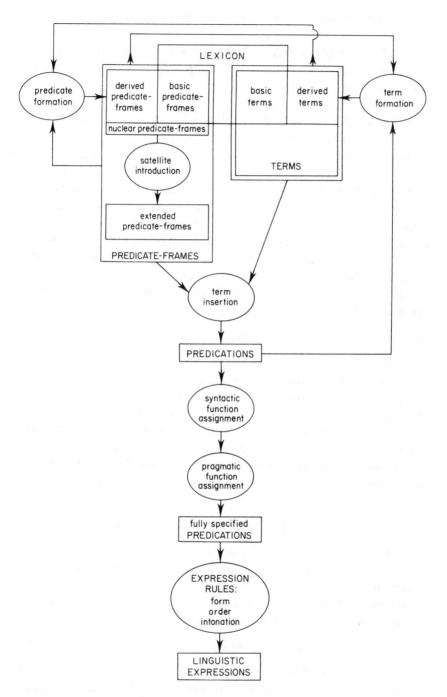

Fig. 1 Organization of a functional grammar

appropriate number of terms. Some terms are given ready-made in the lexicon as basic terms: proper names and pronouns would qualify as such. Most terms, however, are derived through principles of term formation, to be specified below.

All predicates are contained in predicate-frames, structures which specify their fundamental semantic and syntactic properties. Some predicate-frames are again basic and as such contained in the lexicon. Other predicate-frames are derived through rules of predicate formation. Only fully productive formation processes are captured by such rules. Basic and derived predicate-frames together are called nuclear predicate-frames and consist of the predicate and the term positions which are required by that predicate (the arguments of the predicate). Nuclear predicate-frames can be extended by satellite term positions; these are positions for terms which provide further modification and specification of the nuclear predicate-frame as a whole. The following would be an example of a basic predicate-frame as contained in the lexicon of English:

(13)   give$_V$ (x$_1$: animate(x$_1$))$_{Ag}$ (x$_2$)$_{Go}$ (x$_3$: animate(x$_3$))$_{Rec}$

This predicate-frame expresses the following properties of the basic predicate *give*: it is a verbal predicate (V), as distinct from nominal (N) or adjectival (A) predicates; it takes three arguments (x$_1$), (x$_2$), (x$_3$), in the semantic functions of Agent (Ag), Goal (Go), and Recipient (Rec); and the first and the third argument carry selection restrictions to the effect that the terms filling them should designate animate entities.

A predicate-frame such as (13) could be extended by a satellite position in the semantic function of Location to result in the extended predicate-frame:

(14)   give$_V$ (x$_1$: anim(x$_1$))$_{Ag}$ (x$_2$)$_{Go}$ (x$_3$: anim(x$_3$))$_{Rec}$ (x$_4$)$_{Loc}$

Satellites for other semantic functions such as Time, Duration, Reason, Cause, Beneficiary, etc. can be similarly added to nuclear predicate-frames, depending on the semantic properties of these.

Certain predicates have argument positions which may or must be specified by predications. Consider a case such as:

(15)   John believes that Bill loves Sally

Here, the predicate *believe* indicates a relation between one entity, described as "John", and another entity described as "that Bill loves Sally", where the latter description has all the properties of a predication. To account for possibilities of this kind, we assume that the predicate-frame for *believe* has the following structure:

(16)   believe$_V$ (x_1: human(x_1))$_{Po}$ (sub x_2: [PREDICATION] (x_2))$_{Go}$

This predicate-frame indicates that *believe* is a verbal predicate taking two arguments, x_1 and x_2, where x_1 has the semantic function of Positioner (Po)[1]† and is restricted to human terms and x_2 has the semantic function of Goal and is specified by a predication. In a sense, the predication to be inserted into the position indicated here acts as a predicate over the term variable x_2, which symbolizes "that which is believed by x_1". The element "sub" is intended to trigger the subordinating device by means of which the embedded predication will be joined to the main predicate *believe*. Further properties of predicate-frames such as (16) will be discussed in Chapter 2.

For a predicate-frame to result in a predication, its term positions must be filled with terms. All terms are supposed to have the following abstract organization:

(17)   (ωx_i: $\varphi_1(x_i)$: $\varphi_2(x_i)$: . . . : $\varphi_n(x_i)$)   n $\geqslant$ 1

in which ω stands for one or more term operators (for such categories as Definiteness, Number, Quantification, Demonstratives, etc.) and each $\varphi_j(x_i)$ indicates some "open predication in x_i" (= some predication with x_i as its only free variable), acting as a restrictor on the set of proper referents of the term. The following term structures exemplify this organization:[2]

(18)   (d1x_i: John$_N(x_i)$)
       John

(19)   (i3x_j: box$_N(x_j)$: wooden$_A(x_j)$: red$_A(x_j)$: pretty$_A(x_j)$)
       three pretty red wooden boxes

(20)   (d1x_k: man$_N(x_k)$: Past kill$_V$ (x_k)$_{Ag}$ (d1x_l: Bill$_N(x_1)$)$_{Go}$)
       the man who killed Bill

(18) would be stored in the lexicon as a basic term; (19) and (20) would be formed through term formation on the general model of (17). Notice that the different restrictors are "stacked" on to each other through the relation indicated by " : ", which can be read as "such that". In (19) this can be taken to express that the set of potential referents is first restricted to the set of boxes, then to the set of wooden boxes, and so on. From (20) it is

† Notes will be found at the end of each chapter.

clear that a restrictor may be expressed through a relative clause, which in turn may contain other specified terms. Term formation is thus recursive through the restrictors.

If the terms (18), (19), and (20) are inserted into the argument positions of the predicate *give* as represented in (13), the result would be a predication of the following form:

(21) Past give$_V$ (d1x$_i$: John$_N$(x$_i$))$_{Ag}$
      (i3x$_j$: box$_N$(x$_j$): wooden$_A$(x$_j$): red$_A$(x$_j$): pretty$_A$(x$_j$))$_{Go}$
      (d1x$_k$: man$_N$(x$_k$): Past kill$_V$ (x$_k$)$_{Ag}$ (d1x$_l$: Bill$_N$(x$_l$))$_{Go}$)$_{Rec}$

which could underlie a sentence such as:

(22) John gave three pretty red wooden boxes to the man who killed Bill.

The whole predication (21), again, could be inserted into the second argument position of the predicate-frame of *believe* as given in (16), to arrive at the underlying predication for sentences such as:

(23) Peter believed that John gave three pretty red wooden boxes to the man who killed Bill.

The underlying predication (21), however, could also lead to realizations other than (22). Let us illustrate this with a less complex example. All of the following constructions are judged to have the same underlying predication:

(24) John gave the book to Bill

(25) John gave Bill the book

(26) The book was given to Bill by John

(27) Bill was given the book by John

The identity of underlying predication accounts for the fact that these constructions are semantically equivalent to the extent that each of them can be used to describe the same set of states of affairs. The semantic differences between (24)–(27) are judged to lie in different "perspectives" from which each of them presents the state of affairs described. These differences are captured by means of differential assignments of the syntactic functions Subject and Object to the terms of the underlying predication. Subject and Object assignment possibilities differ from language to language, but the possibilities for each language are hypothesized to confirm to the following language-independent hierarchy:[3]

(28)   Ag   Go   Rec   Ben   Instr   Loc   Temp
    Subj $+$ > $+$ > $+$ > $+$ > $+$ > $+$ > $+$
    Obj $+$ > $+$ > $+$ > $+$ > $+$ > $+$

Thus, Agent terms are the first candidates for Subject assignment, then Goal terms, and so on through the hierarchy. It is similar for Object assignment, beginning with Goal terms. The term to which Subj is assigned provides the primary vantage point for the perspective from which the state of affairs is presented. The term to which Object is assigned provides a secondary vantage point. According to this hypothesis, each language has a continuous sequence of Subj and Obj assignment possibilities within hierarchy (28), up to the "cut-off point" for these assignments in these languages. This theory is compatible with the fact that certain languages may have no Object assignment possibilities at all, or even no Subject assignment possibilities (cf. Dik 1980b, ch. 6). The latter is the case in Hungarian (see De Groot, Chapter 3), and probably in Serbo-Croatian (see Dik and Gvozdanović (1981)). These languages lack the type of opposition found in English pairs such as (24)–(25), and have no regular form of passive construction. Languages of this type thus lack the possibility of defining different perspectives on states of affairs in this way. As we shall see, they make up for this by a more systematic use of those differentiations which can be described in terms of pragmatic rather than of syntactic functions. In accordance with the hierarchy given in (28), the Subj and Obj assignment possibilities for English can be summarized as in:[4]

(29)   Ag   Go   Rec   Ben
    Subj $+$ > $+$ > $+$ > ?
    Obj $+$ > $+$ > $+$

The differences between (24)–(27) are captured by applying these assignments in the following way:

(30)   John$_{\text{AgSubj}}$ gave the book$_{\text{GoObj}}$ to Bill$_{\text{Rec}}$

(31)   John$_{\text{AgSubj}}$ gave Bill$_{\text{RecObj}}$ the book$_{\text{Go}}$

(32)   The book$_{\text{GoSubj}}$ was given to Bill$_{\text{Rec}}$ by John$_{\text{Ag}}$

(33)   Bill$_{\text{RecSubj}}$ was given the book$_{\text{Go}}$ by John$_{\text{Ag}}$

In English, Subj and Obj assignment influence the manner in which a predication is expressed in the following way:

Subj and Obj terms go to special positions;

Subj and Obj terms have no prepositional marking;

Subj assignment to Go and later semantic functions results in passive expression of the verbal predicate;

Subject terms trigger agreement with the finite verb;

Subject terms require nominative case in pronouns; all other terms, including Object terms, get accusative case.

After Subj and Obj assignment have been applied, the predication underlying (24) will have the following form:

(34)   Past give$_V$ (d1x$_i$: John$_N$(x$_i$))$_{AgSubj}$
                     (d1x$_j$: book$_N$(x$_j$))$_{GoObj}$
                     (d1x$_k$: Bill$_N$(x$_k$))$_{Rec}$

This underlying predication, however, can still be realized in different forms. All these realizations will contain the constituents *John, gave, the book, to Bill,* but they may differ in stress pattern, as in:

(35)   John gave the book to BILL

(36)   JOHN gave the book to Bill

or they may differ in constituent order, as in:

(37)   John gave the book to BILL

(38)   To BILL John gave the book

Such differences as these correspond to differences in the informational status of the constituents of the predication within the setting in which they are used. These differences are captured in terms of differential assignment of the pragmatic functions Topic (= that constituent about which the predication is meant to predicate something in the given setting) and Focus (= that constituent carrying the most salient information in the given setting). Thus, when predication (34) is to be an answer to the question:

(39)   To whom did John give the book?

then Topic function will be assigned to the AgSubj term *John*,[5] and Focus will be assigned to the Rec term *Bill*. These different assignments will lead to different stress patterns and different constituent orderings in the expression of the predication.

Through all these operations we arrive at the fully specified predication, which in this case will look like:

(40)   Past give$_V$ (d1x$_i$: John$_N$(x$_i$))$_{AgSubjTop}$
$\quad\quad\quad$ (d1x$_j$: book$_N$(x$_j$))$_{GoObj}$
$\quad\quad\quad$ (d1x$_k$: Bill$_N$(x$_k$))$_{RecFoc}$

Such a fully specified predication is taken to contain all the information relevant to the semantic interpretation of the linguistic expression involved on the one hand, and to the formal expression of the predication on the other.

It is important to notice that the order in which the constituents are given in (40) is purely a matter of convention. Predications are regarded as unordered hierarchical structures, which still have to be linearized into the left–right sequence characteristic of actual linguistic expressions. This linearization is brought about by "placement rules", i.e. rules which carry the constituents of predications to certain linearly defined positions. These placement rules belong to the expression component of the grammar and are in fact applied rather late in the derivation of linguistic expressions. Correspondingly, it makes no sense within the framework of FG to speak of the "underlying order of predications", and therefore the question whether or not given languages differ with respect to underlying constituent order does not arise.

Given underlying predications of the general form illustrated in (40), we need rules which will map these predications on to the linguistic expressions by which they can be expressed. These rules are called *expression rules*. The main functions of expression rules are:

(i) to determine the *form* which constituents of a predication may or must take, given their structural and functional properties within the predication;

(ii) to determine the *order* in which constituents may or must be linearized, given their structural and functional properties within the predication.

As to the form of constituents, the following expression devices are most commonly encountered:

Semantic functions are commonly expressed through case distinctions, adpositions (= pre- and postpositions), or both together (as when an adposition governs a specific case);

Syntactic functions are likewise commonly expressed through case and/or adpositions. It is common for Subject and Object terms, however, to take the most unmarked expression form from among the devices available. Thus, in languages which use adpositions for expressing semantic functions, it is very common to find the Subject (and often the Object as well) without any adposition. Thus, the English Recipient is expressed through the preposition *to* (as in *to Bill*), but Recipient-Subject and Recipient-Object take no preposition, as in:

(41)   Bill$_{RecSubj}$ was given the book$_{Go}$ by John$_{Ag}$

(42)   John$_{AgSubj}$ gave Bill $_{RecObj}$ the book$_{Go}$

In languages which use case distinctions for the expression of semantic functions, it is common for the Subject and the Object to take the most unmarked cases from among the total set of cases available in the language. Usually this will be the nominative for the Subject, and the accusative for the Object.[6]

Pragmatic functions are not usually expressed through case distinctions. They may be expressed through adpositions or similar particles, or through special patterns of constituent order or intonation.

The above picture provides a number of special problems, especially with respect to the expression of semantic functions; some of these will be mentioned briefly. First, it has been said that semantic functions are expressed through (mapped on to) cases and adpositions; this does not necessarily imply that each semantic function has its own expression device—indeed, there is usually no one-to-one relation between semantic functions and expression devices. For example, when in some language Recipients are expressed through the dative case, the dative case will usually also be used for coding certain other semantic functions: the number of distinct cases is characteristically smaller than the number of distinct semantic functions to be coded. This means that, given the semantic function, we can determine the case/adposition, but given the case/adposition, we cannot usually unambiguously define the semantic function on the basis of the form of the term in question alone.

In a number of cases there may be doubts about the semantic function to be assigned to some argument, and about the relation between semantic functions and their formal expression. Consider a specific example: verbal predicates with the general sense of "helping someone" may be construed with an accusative in one language but with a dative in another language; or one language may have two "helping" verbs, one taking an accusative and another a dative; or one "helping" verb in a given language may be either construed with an accusative or with a dative, without any clear distinction in meaning. Are we going to say that the accusative and the dative in such cases code different semantic functions, or not?

In general we shall take the following position with respect to this question: "helping" is a real-world relationship between entities A and B, which may be linguistically "construed" or "modelled" in different ways: it may either be construed as an operation of A on B similar to *A hit B* or *A pushed B*; in that case B will have Goal function. Or it may be construed as if A gave or offered something to B, similar to *A gave C to B* or *A talked to B*; in that case B will have Recipient function. It thus seems possible to maintain that the difference between accusative case and dative case does correspond to a difference in semantic function, even though this difference may have hardly any consequences with respect to the events talked about in extralinguistic reality. This also goes to show that the distribution of semantic functions within some predicate-frame is not so much determined by the real world properties of events, as by the interpretations conventionally imposed on such events within a given language. From this point of view there is little sense in talking about some language-independent abstract relation of HELPING, apart from the linguistic interpretations assigned to such a relation in actual languages.[7]

As to the form which the predicate is going to take, this is mainly sensitive to:

which predicate operators (Tense, Aspect, etc.) have been applied to the predicate;

which Subject and Object assignments have been applied;

whether the predicate is to be realized as a finite or as a non-finite predicate.

As to the second point, the following formalization has been proposed (Dik, 1978, ch. 5): when Subject or Object is assigned to some semantic function, the information about which assignment has been applied is communicated to the Verb; this information will then co-determine the form in which the Verb is realized. For instance, when, in English, Subject is assigned to Go, Rec, or Ben, the Verb has to take the passive form;

otherwise it takes the active form. Other languages, however, have much richer voice distinctions.[8]

Another way in which the expression form of the Verb may be influenced by Subject and Object assignment is through agreement: if there is any form of agreement between the Verb and the terms with which it is construed, it is usual for the Subject to be the first, and the Object to be the second candidate for triggering agreement. Such agreement rules can be easily formulated in FG, since the relevant functional information is explicitly available at the point where such rules apply.

As to the specification of constituent order, the general idea is as follows: predicates and terms are regarded as unordered with respect to each other until some rather late point in the generation process. At that point, rules apply which bring the constituents of the underlying predication to the positions defined by "functional patterns", of which each language is judged to possess a limited number (possibly only a single one). The rules which carry constituents to pattern positions are called "placement rules". Since FG does not allow structure-changing operations, a constituent, once it has been placed in some specified position, cannot be moved to another position. Thus, the position of a constituent must be defined in "one go" by the placement rules. The placement rules thus constitute a mapping of sets (= underlying predications) on to sequences (= functional patterns).

The functional patterns needed for defining constituent ordering in different languages generally conform to the following schema:

(43)   P2, P1 (V) S (V) O (V), P3

in which P2 and P3 indicate the positions for Theme and Tail constituents, respectively, P1 indicates a clause-initial position used for special purposes, and S, O, and V indicate positions for Subject, Object, and Verb (both finite and infinite). This schema indicates that Subject and Object generally have specific positions with respect to the Verb, and that the Subject precedes the Object in the unmarked order of most languages. Exceptions to this general schema are discussed in Dik (1980b, ch. 6). Obviously, when a language does not make use of Subject and Object assignment, the S and O positions cannot be relevant to constituent ordering in such a language. This correlates with the fact that such languages in general have more freedom of constituent ordering than languages which do have Subject and Object assignment. This will become clear in the discussions of Serbo-Croatian and Hungarian in this volume.

The special position P1 in (43) is thought to be universally relevant as a position used for special purposes in the following way: (a) most languages have certain categories of constituents which, if present in a predication, must be placed in P1 (in English this holds for question words, relative pronouns, and subordinators); (b) if there is no such constituent in the predication, then P1 can be used for constituents having Topic or Focus function. Note that according to this approach to constituent ordering, there is a fundamental difference between the following constructions:

(44)   That book, John does not read it

(45)   That book John does not read

In (44) the constituent *that book* is in Theme position and functions as a stage-setting introduction to the whole predication. Within that predication, *it* is coreferential with the Theme, and can thus be said to have Topic function within the predication proper. The Theme is characteristically set off from the predication by an intonation break, and the predication is complete in itself (could be used as a complete sentence). In (45), on the other hand, the constituent *that book* is judged to occupy P1 position on account of its Focus or Topic function. There is no intonation break, and the remainder of the sentence is not complete in itself. As we shall see in some of the papers in this volume, it is, in certain cases, not so easy to decide whether a given construction type exhibits an organization parallel to (44) or to (45).

The constituent ordering principles summarized so far are not sufficient to account for all the ordering patterns found in natural languages. There is much evidence that constituent ordering can also be sensitive to the categorial complexity of constituents. With respect to this factor, FG postulates a "language-independent preferred order of constituents" (LIPOC), which says that, other things being equal, constituents prefer to be ordered from left to right in order of increasing complexity, as follows:

(46)   CLITIC – PRO – NP – NPP – V – NP – PNP – SUB

LIPOC predicts that when we have, e.g., a pronoun and a noun phrase of identical functional status within the predication, the pronoun will tend towards an earlier position in the linear order of the clause than the noun phrase; similarly, a subordinate clause will under those circumstances tend towards a later position in the clause and will very often occupy the final position in the clause. Functional patterns conforming to schema (43), rules for placing constituents in special positions such as P1, and the forces exerted by LIPOC, are judged to interact in such a way that for each language they reach a sort of compromise solution, embodied in the particular array of possible ordering patterns in that language.

One problem which so far has not been sufficiently clarified within the context of FG is the question of how the rules determining the form of constituents and the rules determining their order should be interrelated with each other. In a number of cases, the order of constituents is sensitive to the form in which these constituents are realized. This is evident for all those ordering rules which are determined by LIPOC: these rules must know the forms of the constituents before they can take them to their appropriate positions.

In other cases, however, the form which constituents take is dependent on the order in which they occur. For example, there are situations in which the Verb agrees with a given type of constituent when following it but not when preceding it, or situations in which a constituent modifying a series of coordinated terms agrees in certain respects only with the last term in the series. In general, such processes as sandhi or liaison affect the form of constituents, given the order in which they appear.

It seems clear, then, that form- and order-determining rules should be sandwiched in such a way that there may be sequences of (i) form-determining rules, (ii) order-determining rules, and (iii) form-determining rules. This statement, however, is so general that it does not provide automatic solutions for describing the interrelations between form and order phenomena in a given language. In several chapters of this volume, specific instances of this general problem will be discussed, together with alternative solutions for the particular phenomena involved, within the general theory of constituent ordering as sketched here.

This ends our summary of those principles of FG of particular relevance for an understanding of the problems to be discussed in the further contributions in this volume. In Chapter 2, a more detailed analysis is given of the theoretical implications of discrepancies between underlying predication and actual expression for the framework of the theory of FG as developed so far.

Notes

1   A Positioner controls a Position; a Position is a non-dynamic, controlled state of affairs. For the typology of states of affairs underlying these distinctions, see Dik (1978, section 3.4.1.).

2   d = definite, i = indefinite; 1, 2, 3 etc.: number; N = nominal, A =
adjectival predicate; x_i, x_j, x_k, x_l, etc.: variables symbolizing distinct
referents.
3   For extensive discussion of this theory of Subj and Obj assignment, see Dik
(1978, ch. 5).
4   The question mark under Ben in (29) suggests the dialectal and idiolectal
variation in the acceptability of sentences such as: *Mary was bought a dress
by Peter*.
5   There may be reasons to also assign Topic function to *the book* in this case.
For some discussion, see Dik (1978, ch. 6).
6   Ergative systems form an exception to this statement. For discussion, see
Dik (1978, ch. 7; 1980b, ch. 5).
7   For discussion of this point of view with respect to verbs of "teaching", see
Work Group FG (1981).
8   For exemplification and further discussion of voice systems, see Dik (1978,
ch. 5).

References

DIK, Simon C.
    1978   "Functional Grammar." North-Holland Linguistic Series 37. Amster-
        dam, North-Holland.
    1980a Seventeen sentences: basic principles and application of Functional
        Grammar. *In* Edith A. Moravcsik and Jessica R. Wirth (ed.). "Syntax
        and Semantics 13: current approaches to syntax" 45–75. New York and
        London, Academic Press.
    1980b "Studies in Functional Grammar". London and New York, Academic
        Press.
DIK, Simon C. and Jadranka Gvozdanović
    1981   Subject and Object in Serbo-Croatian. *In* Hoekstra *et al.* (1981), 21–39.
HOEKSTRA, Teun, Harry van der Hulst and Michael Moortgat (ed.).
    1981   "Perspectives on Functional Grammar". Dordrecht, Foris.
WORK GROUP FG
    1981   On the Functional Grammar of teaching verbs. *In* Hoekstra *et al.*
        (1981), 203–231.

2 Discrepancies between Predication and Expression in Natural Languages

SIMON C. DIK

Institute for General Linguistics
University of Amsterdam

2.0 Introduction

This chapter contains a general survey of ways in which the form of a linguistic expression can diverge from what one would expect on the basis of the underlying predication and a discussion of how such discrepancies could be accounted for within the framework of FG.

First, we shall consider how complex predications (2.1) and complex terms (2.2) are handled in FG. Next, a general survey will be given of ways in which linguistic expressions may diverge from underlying predications (2.3), followed by some speculations about how these different ways may combine with each other, and whether there might be some sort of (historical?) hierarchy involved in this. Then, we shall see what sorts of descriptive solutions might be proposed for handling discrepancies between underlying predication and expression form within the framework of FG (2.4), and what sorts of criteria can be brought to bear on the comparative evaluation of such solutions. Finally, Section 2.5 gives some illustrative facts from Modern Greek, a language which will not be further discussed in this volume.

2.1 Complex predications

Most phenomena to be discussed in this volume concern the ways in which complex predications can be expressed. Complex predications are predications which contain other predications embedded within them. Complex predications will be distinguished from compound predications, which consist of pairs or series of predications conjoined with each other and which will not be discussed in the present context. Complex predications are also to be distinguished from complex terms, which will be discussed in Section 2.2. Given these distinctions we can be somewhat more precise about the nature of complex predications. Complex predications are predictions in which one or more term positions (= argument or satellite positions) are specified by a predication. Thus, the following construction expresses a complex predication:

(1)   John believes that Bill loves Sally

Here, *believe* is a two-place relation between a person, *John*, and something that person believes, expressed by *that Bill loves Sally*. Accordingly, we shall set up the following predicate-frame for *believe*:

(2)   believe$_V$ (x$_1$)$_{Po}$ (x$_2$)$_{Go}$

In this predicate-frame it is indicated that the first argument of *believe* has the semantic function Positioner, and the second argument the semantic function Goal. The whole predicate-frame designates a set of Positions (Positions are non-dynamic, controlled states of affairs; cf. Dik (1978, ch. 3) for discussion and motivation).

   Given the rules for Subject assignment in English,[1] this predicate-frame correctly predicts that Subject can be assigned to the second argument, so that we may get passive constructions such as:

(3)   That Bill loves Sally is believed by John

(4)   It is believed by John that Bill loves Sally

We must now add some more information on the combinatory possibilities of *believe* to the predicate-frame given in (2): it must be indicated that *believe* takes human Positioners, and that its Goal position can be filled by predications. This we shall express in the following way:

(5)   believe$_V$ (x$_1$: human(x$_1$))$_{Po}$ (sub x$_2$: [PREDICATION] (x$_2$))$_{Go}$

Here, human(x$_1$) is a selection restriction on the possible fillers of the Positioner argument. The status of the restiction on the Goal argument position is somewhat different: *sub* indicates some sort of subordinating device, later to be specified by expression rules, and PREDICATION indicates a position into which a full new predication can be inserted, expressing the content of what is believed. The bracketing structure indicates that such a predication can be taken to specify "that which is believed", symbolized by the term variable (x_2). Notice that the second argument of *believe* will thus be a *term* referring to some entity x_j, where this entity is described by a predication. Given the conventions discussed in Chapter 1, we can now give the full predication underlying sentence (1):

(6)   Pres believe$_V$ (d1x_i: John$_N$(x_i))$_{Po}$

     (sub x_j: [Pres love$_V$ (d1x_k: Bill$_N$(x_k))$_{Po}$ (d1x_1: Sally$_N$(x_1))$_{Go}$](x_j))$_{Go}$

Notice that *love*, just like *believe*, is here analysed as a Position. Further, consider one reason why it is useful to have a distinct term variable, x_j, for the second term of *believe*: anaphorical reference is captured in FG by building anaphorical terms of the form (Ax_α), coreferential to some term indicated by x_α in the context. Now, terms specified by embedded predications can be referred to anaphorically in the same way as terms specified by nominal predicates. Thus, suppose that sentence (1) is continued as follows:

(7)   . . . but he does not like it

Using the convention for anaphorical terms, this could then be represented by:

(8)   . . . but Pres neg like$_V$ (Ax$_i$)$_{Po}$ (Ax$_j$)$_{Go}$

where later expression rules will have to specify the anaphorical terms as *he* and *it*, respectively.[2]

It is clear then that predications are recursive through embedded predications and that embedding of predications into term positions of higher predications results in hierarchical structures. We shall also say that each predication defines a domain and that the domain of an embedded predication is enclosed within the domain of the matrix predication.

Given this terminology we can say that the expression (1) is congruent with its underlying predication, because the domain structure of the expression, which can be indicated as:

(9)   (John believes (that Bill loves Sally))

faithfully reflects the domain structure of the underlying predication. However, in a construction of the form:

(10)   Who does John believe to love Sally?

there is a discrepancy between underlying predication and expression form: the constituent *who*, which semantically belongs to the embedded predication, is placed outside the subordinate clause which expresses this embedded predication. We can say that *who* has been placed outside its proper domain in (10), and thus it is more difficult in (10) than it is in (1) to reconstruct the underlying predication on the basis of the formal properties of the expression.

2.2 Complex terms

In Chapter 1 we saw how terms can be formed according to FG, and in (18)–(20) of that chapter some examples of different types of terms were given. In the underlying structure of a term, there will be one or more "open predications in x_i" (where x_i is the term variable), which act as restrictors on the set of possible referents for the term in question and are successively stacked on to each other through the "such that" relation indicated by " : ". From this it is clear that there is an essential difference between predications as they occur in the underlying structure of terms and predications which are embedded within complex predications: the former are "open" predications, imposing conditions on possible referent properties; the latter are closed predications, which themselves specify a referent. Predications thus play quite different roles in the formation of terms and in the construction of complex predications.

The open predications which act as restrictors in term formation can be expressed in different ways in the form of terms. Usually, the first nominal restrictor provides the Head of the term phrase, and later restrictors are expressed as either phrasal or clausal Modifiers. Phrasal Modifiers may be nominal, as in *a paper box*, adjectival, as in *a wooden box*, prepositional, as in *the chair in the garden*, or participial, as in *the chair standing in the garden*. Clausal Modifiers take the form of (restrictive) relative clauses.

Let us consider the following complex term:

(11) $(d1x_i: man_N(x_i): Past kill_V (x_i)_{Ag}(d1x_j: Bill_N(x_j))_{Go})$

(12) the   man   who killed Bill

In this case, again, we can say that the expression (12) is congruent with its underlying representation, because Head and Modifier are neatly set apart from each other and everything which expresses the content of the second restrictor is in its proper domain.

Quite a few languages, however, have term expressions which cannot be so easily regarded as a direct mapping of underlying structures of the form (11). Thus, for a construction which in English would come out as (13), such languages have constructions which look like (14):

(13)   I need the book which John read

(14)   I need which John read book

Constructions of the form (14) provide great difficulties for probably every approach to the description of relative clauses. They either require a radical revision of standard ways of looking at such clause types (as suggested in Schachter (1973), who proposed his "promotion analysis" on the basis of such cases as these), or they force us to assume that in this case, again, there is lack of congruence between underlying representation and expression form. If the latter course is taken, we should like to have some principled account of how underlying representations of type (11) could lead to term expressions corresponding to (14).

A number of problems connected with this question will be discussed in Rijksbaron's paper on Ancient Greek relative clause formation (Chapter 11).

2.3   Types of differences between underlying structure and expression form

In the discussions contained in this volume we will see that there are a number of different ways in which a linguistic expression can depart from what one would expect on the basis of the underlying structure:

2.3.1   Displacement

We shall speak of *displacement* when a constituent is placed outside the domain defined by the predication to which it belongs. Displacement is a common phenomenon in questions, as in:

(15)   What do you think Mary believes John has bought?

Here the question word underlyingly belongs to the predication *John bought Q-x_i*, but it is placed in the P1 position of the highest clause. This is the phenomenon known as unbounded movement within the framework of Transformational Grammar. Within that framework, two alternative solutions have been proposed for handling this phenomenon: in the first, the question word is brought to initial position in one fell swoop; in the second, the questioned constituent is successively moved up clause by clause, until it reaches its final destination. Given the restrictions imposed on FG, only the equivalent of the first solution would be allowed within this model: we need a placement rule which immediately carries the questioned Goal constituent of *John bought Q-x$_i$* to the clause-initial P1 position.

It is not too difficult to understand how displacement of question words might come about. Many languages strongly prefer or even require questioned constituents to take clause-initial position. If such languages at the same time allow term positions within embedded predications to be questioned then they face a dilemma: either they must give up the principle that question words go to clause-initial position or they must allow the domain structure of the underlying predication to be breached. The latter course appears to be taken in many languages. Displacement, however, is not restricted to questioned terms. Consider the following sentences from Serbo-Croatian (Gvozdanović, Chapter 6).

(16)   Mislio   sam   da   je   vidio dečko most
       thought I-am that he-is seen   boy   bridge
       "I thought that the boy had seen the bridge"

(17)   Mislio sam dečko da je vidio most

(18)   Mislio sam most   da je vidio dečko

In (16) the sentence structure is congruent with the underlying predication: all the constituents of the embedded predication are expressed within the domain of the subordinate clause, which starts with the subordinating particle *da*. However, in (17) the constituent *dečko*, and in (18) the constituent *most*, are outside the domain of the subordinate clause, and thus exemplify a case of displacement. Note that these constituents retain their proper form: nominative and accusative, respectively. For further discussion, see Gvozdanović, Chapter 6.[3]

The interpretation of constructions of the general form of (17)–(18) is not always self-evident. This has to do with the question of whether we must assume that constructions with Theme, Predication organization can occur in subordinate clauses. Most languages have such constructions in main clauses, and it has been argued (Dik, 1978, ch. 6) that in such cases the Theme must be considered as being outside the Predication proper from the very start. Thus, constructions of the form:

(19)   That boy, John saw him on the bridge

are considered as consisting of an isolated term *that boy* in Theme function, followed by a full predication which contains a term coreferential with the Theme (*him*). On this analysis, then, a construction such as (19) does not exemplify a case of displacement: the Theme is outside the predication from the very start. Now, in general it is much more difficult to get this type of organization within embedded predications. Compare English:

(20) As for Paris, the Eiffel tower is impressive

(21) ?I find that, as for Paris, the Eiffel tower is impressive

(22) ?I find, as for Paris, that the Eiffel tower is impressive

Sentences with embedded Theme, Predication constructions thus in general seem less acceptable or even ungrammatical. In certain languages, however, there seem to be good reasons for assuming that such organization *can* occur in embedded predications. This means that, in such languages, it is not immediately clear whether constructions of the form:

(23) I believe the boy that he has seen the bridge

must be regarded as resulting from displacement of *the boy* from the embedded predication, or from embedding a construction in which *the boy* is an independent Theme constituent from the very start.

Several chapters in this volume will touch on aspects of this question as it presents itself in Hungarian (De Groot, Chapter 3), Latin (Bolkestein, Chapter 4), Serbo-Croatian (Gvozdanović, Chapter 6), and Spoken Dutch (Dik, Chapter 5).

How could the occurrence of displacement phenomena be explained? That is, why should languages place constituents outside their proper domain, thus breaking up or at least obscuring the transparency of the relation between expression form and underlying predication? We have no clear answer to this question, but we would like to adduce some considerations which might provide elements for arriving at an explanation.

We saw that displacement is a rather common phenomenon in Q-word questions, corresponding to the strong preference of many languages for having Q-words in clause-initial position. This preference, again, is linked to the fact that questioned terms inherently have the pragmatic function Focus, and that placement of Focus constituents in clause-initial position is a strategy strongly favoured in many languages. Displacement of non-questioned terms might be induced, then, by the parallelism between questions and answers: in many languages, the answer to a Q-word question has the same properties of form and order as the question itself, so that the constituent answering the questioned term is also placed in clause-initial position. Thus, many languages have parallelisms of the following form:

(24)   To whom has John given the book?

(25)   To Peter has John given the book.

On the basis of questions such as (26), then, this parallelism would induce constructions of the form (27), with displacement of non-questioned terms:

(26)   To whom did Harry believe John had given the book?

(27)   To Peter did Harry believe John had given the book.

A second explanatory line might lie in parallelisms such as between:

(28)   John saw Peter leave the office

(29)   John believed Peter to leave the office

In (28) there are good reasons for regarding *Peter* as an independent argument of the verb *see*, followed by a complement containing a predication describing what John saw Peter do. There are many semantic differences between:

(30)   John saw that Peter left the office

(31)   John saw Peter leave the office

which require us to regard *see* as a two-place predicate in (30), but as a three-place predicate in (31).[4] In the case of *believe*, however, there are no comparable differences, so that there is little reason to distinguish two different predicate-frames for this verb. One might think, however, that constructions of the form (31) which are independently required for verbs like *see*, have influenced *believe* to slide into similar patterns (note that verbs of perception and verbs of cognition in a great many languages have similar semantic and grammatical properties).

Another possible explanation for displacement might lie in a presumed tendency of speakers to construe the world in terms of relations between persons and things rather than between persons and states of affairs, or between states of affairs and other states of affairs (cf. Bolkestein, 1976, 280ff.). Compare, in this respect, the following constructions:

(32)   It seems that John is ill

(33)   John seems to be ill

(34)   John is ill, so it seems

In (32) *seem* is contrued as a predicate which takes a predication as an argument and thus assigns some property to some state of affairs. On the other hand (33) has at least the *form* of a predication assigning some property to John. In (34) John is even more clearly the protagonist of the message.

We saw that in certain cases we find displacement in pure form, i.e. a form in which a positional difference is the only difference from the pattern which we would expect on the basis of the structure of the underlying predication. In many instances, however, displacement of constituents is combined with more radical departures from what would be expected on the basis of the underlying predication. Thus, we find cases of "morphological adjustment" and of "non-finite expression" in different combinations with displacement.

2.3.2   Morphological adjustment

We speak of morphological adjustment when some constituent takes on a morphological form other than would be expected on the basis of its functional status within the predication, under the influence of the syntactic environment in which it is expressed. Compare the following two constructions:

(35)   a   I appreciate that she answered my letter so quickly
      b   I appreciate her answering my letter so quickly

In (35a) the embedded predication is realized in finite form, and the Agent-Subject of *answered* takes on the expected nominative form. In (35b) the embedded predication is expressed in a non-finite form, and in this case the Agent of the embedded verb must be realized in possessive or genitive form. We say that its form is morphologically adjusted to the non-finite expression format of the embedded predication.

In the case of displacement, morphological adjustment is triggered by the higher verb in whose domain the displaced argument enters. Consider the following examples:

(36)   a   John believed *her* to like Peter
      b   *She* was believed by John to like Peter

In (36a) the displaced constituent *her*, which semantically must be considered to be an argument of *like*, takes the case which would fit it if it were an Object argument of *believe*. In (36b) *she* has the case form which would fit it if it were a Goal-Subject argument of *believe*. This is reinforced by the fact that the passive verb *was believed* agrees with *she*. Such terms, which have been displaced and morphologically adjusted to the Verb of the higher domain, we shall call "pseudo-arguments" of that higher verb.

The examples at the same time exemplify those rules with respect to which morphological adjustment commonly takes place, namely case assignment and agreement. In general the following picture seems justified: a constituent comes into the sphere of influence of some higher verb through displacement; the higher verb exerts a certain force on the displaced constituent to adapt morphologically to its new environment; this force may be resisted, or it may be yielded to. In the latter case, the constituent in question becomes a pseudo-argument of the higher verb. One could imagine that further developments might even lead to a situation in which the pseudo-argument develops into a genuine argument of the higher verb, and thus yields a newly formed predicate-frame, to be added to the lexicon.

Factors relevant to such possible developments will be discussed by Vet (on French, Chapter 7), Dik (on Portuguese, Chapter 8), and Combé (on Spanish, Chapter 9).

2.3.3   Non-finite expression of the embedded predicate

Another common corollary of displacement is that the embedded predicate, left within its proper domain, is expressed in some non-finite (infinitival, participial, gerundival) form, rather than in the form of a finite verb. Compare in this respect the following constructions:

(37)   John believes that Mary has been kissed by Peter

(38)   John believes Mary to have been kissed by Peter

(39)   *John believes Mary that (she) has been kissed by Peter

From these examples we see that when the embedded Subject, *Mary*, is displaced from its embedded predication (and morphologically adjusted, although this is not apparent in this case), the remainder of the embedded predication must, in English, be realized in non-finite form.

This constraint operative in the grammar of English is by no means universally valid: there are many languages in which constituents can be displaced from embedded predications, or displaced and morphologically adjusted, without the remainder of the embedded predication taking on some non-finite form. Some examples from Serbo-Croatian were given in (17)–(18) above. Further cases from Hungarian, Latin, and Portuguese will be discussed later in the relevant chapters.

As far as our data go, it seems correct to say that non-finite expression of the embedded predicate presupposes morphological adjustment of the main argument of that predicate, i.e. we know of no languages in which constructions corresponding to the following are well-formed:

(39)   *John believes she to have been kissed by Peter

(40)   *John believes that she to have been kissed by Peter

In (39) there would be displacement, no morphological adjustment, and non-finite expression of the embedded predicate. In (40) there would be non-finite expression of the embedded predicate, without either displacement or morphological adjustment.

On the other hand, non-finite expression of the embedded predication does not seem to require prior displacement of the main argument of the embedded predicate. Thus, in English *for-to* complements such as:

(41)   John expected for her to be kissed by Peter

there is non-finite expression and morphological adjustment (*her* takes on the form required by *for*), but it is not clear that we must assume that *her* in this construction has been displaced to a position outside the domain of the embedded predication. Similarly, in constructions of the form:

(42)   John believes Sally's having been kissed by Peter

there is a form of morphological adjustment, but this adjustment is triggered by the nominal character of the embedded construction rather than by some requirement imposed by the higher predicate. Again, there seems to be no reason to assume that *Sally's* in (42) has been displaced to a position outside its proper domain.

Another case of non-finite expression of embedded predications, with morphological adjustment, but without clear indications of displacement, is the so-called accusativus-cum-infinitivo construction in Latin, which some have wanted to describe in terms of a Raising (= displacement + morphological adjustment) operation. As Bolkestein (1979) has demonstrated, however, such an analysis cannot be maintained, because there are a number of construction types in which the accusative case cannot be explained in terms of adjustment to the requirements of some higher verb. Such a view might be entertained for cases like (43), but it cannot be maintained in the light of cases like (44) and (45):

(43) dixit   viros   venisse
      he-said men-acc to-have-come
      "He said the men to have come"

(44) viros   venisse   constat
      men-acc to-have-come it-is-certain
      "It is certain for the men to have come"

(45) viros   venisse   dictum est
      men-acc to-have-come said   it-is
      "It was said for the men to have come"

On the basis of such cases it must be assumed that the accusativus-cum-infinitivo construction in Latin is simply an alternative way for expressing the content of an embedded predication. Again, the morphological form of the accusativus cannot be thought to be triggered by the influence of some foreign domain to which some constituent has been brought through displacement.

It should be added here that there is no clear evidence either that the Latin accusativus-cum-infinitivo construction *historically* derives from a construction type in which there was clear displacement+morphological adjustment+non-finite expression. Nor is there any evidence, however, which could demonstrate that such a development could not have occurred.

As far as we have been able to determine, then, the following schema gives a fair picture of the possible combinations of displacement, morphological adjustment, and non-finite expression in the expression of embedded predications:

	DISPLACEMENT	MORPHOLOGICAL ADJUSTMENT	NON-FINITE EXPRESSION
(46) a	+		
b	+	+	
c	+	+	+
d		+	+

The tentative generalizations embodied in this schema are the following:

(i) there is no non-finite expression without some form of morphological adjustment; therefore:

(ii) non-finite expression does not occur with *only* displacement, although it may occur without displacement.

A last type of discrepancy between underlying predication and actual expression form was mentioned in Chapter 1, example (7). This concerns the so-called AB URBE CONDITA construction of Latin. This construction type provides us with expressions which could be literally rendered as:

(47) After the destroyed city the soldiers built a camp in the neighbourhood

where the intended meaning is clearly something like:

(48) a After the destruction of the city . . .
      b After having destroyed the city . . .

Thus, the intended meaning relates to some event, for which the underlying structure would take the form of a predication, whereas the actual expression has the form of a description of some entity having a certain property. This type of discrepancy between underlying representation and expression form is described in terms of an expression rule involving a shift of category in Bolkestein's paper on this construction in this volume (Chapter 10).

2.4 Possible solutions

Suppose that we find, in a given language, pairs of constructions related to each other in ways similar to the following English pairs:

(49) a John saw that Peter arrived at the office
      b John saw Peter arrive at the office

(50) a John believed that Peter had arrived
      b John believed Peter to have arrived

The question is: how are we to handle such pairs? The first question to be asked is the following: should the a and b sentences be derived from one underlying predication, or not? If not, then we must assume that there are at least two distinct predicate-frames for such verbal predicates as *see*, *believe*, etc. In that case, there are again two possibilities: either the two distinct predicate-frames must both be considered as basic, and thus as occurring in the lexicon side by side. Or one of them could be derived from the other through some rule of predicate formation. Predicate formation rules are rules which take predicate-frames as input and deliver derived predicate-frames as output. See Fig. 1 (p. 5) for their position in the overall model of the grammar.[5]

Predicate-frames are thought to designate sets of states of affairs. Thus, if it can be demonstrated that the a- and b-constructions in pairs such as (49)–(50) designate different sets of states of affairs, then it follows that they must be based on different underlying predicate-frames. If this cannot be demonstrated, then it does not necessarily follow that they are based on one underlying predicate-frame: they might still have different, but synonymous underlying frames. However, the chance that one underlying predicate-frame must be postulated in such a case naturally increases.

Note that semantic differences of perspective, or pragmatic differences pertaining to Topic and Focus distribution do not count as creating differences with respect to the states of affairs designated: such differences, according to FG, do not affect the basic identity of the underlying predicate-frame. Conversely, stating that two constructions are built on the same underlying predicate-frame is not to say that they are fully synonymous: they are then synonymous up to those semantic and informational differences which are taken care of through the assignment of syntactic and pragmatic functions.

How do we find out whether or not two constructions designate the same set of states of affairs? One method is to try to find situations in which someone committed to the truth of (a) is not necessarily committed to the truth of (b). Consider the following pair:

(51) a   John saw that Pollini played Chopin
      b   John saw Pollini play Chopin

Now, think of a situation in which John is browsing through the art pages of some magazine. In such a situation someone believing that (51a) is truly said of John, is not committed to hold (51b) true as well. This shows that there are states of affairs which can be described by (51a) but not by (51b). This is sufficient to conclude that the two constructions must have different underlying predicate-frames. But it is easy to find further confirmation for the difference between (a) and (b) in this case. Consider the following pairs:

(52) a   John saw that Pollini had played Chopin
      b   *John saw Pollini have played Chopin

(53) a   John saw that Pollini played Chopin, but he did not see
Pollini

   b   *John saw Pollini play Chopin, but he did not see Pollini

We can see now that the (b) construction in this case requires that John
actually (immediately) perceive the other entity mentioned, whereas in
the (a) construction it may be the case that John only indirectly learns
about some fact being the case.

Once we know this, we can apply another method which often yields
information on identity or difference between underlying predicate-
frames: study the selection restrictions on the major terms in the constructions involved, and try to find differences between them (for applications
of this method see Bolkestein, 1980).

Again, this method will yield certain results in the case of the verb *see*,
pointing to differences in underlying predicate-frame. Compare:

(54) a   John saw that the invisible ink worked
   b   ?John saw the invisible ink work

(55) a   John saw that hatred tore apart the parties
   b   ?John saw hatred tear apart the parties

On all these counts, then, we conclude that *see* requires two distinct
predicate-frames which can be roughly represented as follows:[6]

(56) see_V (x_1 : anim(x_1))$_{Exp}$ (x_2 : [. . .] (x_2))$_{Go}$

(57) see_V (x_1 : anim(x_1))$_{Exp}$ (x_2)$_{Go}$ (x_3 : [. . . (x_2) . . .] (x_3))$_{Compl}$

Thus, *see* in (56) is a two-place relation between an animate entity and
some state of affairs; *see* in (57) is a three-place relation between an animate
entity, another entity, and some state of affairs in which the second entity
participates. In the second case, but not in the former, it is required that
the Experiencer actually perceive the Goal.

None of the methods used in differentiating the two predicate-frames
for *see* will yield comparable differences in the case of the pairs (50a, b)
with *believe*. Thus, we may provisionally assume that these two constructions are based on the same underlying predicate-frame (for more discussion of this, see Dik, 1979).

If two different construction types are to be derived from the same
underlying predicate-frame, the question is how this is to be done. If the
difference between the two constructions is a matter of pure displacement.

then this difference can be accounted for rather simply at the stage where constituent order is determined (here we must reckon with the possible complication with respect to the Theme, Predication construction, discussed in Section 2.3).

If, however, there are more profound differences between the two constructions, this solution will not be sufficient. For English constructions with *believe* it can be shown that in such cases as the following the displaced constituent fully acts as if it were an argument of the higher *believe* verb:

(58)   John believed *Mary* to have been kissed by Peter

(59)   *Mary* was believed by John to have been kissed by Peter

For this reason it has been proposed (Dik, 1979, 1980a) to account for these constructions in terms of special assignments of Subject and Object function. On this approach, it is assumed that in (58) the Object function relevant to the *believe*-level is exceptionally assigned to the Subject of the embedded predication, and that in (59) the Subject function relevant to the *believe*-level is exceptionally assigned to the Subject of the embedded predication.

According to this method, the underlying predication of (58) will get the following form:

(60)   believe$_V$ (d1x$_i$: John(x$_i$))$_{PoSubj}$
       (d1x$_j$: [kiss$_V$ (d1x$_k$: Peter(x$_k$))$_{Ag}$ (d1x$_l$: Mary(x$_l$))$_{GoSubjObj}$] (x$_j$))$_{Go}$

Thus, *John* is characterized as the Positioner and the Subject with respect to *believe*. The Goal of *believe*, marked by x$_j$, is specified by a predication defined by a *kiss*-relation between *Peter* as Agent and *Mary* as Goal. Within this predication, *Mary* has received Subject function; this accounts for the passive realization of the complement: . . . *to have been kissed by Peter*. The Obj function relevant to the *believe*-level could have been assigned to the Goal of *believe* (i.e. to the whole predication specifying that which is said to be believed). This would have led to a realization of the form:

(61)   John believed that Mary had been kissed by Peter

In (60), however, the Obj function relevant to the *believe*-level has exceptionally "penetrated" into the embedded predication, and has been assigned to the Subj of that predication, *Mary*. Thus, this constituent exceptionally has two distinct syntactic functions: Subj within its own domain with respect to the predicate *kiss* and Obj within the higher domain with respect to *believe*. The extra Obj function will now trigger expression rules to the effect that the constituent *Mary* takes on the form and the position which are in agreement with its status as Obj of *believe*. In a similar way, the outcome would be (59) when Subj rather than Obj function—relevant to the *believe*-level—is assigned to the embedded Subj *Mary*.[7]

This method leads to descriptively correct results in the case of English *believe* constructions, but it cannot be applied in the same way to similar constructions in other languages. As De Groot demonstrates in Chapter 3, Hungarian does not make use of the Subject and the Object function. Nevertheless, it has cases of displacement (which can be described in terms of rules sensitive to Topic and Focus function) which, in certain conditions, also require morphological adjustment. It follows that morphological adjustment cannot always be captured in terms of special Subject and Object assignment conventions. In De Groot's solution to this problem, morphological adjustment is brought about by expression rules which assign case at a late moment, after displacement has taken place. This requires at least some form-determining expression rules to operate after constituent order has been determined. Similar possibilities are considered with respect to certain phenomena in Portuguese (Dik, Chapter 8).[8]

Further work will be needed to show to what extent more structure can be detected in the typology of these sorts of phenomena as they are found in different languages. A number of phenomena certainly suggest that there is some hierarchy involved, in which constructions of this type start out as faithful mappings of their underlying predications, start departing from this through displacement and morphological adjustment, developing into pseudo-arguments of the higher predicate, then penetrate even deeper into the grammar through exceptional Subject and Object assignment, and maybe develop from there into distinct constructions which may finally need their own underlying predicate-frame, either derived through predicate formation, or entered into the lexicon in its own right.

2.5 A final illustration

For a final illustration of the sorts of problems to be discussed in this volume, consider the properties of the verb θέlo "I want" in Modern Greek. This illustration is based on the analysis presented in Kakouriotis (1980). I have adapted this analysis to FG terminology, but this does not imply a departure from the basic facts as they are presented by Kakouriotis.

θélo can, in the first place, be construed as a two-place predicate taking some animate first argument and a second argument specified by a predication. The predication can be expressed by means of a subordinate clause introduced by *na* "that":

(62) θélo   na   enas astifílakas frurí   ton ipurγó
      I-want that a   policeman guards the minister

The embedded Subj, however, can also be displaced out if its proper domain:

(63) θélo   enas astifílakas na   frurí   ton ipurγó
      I-want a   policeman that guards the minister
      "I want a policeman to guard the minister".

Notice that *enas astifílakas* in (63) is in the nominative, just as in (62), and that in both construction types the complement following *na* has a finite form. Notice further that, as Kakouriotis (1980) observes, Modern Greek is another language for which the Tensed-S constraint does not hold. The displaced constituent in (63) can morphologically adjust to its higher domain, and appear in the accusative:

(64) θélo   énan astifílaka   na   frurí   ton ipurγó
      I-want a$_{acc}$ policeman$_{acc}$ that guards the minister
      "I want a policeman to guard the minister"

There are no discernible semantic differences between (62), (63) and (64), so it is reasonable to derive these constructions from one underlying predication; (63) can then be taken care of by means of a placement rule which places the embedded Subject outside its proper domain. In (64), we could follow the method described for *believe* above, and assume that the Object function relevant to the *θélo*-level has, in this case, been assigned to the embedded Subject. Or we could assume that the accusative case is determined by some lower-level expression rule which assigns accusative to the constituent which has been displaced into the Object position of the higher verb. In Modern Greek, there are reasons to opt for the former solution, since the displaced constituent in the accusative turns out to have a number of properties characteristic of genuine Objects.

However, (64) can have another interpretation, which can be paraphrased as: "I need a policeman, so that he can guard the minister". In that case, there are several reasons to assume that *énan astifílaka* is a genuine

Goal argument of *θélo* which, correspondingly, must be assumed to have not only a two-place underlying predicate-frame, as in (65a), but also a three-place one, as in (65b):

(65) a $\text{θélo}_V (x_1)_{Exp} (x_2 : [\text{PREDICATION}] (x_2))_{Go}$
      b $\text{θélo}_V (x_1)_{Exp} (x_2)_{Go} (x_3 : [\ldots (x_2) \ldots] (x_3))_{Compl}$

In the latter case, then, *θélo* designates a three-place relation between some person x_1, some other person (or entity) x_2, and some state of affairs x_3 in which x_2 is involved. This frame is thus of the same form as the one which we established for *see* in (57) above.

Although sentences of the form (64) do not codify the difference between (65a) and (65b)—in other words, these sentences are ambiguous between the two underlying structures—Kakouriotis presents a variety of arguments to the effect that there are, indeed, two distinct underlying predicate-frames. Thus, in the case of underlying (65b), but not in the case of (65a), the subordinator *na* can be replaced by *ja na*, which introduces purposive clauses. Consequently, a sentence such as (66) is unambiguous, and can only have the meaning indicated:

(66) θélo énan astifílaka ja na frurí ton ipurγó
      "I need a policeman in order for him to guard the minister"

Further differences are: in the case of (65a), but not in the case of (65b), the predicational clause has Object properties. In (65b), but not in (65a), the complement may be left unexpressed without resulting in an incomplete expression, i.e. the sentence (67) can be used in the sense of "I need a policeman", along the pattern of (65b):

(67) θélo   énan astifílaka
      1-want a   policeman

In (65a), but not in (65b), the complement may be passivized without affecting the semantics of the expression. Thus, (65a) is similar to English *expect*, as in:

(68) a I expect a policeman to guard the minister
      b I expect the minister to be guarded by a policeman

But (65b) is similar to English *persuade*, as in:

(69) a I persuaded a policeman to guard the minister
      b I persuaded the minister to be guarded by a policeman

Finally, there are selection restrictions differentiating the two patterns of
θélo, as in:

(69) θélo   to peδí mu na γíni   enas meγálos epistímonas
      I-want the son my that becomes a   great   scientist
      = "I want my son to become a great scientist"
      ≠ "I need my son, in order for him to become a great scientist"

We thus see that θélo is a verb which occurs in a two-place predicate-frame
from which displacement as well as displacement+morphological adjustment is possible. In addition, a second, three-place predicate-frame has to
be assumed. The expression possibilities of the two underlying frames are
such that genuine ambiguities between the two underlying frames may
occur.

2.6 Conclusion

This chapter has given a survey of the different ways in which languages
can possess discrepancies between underlying predications and their surface
expression forms. We have also seen what sorts of descriptive solutions
for such cases are available within the theoretical framework of FG. It is
hoped that the discussions in this volume will shed some light on the
many problems encountered in this area of grammatical organization,
although they certainly do not pretend to offer any final solution to them.

Notes

1 See Chapter 1 (29).
2 For some further discussion of anaphora, see Dik (1980a).
3 These examples also show that Chomsky's (1973) Tensed-S Constraint does
   not hold for Serbo-Croatian. In this volume we shall encounter several other
   languages in which this constraint does not hold.
4 See section 2.4.
5 See Dik (1980b, ch. 2 and 3) for discussion of the nature of predicate formation rules in FG.
6 I have here assigned the semantic function Experiencer (Exp) to the first
   argument of *see*, although there are some doubts about the status of this
   function (Dik, 1978, 41 ff.; 1980b, 75). Complement (Compl), too, is of
   rather doubtful status. However, in frames of the general form of (57) there
   is often evidence that the third argument does not have the status of Goal.
   For some further discussion, see also Work Group FG (1981).

7   For more detailed discussion, see Dik (1979). This method of handling
    believe constructions has been successfully integrated into Kwee's (1979)
    computer program for a Functional Grammar of English.
8   Compare Chapter 1 (47).

References

BOLKESTEIN, A. Machtelt
    1976   A.c.I.-clauses and *ut*-clauses with verba dicendi in Latin. *Glotta* **54**,
           263–291.
    1979   Subject-to-Object Raising in Latin? *Lingua* **48**, 15–34.
    1980   "Problems in the description of modal verbs; an investigation of Latin".
           Assen, Van Gorcum.
CHOMSKY, Noam
    1973   Conditions on transformations. *In* S. Anderson and P. Kiparsky (ed.).
           "Festschrift for Morris Halle". New York, Holt, Reinhart and Winston.
DIK, Simon C.
    1978   "Functional Grammar". North-Holland Linguistic Series 37. Amster-
           dam, North-Holland.
    1979   Raising in a Functional Grammar. *Lingua* **47**, 119–140.
    1980a Seventeen sentences: basic principles and application of Functional
           Grammar. *In* Edith A. Moravcsik and Jessica R. Wirth (ed.). "Syntax
           and Semantics 13: current approaches to syntax", 45–75. New York
           and London, Academic Press.
    1980b "Studies in Functional Grammar". London and New York, Academic
           Press.
KAKOURIOTIS, A.
    1980   Raising in Modern Greek. *Lingua* **52**, 157–177.
KWEE Tjoe Liong
    1979   "A68–FG(3); Simon Dik's funktionele grammatika geschreven in algol
           68, versie nr. Ø3." Publications of the Institute of General Linguistics,
           University of Amsterdam, no. 23.
SCHACHTER, Paul
    1973   Focus and relativization. *Language* **49**, 19–46.
WORK GROUP FG
    1981   On the Functional Grammar of teaching verbs. *In* Teun Hoekstra *et al.*
           (ed.). "Perspectives on Functional Grammar". Dordrecht, Foris, 203–
           231.

3 Sentence-Intertwining in Hungarian

CASPER DE GROOT

Department of Language and Literature
Tilburg University

3.0 Introduction

Central in the theory of Functional Grammar (FG) (Dik, 1978) stands the predication: the verb and its arguments. For instance:

(1)   give$_V$ (x$_1$: animate (x$_1$))$_{Ag}$ (x$_2$)$_{Go}$ (x$_3$: animate (x$_3$))$_{Rec}$

In this formula is expressed that the verb *give* has three arguments, with the semantic functions Agent, Goal and Recipient, as we can see in an example like:

(2)   John$_{Ag}$ gave Mary$_{Rec}$ a book$_{Go}$

A problem arises when the following sentence is to be described:

(3)   John believed Bill to have killed the farmer

In certain respects, the constituent Bill behaves as Subj of *kill* (Bill killed), in other respects as Obj of *believe* (John believed Bill).

Dik started the discussion of this problem within the framework of FG in "Raising in a Functional Grammar" (Dik, 1979). He discusses two ways of tackling "Raising" and suggests that "a cross-linguistic study of 'raising' possibilities might lead to interesting results". With this chapter I hope to contribute to the investigation of "Raising" in FG by discussing a type of sentence in Hungarian in which parts of one clause can be found in another one. I have borrowed the term "sentence-intertwining" from Zolnai (1926, *Mondatátszövődés*), who first discussed this phenomenon in Hungarian.

In the first section I will give a rough outline of FG of Hungarian, in particular of the assignment of syntactic and pragmatic functions and word order (see Dik, 1978, and Chapter 1 section 1.2). In Section 3.2 I continue with word order, especially with those cases in which a constituent can be placed in a clause other than that in which it belongs according to the predication in which it occurs. Section 3.3 deals with those examples in which this special word order has morphological consequences. In the course of describing these examples of "Raising" it will become clear that the two solutions proposed by Dik are not applicable and therefore I shall postulate a third one.

3.1   Function assignment in Hungarian

3.1.1   *Syntactic function assignment*

Since there is only one voice in Hungarian, the syntactic function Subj can only be assigned to Agent, or, depending on the state of affairs, to for instance Force or Positioner. It cannot be assigned to arguments with other semantic functions, for instance Goal or Recipient. In other words, no alternative assignment is possible. A passive construction corresponding to English

(4)   The book was read by Peter

does not exist in Hungarian. The passive construction does exist in nominal constituents:

(5)   A   Péter által olvasott könyv az asztalon volt
      The Peter by   read   book the table-on was
      "The book read by Peter was on the table"

The construction within the nominal constituent can be obtained, however, without Subj assignment. The structure of the term is

(6) $(d1x_i: book (x_i): [read_V (x_j: Peter (x_j))_{Ag} (x_i)_{Go}]_{Action})$

It can be read as: the book such that Peter read it. Note that the predication is a part of the term and that the second argument of that predication has the same index as the head. An expression rule ensures that the output of (6) will be (7a) or (7b):

(7)   a   the book read by Peter
      b   the book that Peter read

(For the structure of terms, see Dik, 1978, ch. 4.)
Differences in pairs of sentences like

(8) a   A   kert   rajzik   méhektől
The garden swarms bees-from
"The garden is swarming with bees"

b   A   méhek rajzanak a   kertben
The bees   swarm   the garden-in
"The bees are swarming in the garden"

are not due to a Subj assignment to *méhek* "bees" in (8b), but to the fact
that the two sentences designate different states of affairs, resp. Process and
Action.

The syntactic function Obj is ruled by similar limitations: no alternative
assignment is possible, only the Goal is eligible for this function. No pair
of sentences comparable to the following English sentences exists in
Hungarian:

(9) a   Peter gave Mary a book
b   Peter gave a book to Mary

According to the Semantic Function Hierarchy (SFH) (Dik, 1978,
69ff.) the following schema can be set up for Hungarian:

	Ag	Go	Rec	Ben	Instr	Loc	Temp
Subj	+	—	—	—	—	—	—
Obj		+	—	—	—	—	—

"cut-off point"

The fact that there is no alternative assignment of syntactic functions
renders these functions irrelevant for a description of the Hungarian
language, i.e. they are superfluous. The following predication will, with or
without syntactic functions, yield only sentence (11):

(10) ad_V $(Péter)_{Ag(Subj)}$ $(könyv)_{Go(Obj)}$ $(Mari)_{Rec}$
gave   Peter   book   Mary

(11)   péter   könyvet adott Marinak
$Peter_{nom}$ $book_{acc}$ gave $Mary_{dat}$
"Peter gave Mary a book"

For the time being we assume that the correspondence between the
semantic functions and the cases is as follows: Agent, Force etc.[1] will be

expressed by the nominative, the Goal by the accusative and the Recipient by the dative.

The absence of syntactic function assignment in Hungarian also finds support in the fact that terms with only a semantic function are usually not bound to a special position in the sentence (Dik, 1978, 74). Let us consider (10) again.

(10)   adv (Péter)$_{Ag}$ (könyv)$_{Go}$ (Mari)$_{Rec}$

This predication can produce the following sentences:

(12)   a   Péter könyvet adott Marinak
        b   Könyvet adott Péter Marinak
        c   Marinak könyvet adott Péter
        d   Adott Péter könyvet Marinak
             etc.

All the twenty-four possible permutations are grammatical Hungarian sentences. Because there are so many word orders in the Hungarian language, it has been considered for a long time as a free word order language. It is not that free, however: all examples under (12) can only occur in a specific context or situation.

3.1.2 Pragmatic function assignment

While syntactic functions play no role in Hungarian, pragmatic functions are all the more important. I shall not discuss different types of Topic and Focus here, because it is not relevant for the aim of this chapter. Topic and Focus are defined as follows (Dik, 1978, 129ff.):

Topic: The Topic presents the entity "about" which the predication predicates something in a given setting.

Focus: The Focus presents what is relatively the most important or salient information in a given setting.

For Hungarian I assume the following functional pattern (see Dik 1978, ch. 8, on the order of constituents):

(13)   P1 Pφ V X

In this schema P stands for (special) position, V for Verb and X for any number of terms. The functional pattern is understood to present the order of constituents in Hungarian (for word order in Hungarian, see

Horváth and Kiss). The special positions can only be filled with terms carrying some pragmatic function. P1 is reserved for Topic and Pφ for Focus. For instance, (14) is the predication underlying (15):

(14)   ad$_V$ (Péter)$_{AgTop}$ (könyv)$_{GoFoc}$ (Mari)$_{Rec}$

(15)   Péter könyvet adott Marinak
     P1   Pφ V   X

With a different pragmatic function assignment to this predication:

(16)   ad$_V$ (Péter)$_{AgTop}$ (könyv)$_{Go}$ (Mari)$_{RecFoc}$

we would get another expression:

(17)   Péter Marinak adott könyvet
     P1   Pφ V   X

Topic assignment to more than one term is possible, e.g.:

(18)   ad$_V$ (Péter)$_{AgTop}$ (könyv)$_{GoFoc}$ (Mari)$_{RecTop}$

This predication has (19) as output:

(19)   a   Péter Marinak könyvet adott
     b   Marinak Péter könyvet adott
            P1   Pφ V

Thus, a special property of P1 position in Hungarian is that it can accommodate more than one constituent at a time. The alternative word order of Topics within P1 are difficult to account for. For the time being we assume that order within P1 is free. Thus, there would be no difference in meaning or context between (19a) and (19b).[2]

In contradistinction to P1, Pφ does not have that special property since only a single term can fill the Focus-position. Some terms obligatorily go to Pφ for instance those with a question word or with a "csak-operator" (*csak* "only") (see Horváth and Kiss):

(20)   a   Péter melyik könyvet adta Marinak?
         Peter which book   gave Mary-to
         P1   Pφ V   X

     b   Péter csak könyvet adott Marinak
         Peter only book   gave Mary-to
         P1   Pφ V   X

A sentence with both a question word and a "csak-constituent" in Focus-position is ungrammatical:

(21) a *[Ki csak szerdán]$_{Foc}$ dolgozik?
         Who only Wednesday-on works
      b *[Csak szerdán ki]$_{Foc}$ dolgozik?

What has been said for the main clause also applies to the subordinate clause, e.g.:

(22) mond$_V$ (Péter)$_{AgTop}$ ([vár$_V$ (Éva)$_{AgTop}$ (te)$_{GoFoc}$])$_{GoFoc}$
      say   Peter   wait Eva   you

brings forth:

(23) Péter$_{Top}$ azt$_{Foc}$ mondta, hogy Éva$_{Top}$ téged$_{Foc}$ várt
      P1   Pφ V   P1   Pφ V
      Peter$_{nom}$ that$_{acc}$ said   that Eva$_{nom}$ you$_{acc}$ waited
      "Peter said that Eva waited for you"

What we see is that the subordinate clause has the same functional pattern as the main clause. The P1 and Pφ positions of the subordinate clause have the same properties as those of the main clause. P1 can accommodate more than one constituent, e.g.:

(24) János azt mondta, hogy [holnap   Zsuzsa]$_{Top}$ [nem]$_{Foc}$ jön
      John that said   that tomorrow Zsuzsa   not   come
      'John said, that Zsuzsa does not come tomorrow'

The order within the Topic position is free:

(25) János azt mondta, hogy [Zsuzsa holnap]$_{Top}$ [nem]$_{Foc}$ jön

There is a problem here in that it is difficult to ascertain in what position the subordinator *hogy* "that" is. This problem, however, is too complicated to discuss here.[3] Moreover it is not relevant for the description of sentence-intertwining.

Every clause has a Focus-position, which can be filled with a single term.[4] The ungrammaticality of (21a) and (21b) was a result of there being two constituents in Pφ position. The alternative solution, which is grammatical, is as follows:

(26) Ki   az, aki csak szerdán   dolgozik?
      Who that who only wednesday-on works
      Pφ V   P1   Pφ V

Both terms that have to be placed in Focus-position occur in Pφ now, in the main clause and in the subordinate clause respectively. Note that *Ki az* "who (is) it" is a nominal sentence. The nominal predicate is in V position.

According to LIPOC (language-independent preferred order of constituents) (Dik, 1978, 192ff.) subordinate clauses prefer the final position in the clause. In Hungarian, too, this tendency is present; however, a dummy element representing the subordinate clause will also appear in the main clause. Let us consider (22) and (23) again. In (22) we see that the second argument of the verb *mond* is a predication itself and will therefore be expressed by a subordinate clause and a dummy element. This dummy carries the functions (semantic and pragmatic) of the clause which it represents. In our example the functions are Go and Foc. The basic form of the dummy is *az* "that$_{nom}$". The Goal function triggers the accusative, thus *az+t*; the Focus function fixes the position, i.e. Pφ. Sentence (23) shows the result: the dummy element is in the accusative and in Pφ position; the subordinate clause is in final position in the clause.

The following example illustrates what happens if Topic had been assigned to the second argument of the verb *mond* and Focus to the first argument:

(27)   mond$_V$ (Péter)$_{AgFoc}$ ([vár$_V$ (Éva)$_{AgTop}$ (te)$_{GoFoc}$])$_{GoTop}$

(28)   Azt$_{Top}$ Péter$_{Foc}$ mondta, hogy Éva$_{Top}$ téged$_{Foc}$ várt
      that$_{acc}$ Peter$_{nom}$ said   that Eva$_{nom}$ you$_{acc}$ waited
      P1   Pφ   V   P1   Pφ   V

3.2   Displacement

In Hungarian it is possible to place a constituent in a clause other than that in which it belong according to the predication in which it occurs. Examples of displacement are:

(29)   Mari   nem hiszem, hogy ismeri   Chomskyt
      Mary$_{nom}$ not believe-I that knows-she Chomsky$_{acc}$
      "I do not believe that Mary knows Chomsky"

(30)   Az   egyetemet   husz   éves volt   amikor elkezdte
      The university$_{acc}$ twenty years was-he when   started-he
      "He was twenty years when he started university"

It is quite obvious that the constructions with displacement are marked. The speaker will only take a constituent out of its surroundings and put it somewhere else if that particular constituent is pragmatically marked. This explains why the displaced constituents are only found in P1 and Pφ, the positions reserved for Topic and Focus. When we take a closer look at the predication underlying (29) we see that the constituent *Mari* is Topic "twice" in the sense that it has Topic function itself, and that it occurs in a predication which has Topic function:

(31)   Neg$_{Foc}$ hisz$_V$ (én)$_{Po}$ ([ismer$_V$ (Mari)$_{\theta Top}$ (Chomsky)$_{Go}$])$_{GoTop}$
        Not   believe I   know   Mary   Chomsky

Topic has been assigned to the second argument of the verb *hisz* "believe". This second argument happens to be a predication in which Topic has been assigned to the first argument of the verb *ismer* "know".

As shown in Section 3.1.2 the unmarked output of (31) will be:

(32)   Azt$_{Top}$ nem$_{Foc}$ hiszem,   hogy Mari$_{Top}$ φFoc ismeri Chomskyt
        that$_{acc}$ not   believe-I that   Mari$_{nom}$ knows Chomsky$_{acc}$

Azt is the dummy representation of the subordinate clause in the main clause; it is in P1 because it is labelled Topic. What happened in (29) is that *Mari*, as the Topic of the subordinate clause replaces the dummy representation in the main clause. The fact that Topic was assigned both to *Mari*, and to the embedded predication is the condition for this displacement.

That *Mari* and *azt* exclude each other is shown by the ungrammaticality of the following sentences:

(33)   a   *Mari azt nem hiszem, hogy ismeri Chomskyt
        b   *Azt Mari nem hiszem, hogy ismeri Chomskyt

                P1   Pφ V

One may wonder whether *Mari* in (29) is Topic or Theme. Theme specifies the universe of discourse with respect to which the subsequent predication is presented as relevant, it is a pragmatic function external to the predication.[5] We saw that *Mari* and *azt* are in complementary distribution in constructions such as (29) and (32). We also saw that *azt* is in P1 (Topic) position in (32). This is the first indication that *Mari* in (29) is in P1 (Topic) rather than in P2 (Theme) position.

Fortunately there is a formal argument to distinguish between Theme and Topic. If *Mari* would have been Theme, the predication and the output would have been as follows:

(34)   (Mari)$_{Theme}$, Neg$_{Foc}$ hisz$_V$ (én)$_{Po}$ ([ismer$_V$ (ő)$_\theta$ (Chomsky)$_{Go}$])$_{GoTop}$

(35)   Mari, azt nem hiszem, hogy ismeri Chomskyt
     P2   P1 Pφ V

Notice that (35) differs from (33a) in that there is a pause after the first constituent.[6]

The following examples show that the displacement strategy by means of double pragmatic function assignment works perfectly. If Topic is assigned to not only *Mari* but to *Chomsky* as well, the following sentences can be produced:[7]

(36)   Neg$_{Foc}$ hisz$_V$ (én)$_{Po}$ ([ismer$_V$ (Mari)$_{\theta Top}$ (Chomsky)$_{GoTop}$])$_{GoTop}$
    a Azt$_{Top}$ nem hiszem, hogy Mari$_{Top}$ Chomskyt$_{Top}$ ismeri
    b Azt nem hiszem, hogy Chomskyt Mari ismeri
    c Mari nem hiszem, hogy Chomskyt ismeri
    d Chomskyt nem hiszem, hogy Mari ismeri
    e Mari Chomskyt nem hiszem, hogy ismeri
    f Chomskyt Mari nem hiszem, hogy ismeri

A predication can be extended by means of "satellites" which specify further properties of the nuclear state of affairs as a whole. In the following example the state of affairs is State and it is extended by a satellite with Time function. Displacement of a term with Topic function out of the satellite is possible:

(37)   [van$_V$ (ő)$_\theta$ (husz   éves)$_{\theta Foc}$]$_{State}$ (elkezd$_V$ (ő)$_{Ag}$
     be   he   twenty years   start   he

     (az egyetem)$_{GoTop}$)$_{TempTop}$
     the university

This predication produces:

(38)   a [Akkor]$_{Top}$ [husz   éves]$_{Foc}$ volt,   amikor [az egyetemet]$_{Top}$
        Then   twenty years   was-he when   the university
     elkezdte
     started-he
    b Az egyetemet husz éves volt, amikor elkezdte

Akkor (az+kor) in (38a) is the dummy representation of the Topic labelled satellite. *Egyetemet* "university$_{acc}$" is Topic within a Topic-term and can be displaced.

The displacement-rule also works in more complex sentences. For instance:

(39)   megmond$_V$ (én)$_{Ag}$ ([Neg$_{Foc}$ hisz$_V$ (én)$_{Po}$ ([ismer$_V$ (Mari)$_{\theta Top}$
       say   I   not   believe I   know   Mary

       (Chomsky)$_{Go}$])$_{GoTop}$])$_{GoTop}$
       Chomsky

To gain a better insight into the structure of this predication we isolate *Mari* from it together with the predication-brackets and the Topic labels:

(40)   ... (... (... (Mari)$_{Top}$ ...)$_{Top}$ ...)$_{Top}$

The pattern-schema for (39) will be:

(41)   P1 Pφ V X, conj P1 Pφ V X, conj P1 Pφ V X

According to the displacement-rule *Mari* can be placed in any P1 of (41), because Topic assignment has taken place at every level:

(42)   a   Megmondtam, hogy nem hiszem, hogy *Mari*, ismeri Chomskyt
           "I said, that I do not believe, that Mari knows Chomsky"
       b   Megmondtam, hogy *Mari*, nem hiszem, hogy ismeri Chomckyt
       c   *Mari*, megmondtam, hogy nem hiszem, hogy ismeri Chomskyt

Topic can only be displaced out of Topic predications. Topic displacement out of a Focus predication yields an ungrammatical output. For instance;

(43)   *[Mari]$_{Top}$ [azt]$_{Foc}$ hiszem,   hogy [csak Chomskyt]$_{Foc}$ ismeri
        Mary   that   believe-I that   only Chomsky   knows

The dummy representation in Focus-position and a displaced constituent in Topic-position is ungrammatical. Another example is displacement of both a Topic and a Focus constituent:

(44)   *[Mari]$_{Top}$ [csak Chomskyt]$_{Foc}$ hiszem, hogy ismeri

Displacement is not limited to Topic. Under the same condition a Focus constituent can be displaced:

(45) mond$_V$ (János)$_{AgTop}$ ([jön$_V$ (taxi)$_{AgTop}$]$_{Action}$ (öt)$_{TempFoc}$)$_{GoFoc}$
      say   John   come taxi   five

This predication produces the following sentences:

(46) a [János]$_{Top}$ [azt]$_{Foc}$ mondta, hogy [a taxi]$_{Top}$ [ötre]$_{Foc}$ jöjjön
         "John said that the taxi would come at five"

      b [János]$_{Top}$ [ötre]$_{Foc}$ mondta, hogy [a taxi]$_{Top}$ jöjjön
         "John said that the taxi would come at five"

Focus displacement, however, is only possible out of embedded predications which have the status of an argument of the verb. Focus displacement out of satellites is not allowed. For instance:

(47) [van$_V$ (ő)$_\theta$ (husz   éves)$_\theta$]$_{State}$ (elkezd$_V$ (ő)$_{Ag}$
      be   he   twenty years   start   he

      (az egyetem)$_{GoFoc}$)$_{TempFoc}$
      the university

The output without displacement is shown by (48a); an output with displacement as shown in (48b) is ungrammatical:

(48) a [Akkor]$_{Foc}$ volt   husz   éves, amikor [az   egyetemet]$_{Foc}$
         Then   was-he twenty years when   the university

         kezdte el
         started-he

         "He was twenty years when he started university"

      b *[Az egyetemet]$_{Foc}$ volt husz éves, amikor elkezdte

An explanation for this phenomenon may be found in the fact that the verb *van* "to be" does not require a temporal argument or term. Thus when Focus has been assigned to the subordinate satellite, which is an extension of the predication, the Time function must have a dummy representation in the matrix clause. This dummy element prevents Focus displacement out of the embedded predication, because only one constituent can fill the Focus-position.[8] (Note that in (46b) a satellite has been displaced out of the Goal argument of *mond* "to say".)

3.3 Pseudo-arguments

Displacement seems to be nothing more than putting constituents in a pragmatically motivated position. However, what is the status of the displaced constituent? Does it come into the domain of the higher predication, does it become a part of it? In

(29) Mari   nem hiszem, hogy ismeri   Chomskyt
      Mary$_{nom}$ not believe-I that knows-she Chomsky$_{acc}$
      "I do not believe that Mary knows Chomsky"

Mari is an argument of *ismer* "know" and not of *hisz* "believe"; it is in the nominative case as an expression of its semantic function. There is no morphological adaptation to the new environment. On the other hand, it is the Topic of the whole sentence. We cannot say that *Mari* is a pseudo-argument of *hisz* "believe".

There are, however, examples of displacement with morphological adjustment to the new environment. For instance:

(49) akar$_V$ (Elemér)$_{AgTop}$ ([felpofoz$_V$ (én)$_{AgFoc}$ (anyósa)$_{Go}$])$_{GoFoc}$

The output without and with displacement is, respectively:

(50) Elemér azt   akarja, hogy én   pofozzam fel az
      P1   Pφ V   Pφ V
      Elmer that$_{acc}$ wants that I$_{nom}$ 'slap the face of his
      anyósát
      mother-in-law

(51) Elemér engem akar, hogy felpofozzam az   anyósát
      Elmer me$_{acc}$ wants that 'I slap the face of his mother-in-law

When *én* "I" (with double Focus) is placed in Pφ of the main clause, it appears as an "object" of the higher predicate in the accusative case. There is even agreement with the verb. In Hungarian the verb agrees not only with its subject but also with its direct object. It depends on the character of the object which conjugation the verb takes: the indefinite conjugation when the object is indefinite and the definite conjugation when the object is definite.[9] For example:

(52) a Péter   könyvet ad
        Peter$_{nom}$ book$_{acc}$ gives$_{indef-conjugation}$
        "Peter gives a book"

     b Péter   adja   a könyvet
        Peter$_{nom}$ gives$_{def-conjugation}$ the book$_{acc}$
        "Peter gives the book"

First and second person singular and plural pronouns count as "indefinite" with respect to this rule; the third person pronoun counts as "definite". Thus:

(53) a Péter   őt   akarja
Peter$_{nom}$ her$_{acc}$ wants$_{def-conjugation}$
"Peter wants her"

 b Péter   engem akar
Peter$_{nom}$ me$_{acc}$ wants$_{indef-conjugation}$
"Peter wants me"

Note that subordinate clauses with the conjunction *hogy* "that" and *ha* "if" count as "definite".

Thus, what happened in (51) is that the verb *akar* "want" took *engem* "me" as object and it takes the indefinite conjugation. We might say that *engem* is a pseudo-argument of *akar*.

Another example:

(54) a Azt   Anikó szeretné, ha János   menne velük
That$_{acc}$ Anikó would like if John$_{nom}$ goes with-them

 b Jánost Anikó szeretné, ha velük   menne
John$_{acc}$ Anikó would like if with-them goes-he

János in (54b) is in the accusative, as an "object" of *szeret*. Note that (51) concerns the displacement of a Focus argument while (54b) is an example of Topic displacement.

What kind of explanation can be found for these morphological changes? Does it mean that an argument becomes an argument of another verb as well that it becomes a pseudo-argument? The solution preferred by Dik for English *believe* constructions as discussed in "Raising in a Functional Grammar" (Dik, 1979) is of no help. Let us consider the approach by means of syntactic function assignment into the embedded predication for Hungarian.

The idea of this approach is that Subj or Obj assignment may optionally penetrate the embedded predication and pick out some term of that predication as the Subj or Obj of the higher predicate. For example:

(55) believe$_V$ (John)$_{PoSubj}$ ([kill$_V$ (Bill)$_{AgSubjObj}$ (the farmer)$_{GoObj}$])$_{Go}$

which produces (56):

(56) John believed Bill to have killed the farmer

The representation

(57)   Bill_{AgSubjObj}

has to be interpreted as: *Bill* is Obj of *believe*, Subj and Agent of *kill*. The syntactic functions will trigger the corresponding agreement.

For this treatment to be applicable to Hungarian, we would need Obj assignment. Sentence (51) would have the following predication with Obj assigned to the embedded Agent:

(58)   akar_V (Elemér)_{AgTop} ([felpofoz_V (én)_{AgObjFoc} (anyósa)_{Go}])_{GoFoc}
       want   Elmer   slap   I   his mother-in-law

There are two severe objections against this treatment. When Obj is assigned to an argument, a pragmatic function also must be assigned to that particular argument, and the same pragmatic function must be assigned to the embedded predication as well for displacement to apply. Predication (58) without Focus assignment to (én)_{AgObj} will produce:

(59)   *Elemér akar engem, hogy felpofozzam az anyósát

An argument without a pragmatic function will always be placed in the neutral territory after the verb. Sentence (59) is rejected as being ungrammatical by all informants. In other words, the condition of displacement, defined in terms of double pragmatic function, applies in this case as well. An obligatory pragmatic function assignment rule would violate the theory of FG: structure does not govern the informational status of constituents. It is rather the other way round.[10]

The second objection is that the way Obj is used in this case does not conform to the idea that it is a syntactic function, which, together with the Subj, "traces a path" through the state of affairs designated by the predication. It is used as a syntactic notion, which carries a pragmatic cargo merely to trigger some morphological rules!

A treatment with Obj assignment for Hungarian is an *ad hoc* solution, and is rather unwanted, because it requires the introduction of this function for this particular case.

Let us consider the other approach discussed by Dik, namely that the difference between sentences like:

(50)   Elemér azt akarja, hogy én pofozzam fel az anyósát

(51)   Elemér engem akar, hogy felpofozzam az anyósát

would be due to a difference in the underlying predicate-frames: that there are two verbs *akar*, one a two-place verb, the other a three-place verb. For the sentences (50) and (51) the predicate-frames would be respectively:

(60) $akar_V$ (x_1: human (x_1))$_{Ag}$ (x_2)$_{Go}$

(61) $akar_V$ (x_1: human (x_1))$_{Ag}$ (x_2)$_{Go}$ (x_3: [φ (x_2)$_{Ag/Go}$] (x_3))$_{Compl}$

The two-place verb *akar* (60) has an Agent argument which has to be human, and a Goal argument. However, (61) has a third argument with a rather complex structure. It says that this Complement argument can contain an open predication in x_3; this predication must have x_2 (that is, the Goal argument of *akar*) as Agent or Goal. The restriction to Agent and Goal has to be made, or else the following ungrammatical sentence would arise:

(62)   *János   Máriát   akarja, hogy Péter   könyvet adjon
        John$_{nom}$ Maria$_{acc}$ wants   that Peter$_{nom}$ book$_{acc}$ gives

The grammatical sentence is

(63)   János   azt   akarja, hogy Péter   Máriának adjon könyvet
        John$_{nom}$ that$_{acc}$ wants   that Peter$_{nom}$ Maria$_{dat}$ gives book$_{acc}$
        "John wants that Peter gives a book to Maria"

What happened in (62) is that the Recipient of *ad* "give" has been chosen as the Goal of *akar* "want". This brings us immediately to the first objection against this solution.

(1)   The second argument of (61) has been given the semantic function Goal, but does it meet the requirements of the definition of this semantic function? Goal has been defined (Dik, 1978, 41) as characterizing those entities which are affected (or effected) by the operation of some Agent or Force. It is difficult to determine the semantic status of a term, but there is certainly a difference between the Goal arguments of the following sentences:

(64)   a   Elemér engem$_{Go}$ akar
            Elmer me   wants

        b   Elemér engem$_{Go}$ akar, hogy vezessek
            Elmer me   wants that drive-I

Sentence (64b) does not say that Elmer wants me but that Elmer wants me to drive. Thus, *engem* "me" and the subordinate clause together behave

like a Goal. The Complement argument is a complement of the Goal
argument, rather than an independent third argument of the verb *akar*.

(2) The remark about obligatory pragmatic function assignment can be
made for this solution as well: should (61) be chosen, then Topic or Focus
must be assigned to the Goal argument. There are, however, other conditions which support the idea that this so-called Goal is displaced.

Let us consider sentence (51) with predicate-frame (61) again and
examine the consequences for pragmatic function assignment if the second
argument would be Focus. The simplified structure of the predication is:

(65) akar$_V$ (x$_1$)$_{Ag}$ (x$_2$)$_{Go}$ (x$_3$: [felpofoz$_V$ (x$_2$)$_{Ag}$ (x$_4$)$_{Go}$] (x$_3$))$_{Compl}$

Focus can only be assigned to one member of a predication (see Section
3.1.2), thus (x$_1$)$_{Ag}$ and (x$_3$)$_{Compl}$ are not eligible for Focus function here
because we choose (x$_2$)$_{Go}$ for this function. Usually, Focus can be assigned
within a subordinate clause, but in a pattern such as (65) this function,
added to (x$_2$)$_{Ag}$ or (x$_4$)$_{Go}$, results in a ungrammatical output. The explanation which could be given for this fact is that the argument (x$_2$)$_{Ag}$ shares
in the pragmatic status of the argument with the same index in the higher
predication. This index prevents Focus assignment within the embedded
predication.

In this case Topic can be assigned within the embedded predication to
the Goal and, of course, not to the Agent. It cannot be assigned to the
Complement argument itself. This argument with Topic function claims
a dummy representation in the main clause; a sentence like (66) is ungrammatical:

(66) *Elemér azt$_{Top}$ engem$_{Foc}$ akar, hogy felpofozzam az anyósát

All these restrictions indicate that (65) is implausible and that a sentence
like (51) is a sentence with a displaced Focus argument according to the
general principle. When we have the following predication:

(67) akar$_V$ (x$_1$)$_{Ag}$ (x$_2$: [felpofoz$_V$ (x$_3$)$_{AgFoc}$ (x$_4$)$_{Go}$] (x$_2$))$_{GoFoc}$

it immediately explains why these restrictions have to be formulated:
Focus has been assigned to x$_3$ and it is displaced, and that is why x$_4$ is not
eligible for Focus. The second argument of *akar* has the function Focus,
and that is why it cannot get Topic function too (this argument of *akar* is
comparable with the Compl argument of (65)). After all, the displacement
strategy is needed for all other cases while the solution with different
predicate frames is also an *ad hoc* solution.

We thus come to the conclusion that the assignment of the accusative case to *engem* in (51) is an adjustment to be applied after displacement, where displacement itself is triggered by a certain constellation of pragmatic functions.

In view of the above considerations, I will propose a third solution, which is an addition to the general principle of displacement in Hungarian. As shown above, morphological consequences of displacement cannot be explained by syntactic function assignment or different predicate-frames, i.e. differences in semantic functions. Every displacement is a matter of pragmatics, so why should it be treated in a different way when the displaced constituents have the same informational status? For instance:

(68) a   Elemér engem akar, hogy vezessek
          Elmer me   wants that drive-I

      b   Elemér holnap   akarja, hogy vezessek
          Elmer tomorrow wants that drive-I

Sentence (68a) does not say that Elmer wants me and (68b) does not say that Elmer wants tomorrow. The context of both sentences is that we know who Elmer is and that we know that someone will drive a car. In the first sentence *engem* "me" represents the most salient information, in the second one *holnap* "tomorrow". Pragmatic functions, however, govern only positions in Hungarian and not morphological mutations. That is why the solution has to be found in the expression rules. These rules are susceptible not only to semantic functions but also, among others, to selection restrictions.[11]

Let us assume the following expression rules:

(69)   Terms from embedded predications can be optionally displaced to the P1 and Pφ positions of the higher clause when those terms carry the same pragmatic function as the embedded predication, with the exception of Focus constituents from satellites.[12]

(70)   The dummy representation of an embedded predication will be expressed according to the semantic function of the embedded predication.

(71)   A displaced constituent with Agent, Force, Positioner, Processed, Zero or Goal function, which takes the position of the dummy representation of an embedded predication, will be expressed according to the semantic function of this embedded predication

when it meets the selection restrictions of the argument of which the dummy was the representation.

Rules (69)–(71) cover all examples mentioned above. Rule (69) is the displacement rule. Examples of (70) are:

(72) a   Elemér   azt   akarja, hogy elmenjen
          Elmer_{nom} (az+t) that_{acc} wants   that leaves-she

      b   Annak   örülök,   hogy elment
          (az+nak) That_{dat} pleases me that left-she

      c   A   futbalisták   arra   panaszkodtak, hogy a
          The footballplayers_{nom} (az+ra) that_{subl} complained   that the
          talaj   elázott
          field_{nom} was sopping wet

The second argument of *akar* will be expressed by the accusative; that of *örül* by the dative and that of *panaszkodik* by the sublative case.

Examples of rule (71) are:

(73) a   Elemér engem akar, hogy vezessek
          Elmer me_{acc} wants that drive-I

      b   Máriának örülök,   hogy elment
          Maria_{dat} pleases-me that left-she

      c   A   futbalisták   a talajra panaszkodtak, hogy
          The footballplayers the field_{subl} complained   that
          elázott
          was sopping wet

If the displaced constituents do not match the selection restrictions of the argument with the subordinate predication, they will be expressed according to the markers they wear themselves. For instance:

(29) Mari   nem hiszem, hogy ismeri   Chomskyt
      Mary_{nom} not believe-I that knows-she Chomsky

Mari has Zero function and is therefore expressed by the nominative. The second argument of *hisz* "believe" has a selection restriction "- human". Since *Mari* is human, it is not susceptible to morphological adjustment. Sentence (29) with Mari+accusative is ungrammatical:

(74) *Marit nem hiszem, hogy ismeri Chomskyt

Another remark has to be made in relation to expression rule (71). Not all arguments are susceptible to this rule even when they do not conflict with the selection restrictions. Namely, all arguments with other semantic functions than Agent, Force etc. listed in rule (71) are not. Note that displaced arguments with Agent, Force etc., as well as Goal, are represented in the subordinate clause by means of agreement with the verb. Thus, sentence (73a) can only be understood as: Elmer wants that *I* drive. Example (75) shows the agreement between a displaced Goal argument with morphological adjustment and the verb in the subordinate clause:

(75)   A   szoknyán gondolkozom, hogy   Mari megvette-e
       The skirt$_{sup-es}$ wonder-I   whether Mary bought-it-QM
       "I wonder, whether Mary bought the skirt"

Sentence (75) without displacement is

(76)   Azon   gondolkozom, hogy Mari megvette-e a
       (az+on) That$_{sup-es}$ wonder-I   that Mary bought-QM the
       szoknyát
       skirt$_{acc}$

Thus only subjects and direct objects are sensitive to rule (71). Sentence (62) showed that the application of rule (71) to an indirect object resulted in an ungrammatical output:

(62)   *János   Máriát   akarja, hogy Péter   könyvet adjon
       John$_{nom}$ Maria$_{acc}$ wants that Peter$_{nom}$ book$_{acc}$ gives

When a pronoun however, is added to the subordinate clause, referring to the displaced constituent, the sentence is grammatical to some of my informants. Thus:

(77)   ?János   Máriát   akarja, hogy Péter   könyvet adjon neki
       John$_{nom}$ Mary$_{acc}$ wants that Peter$_{nom}$ book$_{acc}$ gives him/her$_{dat}$

Note that the pronoun *neki* "him/her$_{dat}$" can only occur here in final position of the sentence. It cannot appear as a Focus or not even as a Topic. Within the neutral area after the verb it is not free, it must be in final position. This is an indication that this pronoun probably occurs as a Tail, as a correction, as a clarification. Most informants, however, rejected (77) as being ungrammatical, and some of them did not even understand the meaning of this sentence; who ordered what and who gave whom a book?

The fact that only those arguments are qualified for this particular muta-tion which are marked on the verb in the subordinate predication, supports the choice to treat "pseudo-arguments" in Hungarian by means of expression rules.

Another morphological consequence of displacement is agreement between the verb and its new "object". It does not present any complica-tions because the agreement rule follows the other rules. Agreement between the displaced argument and the verb of the embedded sentences will be triggered by means of the semantic function of that argument.

3.4 Conclusion

This chapter considered pseudo-arguments in Hungarian and the treat-ment of this phenomenon within the theory of Functional Grammar. The two solutions discussed by Dik (1979) seemed unsuitable for Hungarian. A third solution, which does not make an appeal to syntactic or semantic functions but to pragmatic functions and expression rules, was proposed. This solution never conflicts with the theory of FG; on the contrary, it shows how consistently the principles of this theory can be used for a description of a language.

Acknowledgements

I would like to thank the Institute of Cultural Relations in Budapest (Kulturális Kapcsolatok Intézete) for the support and the Institute of Linguistics of the Hungarian Academy of Sciences for the hospitality they gave me while I was working on this project.

I am extremely grateful to my informants, for their patience and their willing-ness to judge my examples and for the time they spent searching for new or better ones.

Notes

1 "Agent, Force etc." stands for all different semantic functions of the first argument. I shall not pay attention to the problem "What makes an argu-ment a first argument?", because it falls outside the scope of this chapter.

2 In De Groot (1981) I proposed to consider only the first constituent of the sentences (19a) and (19b) as Topic constituents, because the context and the interpretation of the unmarked sentences is for (19a): Some people gave Mary something; Peter gave a book. For (19b): Peter gave some people something; to Mary he gave a book.

3   Dik (1978, 178 f.) assumes for Dutch and English the subordinator to be in
    P1. If *hogy* "that" is in P1, one would expect that it also can take any place
    within that position. *Hogy* only occurs, however, in initial position of the
    subordinate clause. Notice that a relative pronoun is free within P1:

    (i)   A   könyv, amit   János említett,   elég   érdekes
          The book   which_acc John mentioned rather interesting
          "The book, that John mentioned, is rather interesting"

    (ii) A   könyv, János amit   említett,   elég   érdekes
          The book   John which_acc mentioned rather interesting
          "The book, that John mentioned, is rather interesting"

4   This chapter does not consider the question which elements can go to
    P φ. It can be argued that by absence of Focus assignment some elements
    come into consideration for Pφ position, for instance indefinite "object" and
    converbs. Thus (iii), the answer to "What happened today?", is without a
    Focus, but with an element in Pφ, let us say an "unmarked Focus":

    (iii) Péter könyvet vett
           P1   P φ   V
           Peter book   bought
           "Peter bought a book"

    If Pφ is left empty, the sentence is ungrammatical (with respect to the
    question "What happened today?"):

    (iv)   *Péter [φ] vett   könyvet
           P1   Pφ V   X
           Peter   bought book

5   In De Groot (1981) it is argued that there is also a kind of Theme con-
    stituents within the predication. We are not dealing with that type of
    Theme here.

6   Sentence (35) contains an uncommon construction which can, however, be
    used in this way, although it is more likely that an element will be put into
    P1 referring to the Theme, thus:

    (v)   Mari,   az   nem hiszem, hogy ismeri   Chomskyt
          Mary_nom that_nom not believe-I that knows-she Chomsky_acc
          "Mary, I do not believe, that she knows Chomsky"

7   Note that an example with displacement of both *Mari* and *Chomsky* shows
    us that there are sentences with more than one Topic constituent. (Cf.
    note 2.)

8   A sentence like (48a) is a rare but correct grammatical sentence. A situation
    in which it will be used seldom occurs. It is more likely that a sentence has
    one Focus. Usually the Focus is either one term (e.g. *az egyetemet* in (48a)),
    or the subordinate predication as a whole. (See Bolkestein, Chapter 4,
    Section 4.2.1.3). However, an expression like (48a) does exist.

9   Since the syntactic functions Subj and Obj are not relevant to a description

of Hungarian, the use of "subject" and "object" is not correct. To distinguish between the Subj and Obj in the terminology of FG and the traditional notions subject and object, I will write the latter either in lower case or between brackets.

10   A position for Obj in the functional pattern is of no help. Such a position would coincide with $P\varphi$:

$$(vi) \quad P1 \left\{ \begin{matrix} P\,\varphi \\ O \end{matrix} \right\} \; V \quad X$$

On the other hand, a rule like: Obj goes to $P\,\varphi$, passes over the fact that the constituent with Obj function is *the* Focus of the sentence.

11   An expression rule is for instance: "An Agent will be expressed in the nominative case". A selection restriction is for instance: "The Agent of the verb *to say* has to be 'human' ".

12   This rule applies to a restricted number of cases. For instance embedded predications which form the second argument of a special category of verbs, may follow this rule (cf. Kiss, 1981). When and in which situations these constructions will occur, are questions which will have to be dealt with elsewhere. Much more research, especially with regard to spoken language, is needed in order to answer these questions.

References

DIK, Simon C.
  1978   "Functional Grammar". North-Holland Linguistic Series 37. Amsterdam, North-Holland.
  1979   Raising in a Functional Grammar. *Lingua* **47**, 119–140.
GROOT, Casper de
  1981   On Theme in Functional Grammar. An application to some constructions in spoken Hungarian. *In* Teun Hoekstra, Harry van der Hulst and Michael Moortgat (ed.). "Perspectives on Functional Grammar". Dordrecht, Foris, 75–88.
HORVÁTH, Julia
  1976   Focus in Hungarian and the $\overline{\text{X}}$ Notation. *Linguistic Analysis* **2**, 175–197.
KISS, Katalin, É.
  1978   A magyar mondatok egy szintaktikai modellje (A syntactic model of the Hungarian sentences). *Nyelvtudományi Közlemények* **80/2**, 261–286.
  1981   Structural Relations in Hungarian, a "free" word order language. *Linguistic Inquiry* **12**, 185–213.
ZOLNAI, Gyula
  1926   Mondatátszövődés. (Sentence-intertwining). *Értekezések a Nyelv- és Széptudományok Köréből* **23/8**.

4 Embedded Predications, Displacement and Pseudo-argument Formation in Latin

A. MACHTELT BOLKESTEIN

Department of Latin
University of Amsterdam

4.0 Introduction[1]

As illustrated by various chapters in this volume, complex predications, i.e. predications which contain an embedded predication as one of their arguments, in many languages may be realized syntactically in more than one way. The most "natural" syntactic realization of such a semantic pattern is a sentence in which there is a direct correspondence between the semantic frame and the syntactic construction. This is the case, for example, when the embedded predication is simply realized as a subordinate clause. However, in such predications there may be certain factors (which may or may not be of a pragmatic nature) which cause alternative syntactic patterns to be adopted. Among these is what has been termed (see Dik, Chapter 2) "displacement". In simple "displacement" a nominal constituent of the embedded predication occurs at a position outside the subordinate clause. It consequently occupies a different place in the linear order of the sentence from that which the element would normally occupy according to the rules for word order in the language under consideration. The nominal element involved does not show signs of morphological adjustment to its environment: it has not come within the syntactic domain of the governing predicate.

A second way of ordering such a complex semantic pattern is the phenomenon usually referred to as "Raising". This phenomenon is here described as exhibiting displacement with morphological adjustment to the new environment. I shall also use the term "pseudo-argument formation", to indicate such cases. The pseudo-argument (the "raised" element) will, for example, behave in some respects like an Object, or like a Subject of the governing predicate. In some languages, e.g. English, this procedure will lead to non-finite realization of the embedded predicate, but this is not true in all languages: in Latin pseudo-argument formation occurs both with finite clauses and with non-finite ones. Furthermore, in a particular language pseudo-argument formation may be obligatory with some predicates, and optional with other ones (see Vet, Chapter 7, on certain French predicates; Combé, Chapter 9, on some Spanish ones).

In this chapter I shall investigate a number of constructions found in Latin which exemplify the two strategies just outlined and consider under what specific conditions these constructions are used. In Section 4.1 I shall discuss some constructions in which a nominal constituent occurs in a position which is different from what might be expected, without showing morphological adjustment to its new environment. I shall argue that some of these cases must be viewed as instances of a so-called Theme,Predication organization. In Section 4.2, two types of pseudo-argument formation will be discussed. In 4.2.1 I will investigate the so-called "proleptic" accusative, which is found with embedded predications expressed as a finite clause, and in 4.2.2 I will go into the so-called personal passive or Nominativus cum Infinitivo (NcI) construction. This construction formally resembles the "Raising" construction found with verbs such as *to say* in English: the embedded predicate is realized as an infinitive. I shall try to determine under what conditions both types of construction occur, and propose a common explanation. In both cases the conditions will turn out to be pragmatic rather than syntactic: they are therefore different from the rule assumed to apply with "raising" verbs such as *to believe* in English, cf. Dik 1979.

This fact obviously has certain consequences for the status of the rules assumed to apply in the course of the formation of the Latin sentences involved. In this respect the rules will be quite similar to those proposed for comparable constructions in Hungarian in de Groot (Chapter 3). In a Chapter 10 I deal with a third way for syntactically realizing a predication containing an embedded predication in Latin (usually called the "ab urbe condita" construction). In contrast with the constructions dealt with in the present paper, the latter construction will be shown to be motivated semantically rather than pragmatically.

4.1   Theme,Predication organization v. Displacement

4.1.1   Main clauses

One type of construction which might be regarded as exhibiting displacement without morphological adjustment figures in Latin grammars under various headings, such as that of "emphatic" or "thematic" nominative (K.-St.* II, 586; Sz.,† 29), "isolated", "unconstructed" nominative or nominativus pendens (Sz., 29, 401, 731). Notions used in this connection for describing the semantic effect of the construction are "Hervorhebung" or "Vorausnahme" ("anticipation") of the "most important" concept (K.-St. I, 712; Sz., 29, 401). Instances also figure in discussions of "anakolouthic" sentences or "contaminations" (Sz., 143, 731; K.-St. II, 586).[2]

In this construction some nominal element which often semantically (i.e. relationally) seems to belong within the subsequent predication, occurs in sentence-initial position without being integrated in its syntactic construction. It will, in that case, sometimes be expressed in the nominative caseform, as in (1a) (the nominative can be viewed as being the most neutral caseform in Latin). It may also be expressed in the caseform which corresponds to the caseform required by the predicate to which it semantically seems to have a relation, as in (1b–d). In the same sentence-initial position elements of a different syntactic form may occur with the same semantic effect, namely prepositional phrases introduced by the preposition *de* ("about", "concerning"), as in (1e–g). This latter form is in fact the one which is more frequent (instances may be found in TLL‡ s.v. *de* 76, 64 sqq.); in the grammars it is usually alluded to in different chapters, although similar terms may be used for describing the semantic effect of such prepositional phrases (K.-St. I, 712–713; II, 582; Sz., 29, 363).

(1) a   *ager   rubicosus . . ., ibi*   lupinum fiat
      earth_nom ochreous,   there_adv lupine   be-put_3sg
      "earth full of ochre, there lupine should be put" (Cato *Agr.* 34, 2)

     b   *cancer   ater,   is*   olet
      tumor_nom black,   it_nom stink_3sg
      "a black tumor, that stinks" (Cato *Agr.* 157, 3)

* Kühner and Stegmann (1912).   † Szantyr (1965).
‡ Thesaurus Linguae Latinae (in press).

c   sed *urbana plebs,*   *ea*   vero   praeceps erat
but city   people$_{nom}$, that$_{nom}$ really eager   was$_{3sg}$
"but the city-crowd, that was really eager" (Sall. *C.* 37)

d   *amicos domini, eos*   habeat   sibi   amicos
friends$_{acc}$ . . . them$_{acc}$ consider$_{3sg}$ himself friends
"friends of the boss, those he should consider as his own friends"
(Cato *Agr.* 5, 3)

e   *de*   *brassica,* . . ., quid *in ea* boni   sit
about cabbage . . ., what in it good$_{gen}$ is$_{3sg}$
"about cabbage, what good it contains" (Cato *Agr.* 157, 1)

f   *de Pompeio,* et facio diligenter et faciam quod mones
"about P., I am both doing my best now, and I will do as you
advise" (Cic. *Q.fr.* 3, 1, 9)

g   *de benevolentia* autem . . ., primum illud est in officio, ut . . .
"but as far as good-will is concerned, firstly the following is part
of our duty, that . . ." (Cic. *Off.* 1, 47)

As is shown by examples (1a–e), such sentence-initial words or phrases
are often in the subsequent predication taken up by an anaphoric pronoun
in the caseform required by the governing predicate. Absence of such a
pronoun is claimed to be rare (Sz., 29, 187).[3] On the other hand, there may
be no coreference at all between a sentence initial element of the type
under consideration and any particular constituent of the subsequent
predication, e.g. (1f–g).[4]

The properties exhibited by the underlined NPs in (1) are in agreement
with those argued in Dik (1978a, 132–141; Chapter 5) to be characteristic
for a so-called Theme,Predication organization of sentences. The notion
"Theme" is a *pragmatic* function: it is defined as presenting "a domain
. . . with respect to which it is relevant to pronounce the following predication" (Dik, 1978a, 130). It is especially pointed out that the relation between
the Theme of a sentence and the subsequent predication is not a "structural" one (note that no coreference is required between the former and some
constituent of the latter), but one of pragmatic relevance. This accounts
for the occurrence of instances such as (1 f–g). In Latin handbooks a
Theme,Predication organization such as the above is often treated as
anakolouthic especially when the Theme is expressed in the nominative
and its coreferent carries another caseform (K.-St. II, 586). The structure

of the subsequent predication is, however, itself completely well-formed and unaffected by the explicitation of the Theme.

On the other hand, the caseform of the Theme-element is not unfrequently different from the one required by the predicate actually used in the subsequent predication. It may be a caseform which would have corresponded if some other predicate with similar meaning had been used (Sz., 143, 731).[5] In such cases, explicitation of the Theme is indeed combined with a change in the construction chosen for the subsequent predication. The presence of a long phrase or subordinate clause between the Theme and the main predicate of the subsequent predication increases the chance that the construction will be different from the one expected, as is noted by Sz. (731) and K.-St. (I, 625); see also Dik (1978a, 136; Chapter 5) on the occurrence of "hesitation phenomena" between Theme and predication.

No specific descriptive problems arise from Theme,Predication sentences, as long as—in agreement with Dik's proposal (1978a,133–137)—Theme is viewed not as extracted from the subsequent predication, but as an addition to it. Accordingly, the term "displacement" is not applicable to this type of phenomenon, whether or not the Theme element happens to be coreferential to some element of the subsequent predication, and whatever the distance between the coreferent elements in the linear order of the sentence.

If we survey the available attested instances of a Theme,Predication organization in Latin, it is obvious, that whether the predication thus organized is simple—as in most examples of (1)—or complex—as in (1g)—is completely irrelevant with respect to the phenomenon under consideration. Moreover, in the case of complex sentences, the sentence-initial element may not only be or not be coreferential to an element of the main clause: it may also quite well be coreferential to an argument *within* the embedded predication. This is illustrated in (2a–e) below (further examples in K.-St. I, 625; Sz., 187).

(2) a *ceterae ... disciplinae ...,* *eas* nihil adiuvare arbitror
        other   disciplines$_{nom}$ ..., they$_{acc}$ nothing to-help$_{inf}$ believe$_{1sg}$
        "the other disciplines, I believe that they will be of no help" (Cic. *Fin.* 3, 11)

     b sed quod *de* *fratre,* ubi *eum* visuri essemus,
        but because about brother where him$_{acc}$ will see$_{1pl}$
        nesciebamus
        not-know$_{1pl}$

"but because as far as my brother was concerned, we did not know where we would be seeing him" (Cic. *Att.* 3, 7, 3)[6]

c   nam *de*   *equitibus hostium*, quin nemo   *eorum* . . .,   non
     for   about horsemen enemy, that no-one of-them$_{gen}$ . . ., not
     debere dubitare
     should doubt
     "for as for the horsemen of the enemy, that none of them . . ., they should not doubt" (Caes. *BG* 7, 66, 6)

d   *de*   *hoc homine*, . . . sic   scriptum accepimus   summam
     about this man, . . .   thus written   have-heard$_{1pl}$ very-great
     fuisse   *eius* . . .   temperantiam
     to-have-been$_{inf}$ his$_{gen}$ . . . sobriety
     "as for this man, we have heard that it is thus written that his sobriety was so great" (Cic. *Tusc.* 5, 57)

e   *de*   *Africano* quidem . . ., iurare   possum non *illum* . . .
     about Africanus, . . .   to-swear can$_{1sg}$ not he$_{acc}$ . . .
     fuisse
     to-have-been$_{inf}$
     "concerning A., I could really swear that he has not been" (Cic. *Tusc.* 4, 50)

f   *de*   *forma*, ovem   esse   oportet corpore amplo
     about shape, sheep$_{acc}$ to-be$_{inf}$ ought   body$_{abl}$ big$_{abl}$
     "as far as size is concerned, a sheep must have a big body" (Varro *R* 2, 2, 3)

As is shown by the sentences in (2), Theme elements of complex predications may be coreferential to either the Subj (2a, e), the Obj (2b), an adnominally expressed possessor (2d) or partitive genitive (2c) etc. (or not be coreferential to any constituent at all (2f)). Furthermore, such coreference to arguments of an embedded predication is possible both when the embedded predication is expressed as a finite clause and when it is non-finite, see (2b, c) and (d, e) respectively.[7]

When the sentence-initial element is expressed in the nominative, as in (2a), its pragmatic status of Theme is quite unambiguous. However, when they are expressed in the form of a *de*-phrase, and when at the same time the main predicate is a verb of speech or thought as in (2b–e), the sentences are actually structurally ambiguous, in that such prepositional phrases may also be analysed as being an argument of the main predicate: many predicates of this semantic class occur with arguments of that form, see K.-St. (I, 500, 712) and TLL s.v. *de* 67, 27f.[8] The latter analysis is obviously required when the *de* phrase does not stand in sentence-initial position, or is a relative pronoun, as in (3); in such cases a pragmatic Theme interpretation of the prepositional phrase is excluded:

(3)   ... nisi   *de*   *quo*   exploratum sit   tibi   *eum*   redditurum
          except about whom investigated is$_{3sg}$ you$_{dat}$ he$_{acc}$ will-give-back
          "except a man, about whom it is investigated that he will give
          back to you" (Cic. *Att.* 4, 15, 3)[9]

In other instances, such as (2b–e) intonation would presumably differentiate a Theme,Predication organization from that in which the *de*-phrase is not Theme, but an argument of the predicate.

Although, in general, arguments of predicates in Latin are quite free with respect to their place in the sentence (but see note 25), arguments of this particular form must precede the embedded predication if the latter is present. There is thus a correspondence in behaviour between *pragmatic* Themes on the one hand, and arguments with this particular *semantic function* (provisionally called "Domain") with the semantic class of predicates involved.

In the case of a Theme,Predication organization, in which there is co-reference between the Theme on the one hand and an argument of an embedded predication on the other, the anaphoric pronoun may more easily be absent from the subsequent embedded predication than in the case of main clauses, especially if it would syntactically be Subj of that predicate. Thus instances such as (4) are not exceptional (see also K.-St. I, 712):

(4)   a   *de te* tamen, fama constans nec decipi posse nec vinci
          "about you, however, there is a steady rumour that you cannot be
          cheated nor conquered" (Cic. *Fam.* 10, 20, 1)[10]

      b   de te ... fama constans *te* nec decipi posse nec vinci

In (4a) a pronoun could be added without change of interpretation, cf. (4b). Whether or not a coreferent pronoun is present, sentences such as (4) are structurally ambiguous in the same way as (2b–e).

4.1.2 Embedded predications

A Theme,Predication organization (see previous section) is not only possible of main clauses. With predicates designating speech or thought, the embedded predication designating the content of the speech or thought may itself be provided with an explicitation of its own Theme (Dik 1978a, 135; Chapter 5). In Latin, the position occupied by the Theme-element will in that case be the position immediately preceding the embedded predication (see (5a–d)):

(5) a   sed hoc crucior, *patrem* . . .   *eum*   nunc improbi viri officio
         but this worry$_{1sg}$ father$_{acc}$ . . . he$_{acc}$ now   bad   man service
         uti
         to-use$_{inf}$
         "but I am now worried about this, that your father . . . that he
         now uses the services of a bad man" (Pl. *Stich.* 11)

     b   docuit   *unum* ex his,   *eum* esse   poetam
         taught$_{3sg}$ one$_{acc}$ of those, he$_{acc}$ to-be$_{inf}$ poet$_{acc}$
         "he taught that one of them, that he was a poet" (Vitr. 7, pr. 7)

     c   erat . . .   suspicio *Parthos*   si . . ., iter *eos* . . . esse
         was$_{3sg}$ . . . suspicion Parths$_{acc}$ if . . ., way they$_{acc}$ to-be$_{inf}$
         facturos
         going-to-make
         'there was a suspicion that the P., if . . ., that they would make
         their way" (Cic. *Fam.* 15, 2, 1)

     d   erat rumor *de Transpadanis*, *eos* iussos creare
         "there was a rumour about the T., that they$_{acc}$ were ordered to
         choose" (Cic. *Att.* 5, 2, 3)

     e   *docuit   *unus*   ex   his,   *eum* esse   poetam (see (5b))
         taught$_{3sg}$ one$_{nom}$ from them, he$_{acc}$ to-be$_{inf}$ poet

When the clause-initial element carries the same caseform as a coreferent within the embedded predication, as in (5a–c), its pragmatic status in relation to the embedded predication is obvious: it cannot be analysed as an argument of the governing predicate (Bolkestein, 1979). However, when it has the form of a prepositional phrase introduced by *de*, as in (5d), the sentence is structurally ambiguous because of the possible argument-status of such prepositional phrases (see 4.1.1 (3) and (4)). As pointed out above. *de*-phrases may also occur at a position in the sentence which is neither sentence-initial (i.e. the position of the Theme of the sentence as a whole, as in (2)), nor the position immediately preceding the embedded predication (which is the position of an embedded Theme). Again intonation of the two underlying structures would presumably disambiguate them.

As far as the syntactic forms for expressing Themes of embedded predictions are concerned, they must apparently be either in the caseform corresponding to that carried by their coreferent within the predication, as in (5a–c), or have the form of a *de* phrase as in (5d). The nominative, in other words, would be ill-formed, see (5e). When the Theme-element is coreferent not to the Subj of the embedded predication but to some different constituent or to none at all, the construction of (5d) is the only one available. I have not found attested instances of this; I assume, however, that fictitious sentences such as the following are well-formed:

(6) a mihi dixit *de*   *bello*, hostes   fugisse
        me$_{dat}$ said$_{3sg}$ about war, enemy$_{acc}$ to-have-fled$_{inf}$
        "he told me about the war that the enemy had fled"

     b narravit *de hostibus* castra *eorum* non longe absese
        "he told about the enemy that their camp was not far away"

In the case of predicates governing finite clauses, various constructions are conceivable in which a Theme,Predication organization of the embedded predication might be realized, but attested instances of such constructions are lacking. Thus I do not know whether a Theme-expression could occur within the clause in the position following the conjunction, and what forms it may take (for Dutch instances of this see Dik, Chapter 5). On the other hand, it seems possible that a prepositional *de*-phrase may occur in the position preceding the subordinating conjunction, as in the fictitious examples (7a–a'). Conceivable patterns such as (7b–b'), in which the Theme element carries the caseform required for its coreferent pronoun within the subsequent predication, are not attested. Sentences such as (7c–c') on the other hand, are found regularly:

(7) a militibus imperavit, *de*   *captivis*, ut *eos*   caederent
        soldiers ordered$_{3sg}$ about captives, that them$_{acc}$ kill$_{3pl}$
        "he ordered the soldiers, concerning the captives, that they should kill them"

     a' militibus imperavit *de*   *captivis*   ut (*ei*)   caederentur
                                                 about the captives, that (they$_{nom}$) be-killed
        "he ordered the soldiers about the prisoners that they should be killed"

b   *militibus imperavit, captivos,   ut   eos   caederent
      captives$_{acc}$ that them$_{acc}$ kill$_{3pl}$

b′ *militibus imperavit, captivi,   ut   ei   caederentur
      captives$_{nom}$ that they$_{nom}$ be-killed$_{3pl}$

c   militibus imperavit *captivos*   ut   caederent
      captives$_{acc}$ that kill$_{3pl}$

c′ militibus imperavit *captivi*   ut   caederentur
      captives$_{nom}$ that be killed$_{3pl}$

In (7a′) the coreferent pronoun is Subj. Its explicit presence is not required, but it does not make the sentence ill-formed. Sentences (7b, b′), on the other hand, where, as might be expected in the case of a Theme,Predication organization, a coreferent pronoun is present, seem to me to be ill-formed.

The sentences (7c, c′) are well-formed. They resemble (7b, b′) in that the caseform of the italicized nouns corresponds to the caseform to be expected on the basis of the embedded predicate, but differ in that a coreferential pronoun is absent. In Latin grammars such sentences are sometimes discussed under the heading of "traiectio" (K.-St. II, 614). In view of the fact that (7b, b′) are ill-formed and (7c, c′)[11] are well-formed the question arises whether we are dealing with the same phenomenon— explicitation of a Theme—in such sentences. To answer this question I shall consider the properties of the construction exemplified by (7c, c′) in some more detail. I shall speak of "displacement" in the case of (7c, c′) but not in the case of (7b, b′).

4.1.3   Displacement without morphological adjustment

Instances of sentences such as (7c) may be found in K.-St. (II, 614–615). Some element of a subordinate clause will occur at a position preceding the subordinating conjunction, without being repeated by a coreferent pronoun within the subordinate clause. Attested instances are (8a–d):

(8) a   memorat *legiones*   *hostium*   ut   (**eos*)   fugaverit
        tell$_{3sg}$ legions$_{acc}$ enemy$_{gen}$ how (*them$_{acc}$) have-chased$_{3sg}$
        "he mentions how he has chased away the enemy's legions" (Pl. *Amph.* 136)

b   *salvus   domum* si (**ita/talis   *eo*)   rediero
safe_{nom} home   if (*thus/such *there) have-returned_{1sg}
"if I will safely have returned home" (Pl. *Amph.* 584)

c   scio iam *filius*   quod (**is*)   amet   *meus*   hanc meretricem
know_{1sg} son_{nom} that   (*he_{nom}) love_{3sg} mine_{nom} this lady
"I already know that my son loves this lady" (Pl. *As.* 52)

d   videndum est ...   *res* ...   *in tuto* ut   (**ea   *ita*)
to-be-seen is_{s3sg} ...   business_{nom} ... safely that (*it_{nom} *thus)

conlocetur
be-arranged_{3sg}

"it should be looked after that this business is arranged safely
(Ter. *Heau* 694)

With respect to instances such as (8a–d) K.-St. suggest a similar explanation as in the instances of Theme discussed in Section 4.1.1: the words
preceding the subordination conjunction have "special emphasis" (II, 614).
Although this implies a pragmatic motivation for the phenomenon, (8a–d)
exhibit various properties by which the wordgroups displaced differ from
Themes in an embedded Theme,Predication organization.

Apart from the fact that addition of a coreferent pronoun results in illformedness in the case of (8a–d) and not in (7b), a second difference with
patterns such as (5d or 7a) above is the fact that the phenomenon may
involve not only constituents referring to entities (as nouns do) but also
adjectives, see (8b). The latter type of elements can not occur with the
pragmatic function of Theme.

Thirdly, notice that the element displaced may not only be a whole NP
(8a), but may also be only the Head-part of a nominal phrase. Thus in
(8c) we find a possessive pronoun within the subordinate clause which is
Modifier to a displaced element.[12]

Fourthly, not only may one single constituent be wholly or partly displaced to a position preceding the conjunction without being repeated by
a coreferent pronoun: we may also find more than one element, which need
not together function as one constituent, so displaced. The elements involved may differ in the semantic status which they have in relation to
the predicate of the embedded predication. Thus, for example, in (8b), both
a predicative adjective and a Location argument have been displaced; in
(8d) displacement includes both a Subj and a Location argument.

A fifth difference is that this displacement is not limited to elements from embedded predications which have the status of an argument of the governing predicate. It also occurs with subordinate clauses which function as satellites in the main predication (cf. the conditional clause in (8b)). In the previous section, I have shown that embedded predications governed by verbs of speech may be provided with an explicitation of their Theme: they designate the content of an utterance, after all. In contrast, it is quite difficult to imagine how a constituent could have a pragmatic function Theme in relation to a predication which itself is a satellite (of Time, Place, Reason etc.) in relation to another predication.

Finally, in none of the sentences in (8) could the displaced elements possibly be replaced by a prepositional phrase introduced by *de* Themes, on the other hand, may always be expressed in this alternative form, both of main clauses and of embedded predications.

On the basis of these observations I conclude that in sentences exhibiting displacement as illustrated in (8) we are not dealing with a Theme,Predication organization of the subordinate clause. What then is the correct explanation of this phenomenon? To answer this question, I shall first discuss some other types of construction. These constructions exhibit displacement, but morphological adjustment to the new environment takes place as well (see 4.2). An explanation for this phenomenon is offered in 4.2.1.3, where I shall return to the possible validity of this explanation for the construction discussed above.

4.2   Pseudo-argument formation

Displacement plus morphological adjustment of the displaced element (pseudo-argument formation) is exhibited by a number of Latin constructions which, as I shall show below, mutually differ in several respects. I shall discuss two different types of pseudo-argument formation in 4.2.1 and 4.2.2.

4.2.1   *"Prolepsis": displacement and finite expression of the embedded predicate*

A first type of pseudo-argument formation is exhibited by sentences in which a nominal constituent of the subordinate clause is expressed in the form of an Object (carrying the accusative caseform) of the governing predicate. If the governing predicate is in the passive voice, the element involved will be expressed as its syntactic Subject (i.e. carry the nominative caseform). Examples of this type of pseudo-argument formation are the italicized NPs in (9)–(11):

(9) a *me*   pernosti . . . qualis sim
        me_{acc} $know_{2sg}$ . . . what kind of $person_{nom}$ be_{1sg}
        "you know what kind of person I am" (Ter. *Andr.* 503)

     b Quo leto   censes   *me*   ut   peream?
        what $death_{abl}$ $propose_{2sg}$ me_{acc} that die_{1sg}
        "with what death do you propose that I should die?" (Pl. *Merc.* 483)

     c vides *me*   ut   rapior
        see_{2sg} me_{acc} how $swept\text{-}away_{1sg}$
        "you see how I am being swept away" (Pl. *Rud.* 869)

(10) a haec *me*   ut   confidam faciunt
        these me_{acc} that $trust_{1sg}$ $make_{3pl}$
        "these things make me trust" (Cic. *Q.fr.* 2, 14, 2)

     b nunc ego *Simonem* mi   obviam veniat   velim
        now I $Simo_{acc}$ me_{dat} toward $come_{3sg}$ $want_{1sg}$
        "now I would wish that S. would meet me" (Pl. *Pseud.* 1061)

(11) a non fuit   *Juppiter*   metuendus   ne
        not was_{3sg} $Juppiter_{nom\ masc}$ $to\text{-}be\text{-}feared_{nom\ masc}$ that

        iratus   noceret
        $angry_{nom\ masc}$ $hurt_{3sg}$
        "it needed not be feared that J. would angry hurt" (Cic. *Off.* 3, 104)

     b *eam* veretur ne   perierit
        it_{acc} $fear_{3sg}$ that $be\text{-}lost_{3sg}$
        "she fears that it is lost" (Pl. *Rud.* 390)

The phenomenon illustrated in (9)–(11) occurs mainly with the semantic class of verbs designating speech, thought and perception, as in (9), and also with verbs of wishing and of causation,[13] as in (10a–b), and with verbs designating "to fear" (K.-St., II, 579). These classes of verbs may govern non-finite clauses (AcI-clauses), and/or finite *ut*-clauses; many of them may also govern dependent Question-clauses, as in (9a) (on the relation between complement type and meaning, see Bolkestein (1976a, 158ff.)). In textbooks on Latin the phenomenon under consideration is treated under the headings of "prolepsis" or "anticipation" of the Subject or of the "most dominant" or "prominent" element of the subordinate clause (K.-St., II, 578; Sz., 471). There is no exact definition of what constitutes "the most dominant" (see also Section 4.1 for a different type of construction, described in similar terms in Latin grammars).[14]

The question is how this phenomenon should be accounted for in a formal description of the sentences involved. As in the case of similar phenomena in other languages (see Chapters 3, 6, 7 and 8 on Hungarian, Serbo-Croatian, French and Portuguese respectively), there are in principle three conceivable solutions:

(1) The governing predicate in sentences such as (9)–(11) has more than one semantic predicate frame. In the frames utilized in (9)–(11), the italicized (pro)noun actually has the status of an argument in relation to the governing predicate involved. Accordingly, it fulfils its own specific semantic function in the state of affairs designated by that predicate.

(2) The governing predicates concerned do not necessarily have more than one semantic frame, but the fact that they allow patterns such as (9) is due to alternative Subject and Object assignments along the lines proposed in Dik (1979) for the English verb *to believe*: to the Subject of the embedded predication a second syntactic function is assigned, determined by the governing predicate, even though semantically (as an argument) it belongs to the embedded predicate.

(3) The predicates concerned do not have more than one semantic frame, but a rule of pseudo-argument formation is triggered by some constellation of syntactic and pragmatic factors. This implies that the rule involved applies in a late stage of the formation of Latin sentences, i.e. forms part of the expression rules of the grammar. Expression rules have as their input the results of syntactic and pragmatic function assignment to a predication (see on such rules Dik, 1978a, 157f.; Chapter 1). This third solution seems to be the most plausible one for Hungarian (de Groot, Chapter 3).

The choice between these three alternative analyses may differ among languages. Before trying to decide which solution is the most plausible in the case of Latin, I shall survey a number of properties of the construction under consideration. The solution chosen must agree with these properties.

4.2.1.1 The empirical data. The following properties of the construction under consideration must be accounted for in our description of the rule involved in pseudo-argument formation.

(i) The construction almost exclusively occurs when the pseudo-argument is coreferential to the Subject of the embedded predicate both when the latter is active voice and when it is passive.[15] In other words, we do not find constructions in which the pseudo-argument is coreferential to a constituent which if not displaced would be e.g. Recipient in the dative caseform within the embedded predication as in (12b). When an anaphoric pronoun is present (cf. also (7b)), this is ill-formed as well (cf. 12(c)):

(12) a   scio   quid patri   dederis
           know$_{1sg}$ what father$_{dat}$ have-given$_{2sg}$
           "I know what you have given your father"

     b *scio   *patrem*   quid dederis
         know$_{1sg}$ father$_{acc}$ what have-given$_{2sg}$

     c *scio   *patrem*   quid ei   dederis
         know$_{1sg}$ father$_{acc}$ what him$_{dat}$ have-given$_{2sg}$

It should be realized, however, that when the displaced constituent is co-referent to the Obj of the embedded predication, it is not possible to distinguish between "pure" displacement and pseudo-argument formation, since in that case the case-form of the displaced element (see also condition (iii)) is identical to the caseform it would have within the embedded predication (the accusative), as in (8a) above and in (13):

(13)   *dormientes spectatores* metuis ne   ex   somno excites?
         sleeping   public$_{acc}$ fear$_{2sg}$ that from sleep awaken$_{2sg}$
         "do you fear that you will wake up the sleeping public?" (Pl. *Merc.* 160)[16]

The condition that pseudo-argument formation may only apply to Subjects of the embedded predicate and not, for example, to Recipients is in fact parallel to the rules for *to believe* in English. It differs, on the other hand, from the possibilities in certain other languages, such as Ancient Greek, where pseudo-argument formation may also apply to Objects of the embedded predication, or Hungarian, where pseudo-argument formation, under the conditions relevant, may apply to any nominal element from the embedded predication (see de Groot, Chapter 3).

(ii) The construction is only allowed when the pseudo-argument comes from within a complement-clause, i.e. from within clauses which themselves have the status of an argument in relation to the governing predicate. It is ill-formed when the pseudo-argument relationally belongs to a satellite clause, as for example in (14):

(14) a   *hoc confiteor *te*   ut   abeas
          this confess$_{1sg}$ you$_{acc}$ in order that go-away$_{2sg}$
          "I confess this in order that you will leave"

      b   *mihi adest   *te*   quia   aeger es
          me$_{dat}$ assist$_{3sg}$ you$_{acc}$ because ill$_{nom}$ be$_{2sg}$
          "he is helping me because you are ill"

A similar condition seems to hold in other languages which also exhibit comparable pseudo-argument formation (see for example Gvozdanović, Chapter 6).

(iii) The governing predicates with which the phenomenon occurs always have an alternative pattern without displacement, i.e. a frame with one place less in which the second argument is an embedded predication. On the other hand, they do not all have an alternative two-place frame in which the second argument may be a nominal phrase (to be expressed in the accusative) which may have the same semantic features as the pseudo-arguments involved may have (see also (iv)). Thus, predicates such as *videre* "to see" and *expectare* "to await" occur both with an embedded predication and with [+concrete] nominal Goals as Object, but verbs such as *scire* "to know" or *velle* "to want" do not. This means, that with certain predicates pseudo-arguments may happen to have semantic characteristics which violate the selection restrictions imposed by that predicate. When this is the case the embedded predication clearly cannot be omitted. On this point, pseudo-argument formation seems to be conditioned by different factors in a language such as Hungarian. In Hungarian pseudo-arguments must conform, as far as their semantic features are concerned, to the semantic selection restrictions normally imposed by the governing predicates upon their own nominal arguments. In other words, in Hungarian, as opposed to Latin, pseudo-argument formation does not occur when the governing predicate does not also have a two place-frame in which a nominal second argument with the same semantic features is possible. Still, in Hungarian, the semantic relation between a "real" argument and its predicate is felt to be different from that between a pseudo-argument with the same semantic features and the predicate (cf. de Groot, Chapter 3).[17]

(iv) In spite of (iii), the predicates concerned must at least be "sympathetic" to the accusative caseform, i.e. require the accusative for expressing their second argument (when nominal).[18] A number of predicates in Latin have a two-place frame in which nominal second arguments are required to carry not the accusative but the dative or ablative caseform, for example. If such predicates also have a frame in which the second argument may be a predication, they still do not allow pseudo-argument formation, neither as an Object in the accusative caseform (cf. 15b) nor as a constituent in the caseform normally required by such verbs (cf. 15c):

(15) a   studeo   libertati
           strive-after$_{1sg}$ freedom$_{dat}$
           "I strive after freedom"

      b   *studeo   patriam   ut   salva   sit
           strive-after$_{1sg}$ country$_{acc}$ that free$_{nom}$ be$_{3sg}$
           "I try my best that my country is safe"

      c   *studeo   patriae   ut   salva   sit
           strive-after country$_{dat}$ that free$_{nom}$ be$_{3sg}$

This condition does not hold in Hungarian: in Hungarian when the governing verb is a "dative-sympathizer", there will be a dative pseudo-argument, etc. (see de Groot, Chapter 3).

(v) Non-finite realization of the embedded predication does not occur.[19] This is difficult to illustrate, because many of the governing predicates involved (such as for example *velle* "to want") may also govern non-finite clauses of the AcI-type, without semantic difference between the AcI and *ut*-clauses. With many other verbs, however, a semantic difference is correlated with the difference in type of clause, i.e. with the difference between governing, for example, a dependent Question-clause (with or without pseudo-argument formation) or an (often Declarative) AcI-clause (cf. Bolkestein (1976a, 284f.) on the notion Declarative as relevant for embedded predications). This may be illustrated by the predicate *scire* "to know" in (16a, b);

(16) a   scio   qualis   sis
           know$_{1sg}$ what-kind$_{nom}$ be$_{2sg}$

     =a′   scio   te   qualis   sis
           know$_{1sg}$ you$_{acc}$ what-kind$_{nom}$ be$_{2sg}$
           "I know what kind of person you are"

≠b   scio   te   bonum esse
      know1sg youacc goodacc to-beinf
      "I know that you are a good person"

In view of the semantic difference between (16a′) and (16b), the latter cannot be described as a non-finite realization of (16a′). (For further evidence that "real" AcI clauses must be distinguished from conceivable patterns consisting of an accusative pseudo-argument plus non-finite realization of the embedded predicate, see conditions (vi), (viii) and (ix) below.)

(vi) There is a strict condition with respect to the relative order of the pseudo-argument and the embedded predication, to the effect that the former *must precede* the latter, although there may be any number of constituents in between them. The position of the governing predicate, on the other hand, is free: it may both precede and follow the embedded predication.[20] If the former, it may both precede and follow the pseudo-argument. This condition upon the relative order of pseudo-argument and embedded predication is quite remarkable, in view of the relative freedom of word order in Latin. Two different conclusions may be drawn from it. First, it shows that there is a difference between, on the one hand, "real" Objects (constituents which semantically are arguments of the predicate in relation to which they have their syntactic function Object) and, on the other, pseudo-arguments which have only a syntactic relation. In three-place patterns "real" Objects may stand in a position either preceding or following any other arguments, even when that argument is an embedded predication and therefore might be expected to move towards the end of the sentence in accordance with the rules of LIPOC (Language-Independent Preferred Order of Constituents) proposed in Dik (1978a, 204–5; Chapter 8). In other words, the order in (17a), with a pseudo-argument (*me*), is not well-formed, whereas (17b), with a "real" Obj (*me*), is completely acceptable:

(17) a *fac   ut   sciam   *me*   /*scis   ubi   sim   *me*
         make that know1sg meacc /*know2sg where be1sg meacc
         "make me know" / "you know where I am"

      b ut   proficiscerem me   adhortatus est
         that leave1sg   meacc warned   have3sg
         "he has warned me to leave"

The second conclusion which arises from the restriction illustrated in

(17a) is that the pseudo-argument construction involved differs from the Latin AcI-construction in this respect.[21] Although statistically the accusative Subj in the AcI precedes its predicate more often than follows it (in agreement with the tendency for the Latin main verb to stand in sentence-final position), it will, for various reasons, quite often be the other way round (see 4.2.2.2). Thus both (18a and b) are well-formed, whereas (17a) is not:

(18) a   me   abire   dixit
          me_{acc} to-leave$_{inf}$ has-said$_{3sg}$
          "he said that I was leaving"

      b   abire   me   dixit
          to-leave$_{inf}$ me_{acc} has-said$_{3sg}$
          "he said that I was leaving"

(vii) As pointed out in 4.1.2 in connection with (7b, c), and in 4.1.3, there are no anaphorical pronouns within the embedded predication which are coreferential to the pseudo-argument.[22] This is perhaps not really surprising, in view of condition (i) and the fact that coreferent Subjects in Latin do not require pronominal elements anyway, even in the case of a Theme,Predication organization of the sentence (cf. Section 4.1.1, example (4a)). In the latter case, however, as noted earlier, coreferential pronouns may always be added.

(viii) When a pseudo-argument is present in the main clause, it is not possible for the governing predicate to govern a pronoun which is coreferential—referring either forward or backward—to the embedded predication as a whole. In other words, (19a–c) are perfectly acceptable (for examples see K.-St., I, 625), but (19d) is unacceptable:

(19) a   *hoc*   *me*   adhortabatur, ut   proficiscerem
          this$_{acc}$ me_{acc} warned$_{3sg}$ that leave$_{1sg}$
          "he gave me this advice, that I should leave"

      b   *hoc*   scit,   qualis   sim
          this$_{acc}$ know$_{3sg}$, what-kind$_{nom}$ be$_{1sg}$
          "this he knows, what type of person I am"

      c   scit   *me,*   qualis   sim
          know$_{3sg}$ me_{acc}. what-kind be$_{1sg}$
          "he knows, what type of person I am"

d *hoc   scit   *me*   qualis   sim
thisₐ𝒸𝒸 know₃ₛ𝓰 meₐ𝒸𝒸, what-kind be₁ₛ𝓰

In other words, the governing predicate cannot govern both a "real" Object and a pseudo-argument in the same (accusative) caseform (in (19a) both accusative constituents in the main clause are real arguments of *adhortari*). Note that pronouns referring to AcI-clauses are completely acceptable, cf. (20):[23]

(20) hoc   scit   me   bonum esse
      thisₐ𝒸𝒸 know₃ₛ𝓰 meₐ𝒸𝒸 goodₐ𝒸𝒸 to-beᵢₙ𝒻
      "this he knows, that I am a good person"

(ix) Pseudo-arguments cannot co-occur with a Theme,Predication organization of the embedded predication, in spite of the fact that a position would be available for it, since the pseudo-argument need not occupy this position itself (cf. (vi) above and section 4.1.2). Thus, whereas both (21a) —with *de patre* as Theme—and (21b)—with a pseudo-argument *me*—are well-formed, (21c, c′) are unacceptable (whatever their relative order):

(21) a   scis   *de   patre*, quid *ei*   dederim
          know₂ₛ𝓰 about father, what himdₐₜ have-given₁ₛ𝓰
          "you know, as for my father, what I have given him"

      b   scis   *me*   quid patri   dederim
          know₂ₛ𝓰 meₐ𝒸𝒸 what fatherdₐₜ have-given₁ₛ𝓰
          "you know what I have given my father"

      c   *scis   *me   de   patre* quid ei   dederim
          know₂ₛ𝓰 meₐ𝒸𝒸 about father what himdₐₜ have-given₁ₛ𝓰

      c′ *scis *de patre me* quid ei dederim

(22) a   de   patre, scis   quid ei   dederim
          about father, know₂ₛ𝓰 what himdₐₜ have-given₁ₛ𝓰
          "as for father, you know what I have given him"

     =b   de   patre, scis   me   quid ei   dederim
          about father, know₂ₛ𝓰 meₐ𝒸𝒸 what himdₐₜ have-given₁ₛ𝓰

As we have seen in Section 4.1.1, in the case of complex sentences with a Theme,Predication organization the Theme may be coreferential to an element within the embedded predication, as in (22). This element functions as Theme of the sentence as a whole.[24] In this case pseudo-argument formation is not excluded, cf. (22b). As is mentioned by Gvozdanović (Chapter 6), in Serbo-Croatian too, co-occurrence of pseudo-arguments with a Theme,Predication organization of the clause is not allowed. The behaviour of patterns exhibiting pseudo-argument formation differs from that of AcI clauses with respect to this criterion: as pointed out in 4.1.2, in Latin, the expression of the Theme of an embedded predication at the position directly preceding it, as in (23) and (5d) above, is well-formed:

(23) rumor est de   Caesare, eum profugisse
      rumour is about Caesar, he$_{acc}$ to-have-fled$_{inf}$
      "the rumour goes, that as for Caesar, he has left"

The possibility for Theme to co-occur with an AcI is another illustration of the fact that the accusative noun of an AcI should be analysed as different from pseudo-arguments such as *me* in (21b); cf. also (vii) and (viii).

An explanation of the phenomenon of pseudo-argument formation must be compatible with the observations given in this section. In 4.2.1.2 I shall consider which of the three alternative descriptions is to be preferred.

4.2.1.2 Solutions (1), (2) and (3) reconsidered.   I shall now reconsider the three possible solutions for analysing sentences in which pseudo-argument-formation has taken place, as suggested in 4.2.1: (1) in terms of more than one predicate frame, (2) in terms of alternative Subject and Object assignments, and (3) as a rule to be applied after both Subj (and Obj) assignment and pragmatic function assignment have taken place.

Various observations made in 4.2.1.1 disagree with solution (1). Observation (vi), for example, offers counter-evidence: in Latin, arguments in a predicate frame may be placed in any order with respect to each other and with respect to their governing predicate: their order is presumably determined by contextual (i.e. pragmatic) factors.[25] There is no evidence that Latin word-order rules are sensitive to either the *semantic* function or to the *syntactic* function of arguments. Observation (iii) also shows that with at least some predicates, such as *scire* "to know", the accusative cannot be considered to be an argument of the governing predicate anyway, although with other predicates (such as *videre* "to see") this seems to be an attractive analysis. Furthermore (cf. (viii)), the fact that no pronominalization of the embedded predication is possible in case of presence of a pseudo-argument in the main clause, argues against (1). It suggests that, on the one hand, in the case of pseudo-argument formation the "remainder" of the embedded predication is not itself the type of (pragmatic) entity which can be referred to by a pronoun (as opposed to embedded predications where no pseudo-argument formation has taken place); and, on the other hand, it suggests that the pseudo-argument cannot function as a constituent on sentence level in isolation from the embedded predication. Thus, its behaviour with respect to pronominalization also offers evidence against the view that we are dealing with three-place patterns in which (apart from the Subj) the two other constituents have an equal status in relation to the predicate. Apart from these counter-arguments, existence of a frame in which the pseudo-argument is a real argument would perhaps lead us to expect the possibility of a non-finite realization of the embedded predicate, since we would then be dealing with the ideal conditions for a rule of so-called a "Equi-NP-deletion". We would then have to explain why in such a frame infinitivization apparently does not take place[26] (cf. (v)), although it often does in other three-place patterns in Latin, as in: *te adhortor proficisci* ("you$_{acc}$ I admonish to leave$_{inf}$") instead of *te adhortor ut proficiscaris$_{2sg}$* (id).

These remarks lead to a rejection of solution (1). However, some of the same observations also offer valid evidence against solution (2), i.e. the solution of alternative Subject and Object assignments. If Obj assignment is able to "dip into" the embedded predication in Latin (cf. Dik, 1979), we still need an additional expression-rule which is sensitive to the history of this Object, in order to place such Objects at a position preceding that of the embedded predication to which they relationally belong (this requirement holds for the patterns of English *to believe* as well). Ordering rules in Latin (as opposed to English) are not sensitive only to the syntactic function Object (cf. sentence (17b)). Since it is dubious whether there are any patterns in Latin which should be analysed in terms of alternative Obj assignment, solution (2) would lead to complications.[27] The condition with respect to the relative word order of pseudo-argument and embedded predication (observation vi) rather seems to point in the direction of a pragmatic motivation for such a construction, i.e. towards solution (3). It should be realized, however, that none of the other observations made in the previous section is absolutely incompatible with solution (2): it is not impossible to describe them as conditions upon the applicability of a rule of alternative Obj assignment.

However, apart from the difficulties for solution (2) raised by observation (vi), another *positive* argument in favour of assuming a pragmatic motivation for pseudo-argument formation (solution 3) rather than one in terms of Obj assignment, is offered by observation (ix): the impossibility of co-occurrence with a Theme,Predication-arrangement of the embedded predication. It is, however, not clear precisely how this fact should be interpreted. One interpretation would be to consider the pseudo-argument itself as Theme: as I have argued in 4.1.2, certain types of embedded predications themselves have a first position available for expression of their Theme; see sentences (5a–d).[28]

Objections to this view are, first, that the pseudo-argument is not required to stand at the position directly preceding the embedded predication as a whole, whereas this is the position which Theme-expressions (such as prepositional phrases with *de*) normally occupy (see (21a), (23)). Secondly (see vii), there never is a coreferential pronoun within the embedded predication (something which, although perhaps not required in Latin, in the case of Themes coreferent to Subjects still frequently occurs), and addition of one leads to illformedness. Thirdly, we would expect not only the position to be more strictly determined than it is, but also, for Themes, perhaps the possibility of the nominative case-form rather than the accusative. Fourthly (see i), if pseudo argument-formation is a way for expressing an embedded Theme,Predication organization, this way of expression is only possible for those Themes which happen to be coreferent to Subjects. Consequently Themes which are not coreferential to Subjects—and Themes often are not; see Section 4.1—cannot become pseudo-argument of the main predicate. Such Themes must have the form of prepositional phrases or be in the same caseform which their coreferents within the embedded predication carry. In other words, if we accept this explanation of phenomenon (ix), Themes of embedded predications which are coreferent to the Subject of the predication involved apparently behave quite differently from Themes which are not. If the two phenomena are not in complementary distribution because they are both a way to explicitate the Theme of the embedded predication, then a different interpretation of the fact that co-occurrence of pseudo-argument formation with expression of the Theme of the embedded predication is not allowed could be that, in view of the pragmatic condition of relevance, the pragmatic function Theme can only be expressed with respect to a *complete* predication. In the case of pseudo-argument formation, as we have seen above, the "remainder" of the embedded predication does not have the status enabling it to be referred to by an anaphoric pronoun on sentence level; see (viii) and (13a–b). It may be due to the same fact that it cannot be preceded by explicitation of Theme either.

4.2.1.3   Pragmatic conditions on pseudo-argument formation. If pseudo-arguments are not pragmatically Themes of the embedded predication, what are they? Two other pragmatic functions may be relevant in this respect, that of Topic and that of Focus. *Topic* is defined by Dik (1978a, 141) as "the entity which marks that constituent of a predication about which the predication can be taken to predicate something". (N.B. there is a difference with the definition of Subject, namely as "the entity from whose point of view the state of affairs is presented" (Dik, 1978a,142–143). *Focus* in its turn is defined as "that pragmatic function which characterizes constituents which present the relatively most important or salient information with respect to the pragmatic information of the Speaker and the Addressee" (Dik, 1978a, 149). Both Topic- and Focus-function are, in other words, carried by elements within the predication.

If we look at the available instances[29] of pseudo-argument formation from this perspective, many pseudo-arguments clearly have the pragmatic status of Topics within the embedded predication: this is obviously the case in all sentences in which the embedded predication is a dependent Question clause, introduced by a question word. By far the greatest number of the instances of pseudo-argument formation concern just this type of clause (K.-St., II, 578; Sz., 471), exemplified by (9a) above. In such clauses, Focus-value is undeniably bound up with the question-word: question-answer patterns are in fact one of the main criteria for distinction between the two pragmatic functions under consideration (Dik, 1978a, 149–153).

Thus, a sentence such as (24a) may be said to have the underlying predication (24b); after Subj-assignment[30] (24c) and pragmatic function distribution, this becomes (24d):

(24) a   te   quid facias demonstrat
           you$_{acc}$ what do$_{2sg}$ show$_{3sg}$
           "he shows what you are doing"

      b   demonstrare $(x_i)_{Ag}$ $(x_j:$ [facere $(x_k)_{Ag}$ $(Qx_l)_{Go}](x_j))_{Go}$

      c   demonstrare $(x_i)_{AgSubj}$ $(x_j:$ [facere $(x_k)_{AgSubj}$ $(Qx_l)_{Go}](x_j))_{Go}$

      d   demonstrare $(x_i)_{AgSubj}$ $(x_j:$ [facere $(x_k)_{AgSubjTop}$ $(Qx_l)_{GoFoc}]$ $(x_j))_{Go}$

If the governing verb is a two-place verb "sympathizing with the accusative" such as *demonstrare*, the constellation SubjTop at the argument x_k

within the embedded predication (x_j) optionally triggers an ordering rule which displaces the element x_k to any position preceding the embedded predication. If the governing verb has an Agent Subj and will be expressed in the active voice, a rule of casemarking will subsequently assign the accusative to x_k. If Subj is assigned to x_j instead of to x_i in (24c), x_k, after having been similarly displaced, will in that case subsequently be marked by the nominative caseform. Unlike de Groot (Chapter 3) on similar sentences, I do not attribute a specific pragmatic status to the embedded predication x_j as a whole, because I am not convinced that this is relevant information in the case of the construction involved. In Section 4.2.2.2, however, I shall come back to the various alternative pragmatic function arrangements possible in complex sentences.

The majority of cases of pseudo-argument formation concern dependent question-clauses. However, the phenomenon also occurs in case of other types of embedded predications such as *ut*-clauses governed by *censere* (9b), *facere*[31] and *velle* (10a, b), and complements introduced by *ne* with verbs such as *vereri* "to fear" (11b). In such subordinate clauses the arrangement of pragmatic functions is less obvious and often only traceable from a closer investigation of the wider context. In many instances here as well, the pseudo-argument involved turns out to be the Topic.

Occasionally, however, a pseudo-argument seems to be Focus rather than Topic. The perfect proof that pseudo-arguments may have Focus-status, would, of course, be sentences such as (25), in which the pseudo-argument is itself a question-word or forms the answer to a question:

(25) a *Quem*   times ne   desit?   ::*Amicum* (timeo
        Whom$_{acc}$ fear$_{2sg}$ that be-absent$_{3sg}$? ::Friend$_{acc}$ (fear$_{1sg}$

        ne desit)
        be-absent$_{3sg}$)

        "Who are you afraid that will be missing? :: My friend (I am afraid that will be missing)"

     b *Quos*   effecit ut   scirent?::*Hostes*   (effecit
        Who$_{acc\ pl}$ made$_{3sg}$ that knew$_{3pl}$::The enemy$_{acc\ pl}$ made$_{3sg}$

        ut   scirent)
        that knew$_{3pl}$

        "Who did he let know? The enemy (he did let know)"

Such sentences would obviously also be hard to fit in with a hypothesis that "pseudo-arguments are Themes". In fact, I have not encountered attested instances of sentences such as (25a, b) or of sentences in which a pseudo-argument is explicitly indicated to have (contrastive) Focus by means of the formulation *non solum* . . ., *sed etiam* ("not only . . ., but also") or by means of a particle such as *quidem*, as in the fictitious sentences (26)[32]:

(26) a scio   non solum *te*   sed etiam *filium tuum* qualis sit
         know$_{1sg}$ not just   you$_{acc}$ but also son$_{acc}$ your how   be$_{3sg}$
         "I know not only how you are, but also how your son is"

      b alii   adsunt;   *te*   quidem nescio ubi   sis
         the others$_{nom}$ be present$_{3pl}$; you$_{acc}$ not-know$_{1sg}$ where be$_{2sg}$
         "the others are there; where you are, I don't know"

Although not attested, sentences (26a–b) do not seem less acceptable to me than (25a, b).

Apart from the possibility that pseudo-arguments are those constituents from the embedded predication which are pragmatically either Topic (as in most cases) or Focus, it is of course conceivable that a pseudo-argument is neither, as in the fictitious example (27):

(27) *Cui*   data   est?::   *Metuo *dominum* ne   inimico   eam
        Who$_{dat}$ given$_{nom}$ be$_{3sg}$?:: I fear   master$_{acc}$ that enemy$_{dat}$ her$_{acc}$
        vendidit
        have-sold$_{3sg}$

        "To whom has she been given?:: I fear that her master has sold her to your enemy"

In sentence (27), *Cui* and *inimico* carry Focus-value, and *eam* is Topic: the pseudo-argument *dominum* is neither. Again, attested examples of such a pragmatic function arrangement have not come to my attention. Nor do they strike me as very likely to occur in Latin. If they did occur, they would create problems for the view that pseudo-argument formation is motivated by a specific constellation of syntactic and pragmatic functions: either that the Subj of the embedded predicate carries the pragmatic function Topic and another constituent of the embedded predication that of Focus; or that the Subj carries Focus. In both cases the embedded predication may be said to be pragmatically "split up".[33]

The above conclusion implies that the rule which forms pseudo-arguments of the type we have been discussing comes quite late in the formation of sentences: it comes *after syntactic function assignment* and *after pragmatic function distribution*. The rule is apparently triggered by this constellation of syntactic and pragmatic functions, but only if the governing predicate happens to be one which is "sympathetic to the accusative": this latter type of information, in other words, must be available before the rule applies. Which syntactic status and (caseform) the pseudo-argument receives depends on the syntactic function assigned to the arguments of the governing predicate: if the first argument is Subject, the pseudo-argument will be expressed in the accusative caseform; if it is not Subject, the pseudo-argument will be expressed in the nominative caseform.

If we classify the ordering rule plus the rule assigning the caseform as a rule of syntactic function-assignment, we create the suggestion that this rule takes place at an earlier stage in the formation of sentences, before pragmatic function assignment. If it did, however, we would be unable to account for the various phenomena connected with pseudo-arguments discussed above.

As we have seen in Section 4.1.3, there are also cases in Latin of displacement without morphological adjustment to the new environment which cannot be interpreted as exhibiting an embedded Theme,Predication organization (examples 8a–d). It would of course be attractive if it was possible to assume that these cases are in fact conditioned by the same pragmatic function arrangement, namely by special pragmatic prominence in the sentence as a whole of an element of the embedded predication, and that the rule which assigns the accusative (or nominative) caseform to the displaced element applies optionally after the rule which determines the relative order of the constituents involved. I have not investigated in detail whether the pragmatic conditions in the case of "pure" displacement are the same as in the case of pseudo-argument formation. However, the fact that (as we have seen) pure displacement is not limited to Subj of the embedded predicate, or even to constituents which have the status of an argument within the embedded predication, and that more than one element may be displaced or only a part of a constituent (4.1.3 (8a–d)) suggests that the motivation for this type of displacement is different from that causing pseudo-argument formation. Further investigation is needed to determine exact function of the former phenomenon.[34]

I shall now discuss a second type of pseudo-argument formation which is common in Latin. In this connection, I shall make a few general remarks on possible pragmatic function-distrubutions within complex sentences (in Section 4.2.2.2).

4.2.2   The "personal passive" or "Nominativus cum Infinitivo" (NcI) construction

A second type of displacement in Latin in which the displaced element undergoes morphological adjustment to another predicate than that to which it semantically belongs is the so-called Nominativus cum Infinitivo (NcI)-construction.[35] This construction is one of the two ways in which certain Latin sentences containing Accusativus cum Infinitivo (AcI)-clauses may be passivized. The two ways which are possible in principle for passivizing an AcI are exemplified by (28b–c):

(28) a dico   milites   mortuos esse   AcI
         say$_{1sg}$ soldiers$_{acc\ pl}$ dead$_{acc\ pl}$ to-be$_{inf}$
         "I say that the soldiers have died"

      b dictum   est   milites   mortuos esse   AcI
         said$_{nom\ sg}$ be$_{3sg}$ soldiers$_{acc\ pl}$ dead$_{acc\ pl}$ to-be$_{inf}$
         "it is said that the soldiers have died"

      c milites   mortui   esse   dicuntur   NcI
         soldiers$_{nom\ pl}$ dead$_{nom\ pl}$ to-be$_{inf}$ be-said$_{3pl}$
         'the soldiers are said to have died"

In (28c) it is clear that the nominal constituent *milites* is semantically an argument of the predicate *mortui esse* "to be dead". Syntactically, however, it behaves as a Subject to the governing predicate *dicere* "to say". Semantic classes of predicates which allow both a regular passive and an NcI as in (28c) are verbs of speech and verbs of thought (the embedded predication with such verbs, in other words, may be a Declarative or an Imperative clause (Bolkestein, 1976a)). Other predicates which govern an AcI, e.g. *velle* "to want", cannot be passivized at all and consequently do not occur with the NcI; naturally, the same holds for one-place predicates governing AcIs, e.g. *aequum est* "it is just". Verbs of emotion, which also govern AcI-clauses, e.g. *gaudere* "to enjoy", rarely occur with a NcI, even if they allow of passivization.[36]

I shall assume here that a solution in which two predicate frames are attributed to a governing verb such as *dicere* is to be rejected (solution 1 of Section 4.2.1.2) and that the Latin AcI-construction cannot be analysed satisfactorily in terms of some form of Object-assignment to the accusative NP which is Subj of the AcI-clause. (See Section 4.2.1.1, especially (vi),

(vii) and (ix); for a number of other arguments against such an analysis see also Bolkestein (1979).)

The question to be investigated is whether there is a difference in the conditions under which the (b) form or the (c) form is chosen for passivizing (28a). In other words, is it simply a question of a different assignment of syntactic functions over the nominal elements involved (see solution (2), Section 4.2.1.2), similar to what was proposed with regard to the English verb to *believe* in Dik (1979), i.e. independent of pragmatic factors; or are there perhaps certain pragmatic factors which influence the choice of passive construction? In the latter case, the rule which assigns the nominative case-form to *milites* in (21c) applies after a certain syntactic and pragmatic constellation has been assigned to the underlying predication. It must then be viewed as an expression rule, and consequently as quite similar to the rule responsible for "prolepsis" in Latin (4.2.1) and Hungarian (de Groot, Chapter 3).

4.2.2.1 Empirical observations. In Latin Grammars (e.g. Kühner-Stegmann, I, 708; Sz., 363) a number of conditions are mentioned in which the choice of an NcI-construction is claimed to be less "natural' 'than the choice of a passive such as (b), in which the embedded predication is maintained as an AcI-clause. This judgment about the "naturalness" of one construction as opposed to the other is intuitive and not supported by statistical data.[37] It seems to agree, however, with my own observations, based on some two hundred attested instances. Some of these conditions are reminiscent of certain conditions listed in 4.2.1.1. They are the following:

(i) When the governing predicate is in the perfect passive tense, or in gerundi(v)um-construction, i.e. when we are dealing with so-called compound verbal forms consisting of a participle or participle-like form of the predicate plus a form of *esse* "to be", the AcI is claimed to be preferred above the NcI. However, it is not difficult to find instances of the latter. Examples of AcI and NcI in the case of compound verb forms are (29) and (30) respectively:

(29) a quam Gallos   obtinere   dictum   est
         which Gauls_{acc pl} to-occupy_{inf} said_{nom sg} be_{3sg}
         "about which it is said that the G. occupy it" (Caes. *BG* 1, 1, 5)

      b in hac habitasse   platea dictum est   Chrysidem
         in this to-have-lived_{inf} ally   said_{nom} be_{3sg} Chrysides_{acc}
         "in this ally it is said that C. has lived" (Ter. *Andr.* 796)[38]

(30) a   quae   ab aliquo . . .   dicta   sunt fore
         which$_{nom}$ by someone . . . said$_{nom\ pl}$ be$_{3pl}$ to-will-happen
         "things which by someone are said to be going to happen" (Cic.
         Top. 93)

      b   quia   ⟨patria⟩   tanta sapientia fuisse
         because ⟨the country$_{nom\ fem}$⟩ of such wisdom to-have-been$_{inf}$

         . . . putanda   est
         . . . to-be-believed$_{nom\ fem}$ be$_{3sg}$

         "because the country should be believed to have had such a
         great wisdom" (Cic. *De or.* 1, 196)

Although not ill-formed, instances such as (30) are statistically much less
frequent.

(ii)   When the governing predicate itself is governed by an "auxiliary"
or modal verb such as e.g. *posse* "may, can" or *debere* "must", the NcI is
claimed to be much less frequent than the AcI. Again the latter is not
wholly excluded, cf. (31) and (32):

(31) a   negarine   ullo modo possit . . .   quemquam . . .
         to-be-denied in any way be-possible$_{3sg}$ . . . anyone$_{acc}$ . . .

         effici   posse?
         to-be-made can$_{inf}$

         "can it be denied in any way that anyone could be made" (Cic.
         Fin. 3, 29)

      b   ex   quo   iudicari   potest virtutis esse . . . cursus
         from which to-be-judged can$_{3sg}$ of virtue to-be . . . the course$_{acc\ pl}$
         "from which it may be judged, that the course of virtue is . . ."
         (Cic. *Phil.* 5, 48)

(32) a   an . . . futura   quae sint, ea   vera
         . . . future things$_{acc\ pl}$ which be$_{3pl}$, those$_{nom\ pl}$ true$_{nom\ pl}$

         esse   possint intellegi
         to-be$_{inf}$ can$_{3pl}$ to-be-understood

         "or can things that are going to be in the future be understood
         to be true" (Cic. *Fat.* 32)

b   si dici   possit ex   hostibus   equus   esse
    if to-be-said can$_{3sg}$ from the enemy the horse$_{nom\ sg}$ to-be

captus
taken$_{nom}$

"if the horse can be said to have been taken from an enemy"
(Cic. *Inv.* 1, 85)

Here as well, this difference is a matter of relative frequency: (31a, b) are more frequent than (32a, b).

(iii) When the governing predicate is combined with certain adverbial expressions, such as e.g. a sentential Disjunct, or accompanied by a Recipient-constituent in the dative case-form or an Agent in the ablative introduced by *ab*, again the AcI is preferred above the NcI-construction; see (33). Occasionally, however, a NcI is found as well; see (30a) and (34):

(33) a   non sine causa   dicitur   ad officia referri   omnes
          not without reason be said$_{3sg}$ to duty   to-be-referred$_{inf}$ all

nostras cogitationes
our   thoughts$_{3pl}$

"not without reason it is said that all our thoughts are brought back to duty" (Cic. *Off.* 3, 60)

b   nuntiatum   est   nobis a M. Varrone venisse
    announced$_{nom\ neu}$ be$_{3sg}$ us   from M. Varro to-have-come$_{inf}$

eum Romam pridie
he$_{acc}$ to Rome the day before

"the message reached us from V. that he had come to R. the day before" (Cic. *Ac.* 1, 1)

(34) a   quae (res)   inesse   in homine perspiciantur   ab
          which (things)$_{nom\ pl}$ to-be$_{inf}$ in man   be-perceived$_{3pl}$ by

iis   qui ...
those who ...

"things which may be perceived to exist in man by those people who ..." (Cic. *Leg.* 1, 62)

b   dicitur   mihi servus fugitivus   cum Vardaeis esse
    be-said$_{3sg}$ me   slave$_{nom}$ run-away ... with the V.   to-be$_{inf}$
    "Your runaway slave is said to me to be with the V." (Cic. *Fam.* 5, 9, 2)

Some expressions the presence of which influences the choice of an AcI are *contra, merito, vix, recte, non dubie*, truth-value specifying and evaluative expressions.[39]

(iv) The NcI-construction is incompatible with the occurrence of anaphoric pronouns which are coreferential to the embedded predication as a whole, as in (35a) (4.2.1.1 (viii)):

(35) a vere etiam illud dicitur,   facillime consequi homines . . .
          truely even that be-said$_{3sg}$ easily   arrive-at people$_{acc\ pl}$
          "this remark is also true, that people easily arrive at . . ." (Cic.
          de Orat. 1, 150)

      b *illud* etiam dicuntur /dicitur,   milites   mortui
          this$_{sg}$ also   be-said$_{3pl}$/be-said$_{3sg}$. soldiers$_{nom\ pl}$ dead$_{nom\ pl}$
          esse
          to-be$_{inf}$

A construction such as (35b) is ill-formed, both when the governing predicate is plural, agreeing with the noun *milites*, and when it is singular, agreeing with the resumptive pronoun.

Apart from the above observations which are found in textbooks on Latin, the NcI exhibits some further characteristics which also must be accounted for in a description.

(v) Firstly, statistically, there is a very strong tendency for the Subj of the NcI—when explicitly expressed—to precede the infinitive, i.e. the predicate to which it semantically belongs.[40] At the same time the nominative may either precede the governing predicate or follow it. In the case of the AcI-construction on the other hand, the Subj of the AcI precedes the infinitive more often than follows it, but instances of the Subj following the infinitive are not at all uncommon, e.g. (29b) and (33a,b).

(vi) A second statistical tendency is the fact that when the passive governing predicate stands in sentence-initial position—which is a marked position for finite verbs in Latin, the pattern position for finite verbs being sentence-final[41]—the construction will almost always be an AcI, and not a NcI. Thus (33b) is much more frequent than (34b), which is rare and is one of the few exceptions to this tendency.

(vii) Finally, as pointed out previously, it is quite possible to explicitate the Theme of a non-finite predication by means of a PP introduced by *de* either at the beginning of the sentence as a whole, or at the position immediately preceding the embedded predication, Section 4.1.2, examples

(2b–e) and (5d) above; I have however not found an embedded Theme, Predication organization co-occurring with a Nominative cum Infinitivo construction. Thus sentences such as (36a) and (37a) are unattested in Latin, whereas the corresponding AcI-constructions—(36b) and (37b)— are well-formed:

(36) a *dicuntur *de*   *militibus ei*   mortui   esse
         be-said$_{3pl}$ about soldiers they$_{nom\ pl}$ dead$_{nom\ pl}$ to-be$_{inf}$
         "it is said that, with respect to the soldiers, they are dead"

      b dicitur   *de*   *militibus eos*   mortuos esse
         be-said$_{3sg}$ about soldiers they$_{acc\ pl}$ dead   to-be$_{inf}$

(37) a *dicuntur *de*   *bello milites*   mortui   esse
         be-said$_{3pl}$ about war soldiers$_{nom\ pl}$ dead$_{nom\ pl}$ to-be$_{inf}$
         "it is said about the war that the soldiers are dead"

      b dicitur   *de*   *bello milites*   mortuos esse
         be-said$_{3sg}$ about war soldiers$_{acc\ pl}$ dead$_{acc\ pl}$ to-be$_{inf}$
         "it is said about the war that the soldiers are dead"

Both if we interpret the above PPs as explicitating the Theme of the embedded predications and if we analyse them as arguments of the governing verbs, (36a) and (37a) are ill-formed. The sentences are not ill-formed, of course, if the PPs are placed at the beginning of the sentence as a whole and consequently have to be interpreted as Themes of the sentences as a whole.[42] (See (xi) in Section 4.2.1.1.)

What possible explanation is there for the above series of phenomena? Clearly, the two passive formations do not occur with the same frequency in all circumstances, even though there are almost no contexts, apart from those discussed in (iv) and (vii), which totally exclude one of the two constructions from being used.

Some of the above phenomena, such as (v), suggest that the decisive factor may be connected with differences in the distribution of pragmatic functions over the sentence as a whole. Tendency (v) for example, could be due to the fact that, in case of a NcI-construction, the Subject-element of the embedded predication has a specific pragmatic status within the sentence as a whole (for example that of Topic or of Focus) which it does not have in case of an AcI construction.

Before reconsidering the empirical data in this light, it will be usedful to discuss in more detail what pragmatic function arrangements are conceivable in complex sentences.

4.2.2.2   Topic and Focus patterns within complex sentences.   In a sentence which contains an embedded predication which is not a dependent question-clause but, for example, a Declarative or Imperative one, various Topic and Focus arrangements are conceivable. Take, for example, a predication such as (38). This predication, after syntactic function assignment, may serve as underlying predication in an answer to any of the questions given in (39a–e):

(38)   dicere (legatus)$_{AgSubj}$ (x$_i$: [mortuus esse (Caesar)$_{\emptyset Subj}$] (x$_i$))$_{Go}$

(39)   a   *Quis*   dixit   Caesarem mortuum esse?::   *Legatus*
            Who$_{nom}$ said$_{3sg}$ Caesar$_{acc}$ dead$_{acc}$ to-be$_{inf}$?::   The legate$_{nom}$
            (dixit etc.)
            (said$_{3sg}$ etc.)
            "*Who* said that C. was dead?: *The legate* (said that etc.)"

       b   *Quid* legatus dixit?::((Legatus) dixit) *Caesarem mortuum esse*
            "*What* did the legate say?:: (The legate said)*that C. was dead*"

       c   *Quid fecit* legatus?:: (Legatus) *dixit* etc.
            "*What did* the legate *do*?::(The legate) *said that* etc."

       d   *Quem* dixit legatus mortuum esse?::(Mortuum esse) *Caesarem* (legatus) dixit)
            "*Who* did the legate say that was dead?::(He said that) *Caesar* (was dead)"[43]

       e   *Quid accidisse* Caesari dixit legatus?::(Legatus dixit) Caesarem *mortuum esse*
            "*What* did the legate say that *happened* to Caesar?::(He said that) Caesar *was dead*"

In other words, in an appropriate context or situation, given a sentence with the underlying predication presented in (38), each constituent of that predication may be the one which gives the most salient information, i.e. have the pragmatic function of Focus. In (39a–e) I have indicated this pragmatic function by italics. In (39a–c), the Focus constituent belongs to the main clause: in (39a) Focus is on the AgSubj *legatus*, in (39b) Focus is on the GoObj, x_i, i.e. on the whole embedded predication. Furthermore each of the constituents within the embedded predication may be Focus as well: in (39d), the Subj of the embedded predicate, *Caesarem*, carries Focus, and in (39e) Focus is on the embedded predicate *mortuum esse*. Correspondingly, in each sentence, a different part of the predication represented in (38) will carry the pragmatic function Topic. It is not easy to decide whether in (39a–e) all not-Focus elements are in fact Topic, or whether in each sentence only one not-Focus element is Topic. (An argument in favour of the first alternative seems to be, that in Latin in an answer to a question none of them needs to be expressed explicitly.) Focus is easier to identify than Topic. Thus, it might be argued that in (39a) Topic is either the whole sequence *dixit Caesarem mortuum esse*, or some part of it, for example *Caesarem*, and that in (39b) Topic may be either the whole sequence *dixit legatus* or some part of it, e.g. *legatus*, etc. In Functional Grammar, Topic is usually attributed to one constituent of a predication. At the same time, however, the possibility is left open, that in one sentence there may be more than one Topic (Dik, 1978a, 143).

Leaving out indication of Topic, I indicate Focus by italics in the following predications corresponding to (39a–e). In (c') I have attributed Focus only to *dicere*, although perhaps it should be assigned to the whole combination of *dicere* plus its embedded predication:

(39) a' dicere (*legatus*)$_{\text{AgSubjFoc}}$ (x_i: [mortuus esse (Caesar)$_{\text{θSubj}}$] (x_i))$_{\text{Go}}$

    b' dicere (legatus)$_{\text{AgSubj}}$ (x_i: [*mortuus esse (Caesar)$_{\text{θSubj}}$*] (x_i))$_{\text{Go Foc}}$

    c' *dicere*$_{\text{Foc}}$ (legatus)$_{\text{AgSubj}}$ (x_i: [mortuus esse (Caesar)$_{\text{θSubj}}$] (x_i))$_{\text{Go}}$

    d' dicere (legatus)$_{\text{AgSubj}}$ (x_i: [mortuus esse (*Caesar*)$_{\text{θSubjFoc}}$] (x_i))$_{\text{Go}}$

    e' dicere (legatus)$_{\text{AgSubj}}$ (x_i: [*mortuus esse*$_{\text{Foc}}$ (Caesar)$_{\text{θSubj}}$] (x_i))$_{\text{Go}}$

From (39a'–e'), it is clear that at least two basically different pragmatic function arrangements must be distinguished: (1) a pragmatic function arrangement in which the embedded predication *as a whole* has the pragmatic function Focus, as in (39b), or *as a whole* is not-Focus, as in (39a); and (2) a situation in which some element from within the embedded predication—be it the Subj, as in (39d), or the embedded predicate, as in (39e)—is Focus of the sentence as a whole and provides its most salient information. Accordingly in such a situation, the embedded predication does not function as a unified entity from a pragmatic point of view.

This distinction into two basically different pragmatic arrangements does not exclude the possibility that in a situation such as (1) the embedded predication may internally have a (secondary) pragmatic function distribution. In fact, the various possibilities outlined in (43–44) below suggest that this is the case. However, the relevant difference between (1) and (2) is that in (1), in the sentence as a whole in its context, the embedded predication functions *as a unified entity* from the pragmatic point of view, whereas in (2) it does not. Consequently, in (2) no secondary internal pragmatic function arrangement within the embedded predication is possible.

Now, consider a predicate such as *dicere*, which in the active voice requires the AcI-construction for realizing a (Declarative) embedded predication. When *dicere* is in the active voice, as in examples (39a–e), no alternative syntactic constructions are available for differentiating the two basically different pragmatic function arrangements distinguished as (1) and (2). Supposedly, intonation and word order differences are the formal means by which it may be made explicit to which of the above questions the sentence might form an answer.

When on the other hand the governing predicate must govern a finite clause and is "sympathetic to the accusative" (Section 4.2.1), an alternative syntactic construction is in fact available for marking the fact that the embedded predication is pragmatically "split up" namely by placing the Subject of the embedded predication—which may be (4.2.1) either Topic or Focus—in a position preceding the embedded predication and making it look like an Object of the governing predicate by casemarking. Note that in an AcI, the Subject of that predication takes the accusative case-form anyway, so no comparable procedure can be applied.

When, however, a predicate governing a non-finite clause (such as *dicere*) must be expressed in the passive voice because Subj function is assigned to the embedded predication, two syntactic constructions are again available for realizing the underlying predication: one in which the AcI remains an AcI (28b), and another one in which the Subject of the embedded predication is expressed in the (now available) nominative as a pseudo-argument of the governing predicate (28c).

It was suggested in the previous section, that in view of the word-order differences (in the NcI the nominative almost always precedes the infinitive (4.2.2.1 (v)), we may be dealing with a pragmatically motivated phenomenon. This hypothesis can now be explicitated to the effect, that the NcI will be used when the embedded predication does not function *as a whole* pragmatically, but is "split up" by the fact that one of its elements has the status of Focus in the sentence as a whole. The AcI, on the other hand, must be used either when the embedded predication as a whole has the pragmatic function of Focus in the sentence or when an element *outside* the embedded predication has Focus-function. According to this hypothesis, the NcI should be excluded in certain contexts: it should not, for example, be possible as an answer to (39a) or (39b), but it should be able to form an answer to (39d) and (39e). On the other hand—(39d) and (39e) being well-formed[44]—the AcI is clearly not excluded in those pragmatic situations in which an NcI is possible. The NcI, in other words, is optional. This is not surprising, in view of the fact that the AcI construction serves both types of pragmatic function arrangements anyway when the governing predicate is active in voice.

A preliminary illustration of the implications of my hypothesis is offered by the presumably ill-formed resp. well-formed sequences in the following sentences, in which Focus is italicized:

(40) a   *A quo*   mortuos   esse   milites   dicitur?::   **A*
By whom dead$_{acc\ pl}$ to-be$_{inf}$ soldiers$_{acc\ pl}$ be-said$_{3sg}$?::   By

legato milites   mortui   esse   dicuntur.
legate soldiers$_{nom\ pl}$ dead$_{nom\ pl}$ to-be$_{inf}$ be-said$_{3pl}$

"*By whom* is it said that the soldiers are dead?::*By the legate* the soldiers are said to be dead"

b   **A quo*   milites   mortui   esse   dicuntur?
By whom soldiers$_{nom\ pl}$ dead$_{nom\ pl}$ to-be$_{inf}$ be-said$_{3pl}$?

"*By whom* are the soldiers said to be dead?"

c   *Quid* dicitur?::   **Milites   mortui   esse*   dicuntur
What be-said$_{sg}$?::   Soldiers$_{nom\ pl}$ dead$_{nom\ pl}$ to-be$_{inf}$ be-said$_{3pl}$

"*What* is said?:: The soldiers are said to be dead"

d   *Quos*   mortuos   esse   dicitur?::   *Milites*   mortui
Who$_{acc\ pl}$ dead$_{acc\ pl}$ to-be$_{inf}$ be-said$_{3sg}$?:: Soldiers$_{nom}$ dead$_{nom}$

esse   dicuntur
to-be$_{inf}$ be-said$_{3pl}$

"*Who* is it said that are dead?:: *The soldiers* are said to be dead"

d' *Qui*   mortui   esse   dicuntur?
Who$_{\text{nom pl}}$ dead$_{\text{nom pl}}$ to-be be-said$_{\text{3pl}}$

"*Who* is said to be dead?"[45]

e   *Quid accidisse* militibus dicitur?:: Milites *mortui esse* dicuntur

"What is said to have happened to the soldiers?:: The soldiers
are said *to be dead*"

In (40a–c) the embedded predication is not "split up" pragmatically but
functions as one entity: in (40a–b) Focus is on the Agent, in (40c) it is on
the embedded predication as a whole; therefore we may not have an NcI
in these cases.[46] In (40d) and (40e) an element *within* the embedded
predication has the pragmatic function Focus: therefore the NcI may now
be used.[47]

We shall now return to the empirical observations listed in Section
4.2.2.1 to see whether the observed properties and statistical tendencies
exhibited by the NcI-construction are indeed compatible with the above
hypothesis.

4.2.2.3   Reconsideration of the empirical data: an explanation.   In 4.2.2.2
it was suggested that the NcI-construction is used in those cases in which
the embedded predication is pragmatically "split up" in a Focus-part and
a non-Focus part—which may be either (part of the) Topic or contain the
Topic— and that the construction consequently cannot be used in contexts
in which the embedded predication pragmatically functions as an entity
with the function Focus or when Focus is a constituent outside the embedded predication. This assumption enables us to explain many of the
differences in statistical frequency of the AcI versus the NcI in the contexts
mentioned in 4.2.2.1 under (i)–(vii).

Thus, for example, if we reconsider phenomenon (ii)—in case of the
presence of modal verbs there is a statistic preference for using the AcI—
we may now see why this is the case. If we add a modal verb such as
debere or *posse* to an underlying predication such as (38) above, we get the
following underlying predication:

(41)   debere [dicere (legatus)$_{\text{Ag}}$ [mortuus esse (Caesar)$_{\text{θ}}$]$_{\text{Go}}$]$_{\text{θ}}$

In (41) the predication represented in (38) itself forms an argument (with
the "empty" semantic function zero (∅)) of the one-place predicate *debere*.

(For evidence in favour of analysing *debere* as one-place in spite of its syntactic construction, see Bolkestein (1980, 120f.); whether we accept this analysis or prefer another underlying structure is irrelevant to the present issue.)[48]

It is clear that whatever solution we choose for describing (41) the underlying predication contains one more semantic element than (38). This element may in its turn, in a speech-situation, be the one which conveys the most salient information, that is, the one which carries the pragmatic function Focus. If the modal verb does indeed carry this function, the embedded predication governed by *dicere* namely (*mortuus esse (Caesar)*) is not "split up" pragmatically. Accordingly, the predication cannot be expressed as an NcI-construction (see note 46). In other words, the statistical probability that the pragmatic function Focus will be carried by an element *within* the embedded predication becomes smaller, when the number of semantic or lexical elements in the governing clause is higher. On the other hand, there is of course no requirement in a predication such as (41) for either the modal verb to carry Focus, or if it does not, for Focus to be carried by *dicere* (although this will frequently be the case): no element of (41) is excluded from being Focus. Therefore we still find instances such as (32) above, in which an NcI co-occurs with a modal verb. However, if we investigate the contexts of the attested instances, they turn out to agree with the hypothesis formulated above. In, for example, (32b), the phrase *ex hostibus* "from the enemy" from within the embedded predication is (contrastive) Focus of the sentence as a whole, and *equus* "the horse" is Topic in this case in the whole stretch of discourse involved. I have seen no "exceptional" case of an NcI governed by a modal verb which may not be explained along these lines: they always exhibit a pragmatic function arrangement in which the NcI is split up in a Focus-part and a non-Focus part (which contains the Topic or is part of it).

When we turn to phenomenon (iii)—the impossibility of co-occurrence of an NcI with sentential Disjuncts, i.e. expressions indicating for example the speakers evalution of the subsequent predication—the same line of reasoning may be followed. Here, it is even more frequently the case that the most salient information conveyed by speaker is in fact his own evaluation: a good example of this is (33a) above. The few exceptions to the general statistical tendency for the NcI not to be found in such instances may again be explained as due to the fact that some element from within the embedded predication has specific pragmatic "prominence" in the sentence as a whole.[49]

Similarly, the greater frequency of the AcI-construction in case of co-occurrence with dative Recipients in the main clause, or with passive Agents, as in (33b) above, may be explained in the same way: such sentences may for example be used as an answer to questions about the identity of the Recipient, respectively the Agent, as in (42a–b):

(42) a *Cui*   nuntiatum   est venisse   eum?:: *Nobis*
         Who$_{dat}$ announced$_{nom}$ be$_{3sg}$ to-have-come he$_{acc}$?:: Us$_{dat}$

         "To whom has it been announced that he has arrived?:: To us"

      b *A quo*   nuntiatum   est venisse   eum?:: *A*
         By whom announced$_{nom}$ be$_{3sg}$ to-have-come he$_{acc}$?:: By

         M. Varrone
         M. Varro

         "By whom is it announced that he has come?:: By M.V."

In (42a–b) Focus is carried by the Recipient, respectively the Agent of the predicate *nuntiare*. This implies that in these sentences the embedded predication itself is not split up pragmatically. Consequently it may not be expressed as a NcI-construction. It may be predicted that in statistically "exceptional" cases of the NcI such as (34a–b), the most salient information in fact indeed always will turn out to be conveyed by a constituent *within* the embedded predication. This is indeed the case in, for example (34b): Focus is on *cum Vardaeis* "with the V.". (The remark is in fact an answer to a question posed in a letter of one year earlier, asking for information about the whereabouts of a certain runaway slave of Cicero's in certain foreign parts of the Roman empire.)

As regards phenomenon (iv)—to which there are no exceptions—it is interesting to note that pronominal reference to an embedded predication thereby also isolates this embedded predication as a pragmatic unit (which may either be Topic or Focus).[50]

As regards (v) and (vi)—the claim that there are differences in the relative frequency of the various possible word-orders between the NcI and the AcI-construction—it should be realized that this claim is based on the loosely collected number of instances and my own intuition and should be complemented by a more complete statistical survey of the material. With this reservation, the tendencies observed support the hypothesis, as I shall try to show. In (43) and (44) I have roughly indicated the possible word-orders and their difference in relative frequency of occurrence (A = accusative Subj of an AcI; N = nominative Subj of an NcI; I = embedded predicate; Vf = governing predicate in passive voice):

(43)		"frequent"	"less frequent"	"rare"	
NcI	N ... I			I ... N[51]	
AcI	A ... I	I ... A			

(44)		"frequent"		"less frequent"		"rare"		
NcI	N	I	Vf			Vf	N	I[52]
	N	Vf	I			Vf	I	N
AcI	A	I	Vf	I	A	Vf		
	A	Vf	I	I	Vf	A		
	Vf	A	I	Vf	I	A		

I shall not try to answer the question whether the place of the governing predicate (Vf) is relevant for the relative order of the Subj of the embedded predicate and its predicate (I). (A closer investigation might reveal that there is some correlation between the relative order of I and A within an AcI and the occurrence of Vf in sentence-initial position.)

As we see, in the case of an NcI, the nominative N has a stronger tendency to precede its predicate I than A has (see (43)) and also to precede the governing predicate Vf (see (44)).

Now, as pointed out in Latin grammars (K.-St., II, 598; Sz., 403), the statistically most frequent position for the Latin finite verb is sentence-final. Its position may be different if either the finite verb itself or some other constituents are "extra important" (see note 25). Occurrence of Vf at the beginning of the sentence, in other words, points towards special pragmatic prominence either of Vf itself or of the constituent which is placed in sentence final position instead of it. Furthermore, as is also often pointed out, in Latin elements which are Topic tend to occur at the beginning of the sentence. Seen in this light, the fact that, in an NcI, N occurs relatively more frequently near the beginning of the sentence and to the left of I and of Vf may be explained as due to the fact that its pragmatic status is often that of Topic in the sentence as a whole; correspondingly, the Focus of the sentence will lie within the embedded predication, being either the embedded predicate I itself or some other part of the embedded predication. With such a pragmatic function arrangement within the NcI there actually is no motivation for Vf to precede N and I, nor usually for I to precede N. The latter could be expected to happen if N itself carries Focus.[53]

In the case of the AcI-construction, the condition upon the relative order of A and I on the one hand and of A and Vf on the other is less strict. This phenomenon may be accounted for by assuming that A (the Subj of the AcI) does not itself fulfil a relevant pragmatic function with respect to the sentence as a whole: the AcI itself *as a whole* carries such a pragmatic function. Thus, it will preceed or follow Vf, depending on what pragmatic function it has, that of Focus or of not-Focus (see 4.2.2.2). The variability of the relative order of A and I within the AcI may be due to the fact that, within embedded predications of that form, a secondary pragmatic function arrangement may exist (which is independent of the pragmatic function fulfilled by the embedded predication within the whole sentence); within this secondary pragmatic function arrangement, either A or I of the AcI may have the specific pragmatic status of Focus.

Note that, the "pattern"-position of Vf being sentence-final, both Vf N I and Vf A I are "marked" orders: as shown in (44), the latter occurs more frequently than the former. There are several possible explanations for this fact. In agreement with the view expounded above, the explanation may be that it is due to the difference in pragmatic function arrangement of the patterns involved: in the case of an AcI construction, a conceivable pragmatic motivation for putting Vf in the non-pattern position would be either Focus status of Vf itself, or Focus status of the embedded predication as a whole. Neither motivation is relevant in the case of the NcI-construction, since in an NcI Focus is on part of the embedded predication anyway and never either on Vf, or on the embedded predication as a whole.

A different explanation for the relative rarity of Vf N I may be that in the case of the order Vf A I we are dealing with the effect of language-independent preferred order of constituents (LIPOC) (Dik, 1978a, 204). LIPOC claims that the more complex constituents are, the more they have a tendency to occur in a position to the right of the verb and towards the end of the sentence. In the case of the NcI the complexity of the underlying predication is so to speak solved—under the pragmatic conditions stated above—by pseudo-argument formation. Therefore there is no motive for placing the embedded predication to the right of the verb.

According to this view LIPOC in Latin would be relevant in the case of the AcI but not in the case of the NcI. Intuitively it seems to me, however, that in Latin the AcI is not actually felt to be so complex as to obey LIPOC. Note that it quite frequently as a whole precedes Vf, as in (29a, b). Therefore I prefer an explanation for the difference in frequency of sentence-initial Vf between the NcI and the AcI in terms of pragmatic function arrangement.

With respect to observation (vii)—the fact that co-occurrence of a Theme,Predication organization of the embedded predication on the one hand and an NcI-construction on the other is not well-formed—the same argumentation may be followed as in Section 4.2.1 with respect to the absence of co-occurrence of pseudo-arguments and an embedded Theme, Predication organization of the embedded predication involved (see 4.2.1.1 (ix) and the discussion concerning (21) and (22); see also Section 4.2.1.2). It was suggested that Themes require a pragmatic entity ("Thematized") in relation to which they are Theme. If, as we have argued, the NcI-construction is the characteristic construction for those embedded predications which pragmatically are broken up into a part which functions as Focus in the sentence as a whole and a non-Focus part which is Topic (or part of the Topic), there is in fact no unified entity in relation to which a Theme can be explicitated.

Thus most of the empirical data discussed in 4.2.2.1 are compatible with the hypothesis that when the NcI is used we are dealing with a specific pragmatic function arrangement of the underlying predication, whereas when the AcI is used this is not necessarily the case. Only for phenomenon (i)—preference for the AcI when the governing predicate is realized as a compound verb-form—there is no obvious explanation. With respect to the gerund and the gerundival construction with *esse*, which have a "modal" meaning (necessity or "obligation"), it may be claimed that here, as well as in the case of modal verbs, the underlying predication contains an extra semantic, though not lexical, element which is a potential carrier of pragmatic Focus (conform the semantic pattern assigned to this construction in Bolkestein (1980, 134ff.)). Among the exceptions to (i) in any case I have found no instances which clearly contradict the hypothesis defended here (e.g. the contexts of (30a, b)).

However, the above explanation does not seem applicable when the governing predicate is simply a perfect tense passive. Perhaps sentences referring to the past contain more lexical material (for example in the form of adverbials of time, place, reason, circumstances etc.) and thus more potential candidates for Focus assignment than sentences referring to the time of speech. The statistical support required for such an explanation falls outside the scope of this chapter.

4.3 Conclusion

In the first part of this chapter it is demonstrated that complex sentences which exhibit a word order different from that expected on the basis of normal word-order rules in Latin, because of the position occupied by a nominal element which relationally seems to belong to the subordinate clause, should be divided into several types. In Section 4.1, it is shown that one type of apparent displacement in fact represents a different phenomenon, namely the pragmatically motivated construction labelled Theme, Predication organization in Dik (1978a, 132–141). Such an organization is, as we have argued, possible both of unembedded and of embedded predications governed by certain semantic classes of predicates. A second type of "pure" displacement is distinguished as different from Theme,Predication patterns, among other things by the fact that there is no possibility of having an anaphoric pronoun coreferent to the displaced element within the subordinate clause. The nature of the conditions which determine the occurrence of this latter pattern requires further investigation.

In the second part of this chapter (Sections 4.2.1 and 4.2.2 respectively) two different constructions in Latin are investigated which may be described as exhibiting pseudo-argument formation: (i) the so-called proleptic accusative construction and (ii) the NcI or personal passive construction. Of both constructions the empirical data were investigated. One property which they turn out to have in common is the requirement for the displaced element to precede the embedded predicate in the linear order of the sentence, whereas the position of the governing predicate is not restricted. As far as this behaviour is concerned, pseudo-arguments turn out to be different from elements which really are arguments of the governing predicate: the latter, whatever their syntactic function, may move around the sentence (presumably subject to placement rules determined by pragmatic conditions, which I have not further investigated here). The second property which both constructions share is the illformedness of co-occurrence of the pseudo-argument with an embedded Theme, Predication organization, as well as with pronominal reference to the embedded predication.

The motivation for pseudo-argument formation is the same in both cases, namely the fact that a constituent within the embedded predication carries Focus in the sentence as a whole. In such a case the Subj of the embedded predication is displaced into the main clause.[54] In Section 4.2.2.2 it is argued that such special pragmatic prominence has the effect of pragmatically splitting up the embedded predication, with the result that it does not function as an entity on the pragmatic level.[55] An alternative pragmatic function arrangement was shown to be possible for complex sentences as well, namely one in which the embedded predication as a whole carries a pragmatic function (Topic or Focus) in the sentence and therefore functions as a unit on the pragmatic level. In the latter case pseudo-argument formation does not take place. A quite different type of condition for pseudo-argument formation is connected with the lexical properties of the governing predicate and is similar for both constructions, namely "passivizibility" in the case of the NcI, and being a predicate "sympathetic to the accusative" in the case of the "proleptic accusative".

As a result of the observed pragmatic conditions for pseudo-argument formation, it must be assumed that the rule effecting it applies *in a later stage* in the formation of sentences than both syntactic function assignment and pragmatic function distribution. Notice that in the case of "prolepsis" the displaced element may either become Object or Subject, depending on whether in an earlier stage Subj is assigned to the first argument of the governing predicate: it looks as if a predicate when governing an embedded predication has a "left over" caseform (the acc. resp. the nom.) ready at hand to attach to any nominal constituent which it meets earlier than its actual argument (the embedded predication): its own position in the sentence is irrelevant to this procedure.

The conditions for displacement in Latin resemble those claimed to exist in Hungarian by de Groot (Chapter 3) and to a certain extent also those in Serbo-Croatian (Gvozdanović, Chapter 6), but are not completely identical to them: (i) in Latin, as opposed to Hungarian, only Subjects may become pseudo-arguments; (ii) the fact that the embedded predication is pragmatically not an entity is itself sufficient to trigger the rule; and (iii) pseudo-argument formation is restricted to nominative and accusative caseforms. The status of the rule to be assumed for Latin in a Functional Grammar framework is quite similar to that of the rule which must be assumed for Hungarian; it is an expression rule, assigning available "left over" caseforms to constituents which for pragmatic reasons are placed in a position different from their "normal" one. Thus the two analysis in fact seem to reinforce each other.

Notes

1   This paper owes much to the stimulating working-sessions which took place
    on the general theme of the present book among the co-authors. It is impos-
    sible to do justice to this form of mutual influence by any amount of
    cross-referencing. I am also grateful to Pieter Masereeuw, his energy spent
    on tracing attested instances.

2   The construction is found in Latin of all periods (Sz., 29). It is usually
    assumed to be a property of the socially lower registers and colloquial style.

3   An instance where a coreferential pronoun is lacking although it could have
    been present is Hor. *Sat.* 1, 2, 101.

4   The Theme may be taken up by a different lexical item (Pl. *Ps.* 64 ff.; (2 f)
    below); instances without pronominal coreferents or near-synonymous
    lexemes in the subsequent predication are Pl. *Rud.* 1228; Cic. *fr.* 3, 1, 10.

5   Instances of such "anakolouths" are Pl. *Men.* 853; *Poen.* 659; *B.Afr.* 25, 1.

6   Concerning this instance K.-St. (I, 713) (wrongly, as I will show) remark that
    the constituent *de fratre* is equivalent to a "proleptic accusative". If it were,
    there could not be a coreferent pronoun within the clause (Section 4.2.1).

7   According to Sz. (363) such "Vorausnahme" of the Subject of an AcI is
    colloquial (see note 2).

8   Cf. e.g. Liv. 39, 12, 1.

9   See TLL s.v. *de* 67, 27f for a list of instances of verbs of speech and thought
    with arguments of the form *de* + noun.

10 Similar instances are Cic. *Br.* 57; *Fin.* 1, 5 (the first with a relative pronoun
    as "Theme"-argument). I call the accusative NP in an AcI-clause a Subj on
    the basis of the fact that there is agreement between it and the infinitive in
    gender and number in the relevant forms, although not, of course, in person;
    an AcI may furthermore contain an active or a passive voice infinitive.

11 Cf. note 6.

12 Another instance with an attribute within the subordinate clause is Ter.
    Eun. 265.

13 With this class of predicates not only a noun may be involved in pseudo-
    argument formation, but a predicative adjective may be displaced together
    with it (e.g. Pl. *Aul.* 797; *Poen.* 453; K.-St., II, 580).

14 K.-St. (II, 578) speak of "Attraktionsartige Verschränkung" of two sen-
    tences, de Groot (Chapter 3) of "sentence intertwining". In Sz. (471 ff.) the
    construction is explained as being due to original parataxis; K.-St. speak of
    the clause forming an "Epexegese" to the nominal constituent (II, 578).
    Evidence against this view is offered in 4.2.1.1, observation (iii).

14 Occasionally pseudo-argument formation occurs in combination with
    "traiectio" (4.1.3), as in Cato *Agr.* 5, 5. If this happens, the pseudo-argument
    precedes the other displaced constituents.

15 This shows that the semantic function of the argument involved is irrelevant.

16 See also e.g. Pl. *Amph.* 524 and *Pers.* 458.

17 Thus, for example, *scio veritatem* "I know the truth$_{acc}$" although **scio eum*
    "I know him$_{acc}$" is ill-formed and *dicere veritatem* "to say the truth$_{acc}$" in
    spite of **dico te* "I say you$_{acc}$".

18 See Bennett (1914, 222) for this observation. If the governing predicate is not "sympathetic to the accusative", according to K.-St. (II, 582), one must use a *de*-phrase. The latter expression however, allows a coreferential pronoun within the subordinate clause (cf. note 6), and must be analysed as a different type of phenomenon.

19 An exceptional case is Cic. *Fam.* 1, 5a, 1 where the governing predicate *cognoscere* "to discover, find out" is one which may govern both AcI-clauses and dependent question-clauses. This instance must be explained as due to a contamination between the two constructions. I consider the AcI as different from pseudo-argument formation plus infinitization (Bolkestein, 1979).

20 I have encountered only one instance where the pseudo-argument follows the embedded predication (Pl. *Pseud.* 694); there, however, it is already announced by a possessive pronoun in the (accusative) caseform preceding the clause. A curious instance of a pseudo-argument within the embedded predication is Ter. *An.* 614.

An instance of two words in between the pseudo-argument and the clause is Pl. *Merc.* 253; an instance of six words is *Varro L* 7, 3, 6. See for attested cases Bennett (1914, 222 ff.).

21 Attested instances of all possible word-orders may be found in Bennett (1910, 367–399). On the notion Subj for the accusative NP see note 10.

22 One instance has come to my attention involving a personal pronoun: Pl. *Truc.* 201.

23 Attested instances of "preparative" pronouns announcing the content of a dependent question clause are Cic. *Lael.* 23; *Catil.* 2, 21; Pl. *Capt.* 958; of announcing an AcI Cic. *Caec.* 25 (plus a *de*-phrase as well); Cic. *Inv.* 1, 77; *Fin.* 5, 77; further instances in Bennett (1910, 398).

24 See, however, note 9 and my remark on the structural ambiguity of *de*-phrases in case of verbs of speech and thought.

An instance of a Theme preceding an AcI is Cic. *Caec.* 25.

25 See the remarks on "normal" and "deviant" word-order patterns in e.g. Sz. (397, 401–402) and K.-St. (II 589 ff., 498), who suggest that word-order is free and varies according to "Betonung" (stress), i.e. is determined by pragmatic factors. (In Caesar 93% of sentences have the verb in sentence-final position (Sz., 403); in other authors the statistics are less convincing and vary).

26 Apart from the case alluded to in note 19.

27 Latin, in other words, has no predicates with a frame comparable to the English verb *to give* (Dik, 1978a; 99–101). Occasional remarks in the grammars suggest that there may be semantic differences between the two case-patterns allowed by e.g. *donare* "to give", with either the Receiver or the "entity given" in the accusative. This suggests that such a verb has two predicate frames instead of alternative Obj-assignment (Dik, 1978a, 100).

28 See note 24.

29 In e.g. Bennett (1914, 222 ff.), K.-St. (II, 578 ff.) and Sz. (471) and the literature cited in the latter.

30 I do not indicate the Obj function here; see note 27.

31 See note 13.

32 It is possible that different kinds of Focus should be distinguished in Latin. Thus "contrastive" Focus and "most salient information Focus" may quite well co-occur in a sentence.

33 See note 55. The fact that pseudo-argument formation does not occur with other than Subjects of the embedded predication may be due to the fact that if it would occur, it would be quite hard to trace the exact semantic function of the element involved within the embedded predication.

34 The objection to pseudo-argument formation of other than Subj mentioned in note 33 does not hold for displacement sec.

35 In K.-St. (I, 708) and Sz. (363) a number of instances of the NcI are found; see also Scherer (1975, 87–88) and Kirk (1938). Confusingly, the term NcI is sometimes applied to a completely different type of construction, exemplified by *putat aeger esse* "he believes to be ill". The infinitive here is a complement of an active voice main verb. In Bolkestein (1979), it is argued that the rule which forms the NcI does not necessarily offer support for assuming the existence of a rule which "Raises" Subj to Obj position in case of the AcI: it operates independently.

36 This fact may have to do with the specific semantic property of "factivity" which embedded predications with such predicates have (for the notion see Kiparsky and Kiparsky (1970)). With factive embedded predications, the specific pragmatic function arrangement which forms the condition for the NcI-construction does not seem to occur very often. The embedded predication will, when factive, as a rule, as a whole have a pragmatic function (of Topic or Focus) in the sentence. See Bolkestein (Chapter 10) on the pragmatic arrangements in factive constructions.

37 An extensive collection of instances of "statistically less frequent" cases of the NcI, is Kirk (1938), who claims to have included all authors from *ad Her.* to Suetonius and gives some numbers too.

38 Cf., with an NcI, *Demaenetus ubi dicitur habitare* "where D. is said to live" (Pl. *As.* 382).

39 Interesting exceptions with the NcI are Caes. *BC* 1, 14, 1 (with *falso* "falsely"); Cic. *Rep.* 2, 38, also with *falso* (not in sentence-initial position); and Vitr. 2, 8, 12 with *falsa opinione*. An instance of the NcI with a passive Agent is Cic. *Fam.* 1, 7, 3 (which at the same time contains a compound verb form as well). See also Cic. *N.D.* 1, 107; 2, 39; 2, 154.

40 The only "exceptions" to this tendency which I have encountered are: Cic. *Leg.* 1, 23; *Q.fr.* 1, 2, 9; *Cat. Mai* 63; Caes. *BC* 1, 14, 1; *B.Afr.* 28, 4; Liv. 4, 21, 5; Plin. *NH* 7, 213; 2, 166; 9, 150; 35, 65; and the three cases mentioned in note 41.

41 Cf. note 25. The only cases of NcI with sentence initial governing predicate which I have found are: Cic. *Top.* 93; *Ac.* 2, 4; *Cluent.* 180; Suet. *Oth.* 7; Vitr. 1, 6, 9; Plin. *NH* 4, 79; 35, 98. In the latter three instances the nominative follows the infinitive (cf. note 40).

42 See note 9. It is remarkable that, when the *de*-phrase has to be analysed as an argument of the governing verb (in view of its position), it still cannot co-occur with the NcI construction. For a Theme coreferential to a constituent

of an AcI, i.e. an embedded predication, see Var. *R.* 2, 2, 3 and Cic. *Fam.* 2, 17.

43 Instances of Question-word questions in which the question word indeed is a constituent of an AcI may be found in K.-St. (II, 496); an attested instance is Sall. *J.* 85,16.

44 Instances such as those referred to in note 43 show that, in the case of active AcIs, sentence Focus may quite well be on a constituent of the embedded predication.

45 See note 43 for an instance of (40d); attested instances of (40e) are e.g. Pl. *Trin.* 692; Cic. *Br.* 189; *Clu.* 104.

46 In many cases in which the embedded predication is realized as an AcI, the "most salient information" (Focus) is indeed clearly carried by a constituent outside the embedded predication (e.g. with an AcI Cic. *Fin.* 5, 28 *qui potest intellegi* "*how* can it be understood" and *quo facilius intellegi potest* "the more *easily* it can be understood" Cic. *Rep.* 2, 20). The NcI-construction would not be possible here. Cf. as well Cic. *Agr.* 2, 42; *Fin.* 5, 77; *N.D.* 2, 73.

47 Instances where the NcI contains a constituent which carries "contrastive" Focus (note 32) are not hard to find: Cic. *Inv.* 2, 24 (with *aut . . . aut*, "or . . . or"); *Att.* 1, 13, 6 and *Fam.* 9, 21, 3 (with *et . . . et*, "and . . . and").

48 A different analysis might prefer to treat *debere* as a two-place predicate, parallel to its syntactic appearance, or as forming a new predicate together with its infinitive, i.e. *debere dicere* as the result of a predicate formation rule (see Vet Chapter 7 for a discussion of some French predicates posing a similar problem).

49 This indeed holds for the instances mentioned in note 39 as well.

50 When the pronoun refers "backwards", the pragmatic function of the embedded predication will often be that of Topic, when it refers "forwards" (i.e. when it is "preparative"), the embedded predication will often be Focus in the sentence as a whole. See note 23 for some attested instances of pronouns coreferential with embedded predications. See also ch. 10.

51 See note 40.

52 See note 41.

53 The instances of N following instead of preceding I mentioned in note 40 as statistically less frequent either concern a "superfluous" N (because already known or announced previously by e.g. pronouns such as *ipse* "self" or *ille* "that one"), a "trivial" N (such as *homines* "people"), or instances of N with (often contrastive) Focus.

The instances of Vf in sentence-initial position (note 41) do not clearly exhibit one common pragmatic function distribution.

54 I have no other explanation for the fact that pseudo-argument formation applies only to *Subjects* of embedded predications in Latin than the one tentatively suggested in note 33. In this respect my analysis has no advantage over an analysis which assumes that we are dealing with a specific form of embedded Theme,Predication organization.

55 Allwood (1976) observes that pragmatic factors may lead to a "breaking up" of "referential" (i.e. semantic) units: this view agrees with the claim made in the present paper. I am grateful to R. Pfister of Munich for drawing my attention to the observations on the NcI in Reisig-Haase (1888, 820f.). Part

of their account is compatible with my suggestions, and could well be reformulated in such terms.

References

ALLWOOD, J. S.
   1976   The complex np constraint as a non-universal rule and some semantic factors influencing the acceptability of Swedish sentences which violate the cnpc. *In* J. Stillings (ed.). "U/MASS Occasional Papers in Linguistics," Vol. II. Amherst.
BENNETT, C. E.
   1910   "Syntax of Early Latin I, The verb". Repr. Georg Olms Verlag, Hildesheim.
   1914   "Syntax of Early Latin II, The cases". Repr. Georg Olms Verlag, Hildesheim.
BOLKESTEIN, A. M.
   1976a The relation between form and meaning of Latin subordinate clauses governed by verba dicendi. *Mnemosyne* **39**, 156–175; 268–300.
   1979   Subject-to-Object raising in Latin?. *Lingua* **48**, 15–34.
   1980   "Problems in the description of Modal verbs: an investigation of Latin". Van Gorcum, Assen.
DIK, S. C.
   1978a "Functional Grammar". North-Holland Linguistic Series 37. Amsterdam, North-Holland.
   1979   Raising in a Functional Grammar. *Lingua* **47**, 119–140.
KIPARSKY, P. and C. Kiparsky
   1970   Fact. *In* D. D. Steinberg and L. A. Jakobovits (ed.). "Semantics". Cambridge, Cambridge University Press, 345–369.
KIRK, W. H.
   1938   Passive verba sentiendi and dicendi with declarative infinitive. *CPh* **33**, 182–187.
KÜHNER, R. and C. Stegmann
   1912   "Ausführliche Grammatik der Lateinischen Sprache, II: Satzlehre". Hanover, repr. Verlag Hahnsche Buchhandlung 1971, in two vols (*abbrev.* K.-St.).
REISIG, C. K. and F. Haase
   1888   Vorlesungen über lateinische Sprachwissenschaft (von C. K. Reisig mit den Anmerkungen von F. Haase, Neu bearbeitet von J. H. Schmalz und G. Landgraf) repr. 1972 Martin Sändig oHG: Walluf bei Wiesbaden.
SCHERER, A.
   1975   "Handbuch der Lateinische Sprache". Heidelberg, Carl Winter.
SZANTYR, A.
   1965   "Lateinische Grammatik II. Syntax und Stilistik". Munich, Beck (*abbrev.* Sz.).
THESAURUS LINGUAE LATINAE
   (In press.) (*abbrev.* TTL). Leipzig, Teubner.

5 Embedded Themes in Spoken Dutch: Two Ways Out

SIMON C. DIK

Institute for General Linguistics
University of Amsterdam

5.0 Introduction

Theme,Predication organization is a very common phenomenon in Dutch main clauses, especially in spoken Dutch. However, the particular form in which this construction type occurs in main clauses cannot be used in subordinate clauses. This would imply that, if no further measures were taken, the pragmatically relevant structuring which is characteristic for the Theme,Predication construction in main clauses, could not be used within the domain of subordinate clauses.

This chapter shows that in spoken Dutch this problem is regularly circumvented by means of two different escape strategies. The first strategy consists in using main clause organization within the domain of the subordinate clause, through which it becomes possible to have Theme, Predication within a subordinate domain in the same way as this construction can be used within the domain of main clauses. The second strategy consists in starting the subordinate clause with the appropriate subordinator, then giving the Theme, and then repeating the subordinator followed by the Predication.

It should be noted that the constructions resulting from both these escape strategies would be judged as ungrammatical when presented and considered in isolation. They typically do not figure in Dutch grammar books. On the other hand, any transcript of a more or less spontaneous conversation will provide a couple of examples of the constructions involved, and when they are used, they conform to clearly rule-governed patterns. They thus reveal something about the ways in which speakers of

Dutch avail themselves of the grammatical resources of their language in solving certain communicative problems.

In this chapter a distinction is made between constructed and actually attested examples: the former are indicated by numbers (1), (2), (3) etc. in the usual way; the latter are indicated by letters (a), (b), (c) etc. The actually attested examples have been culled from transcripts of spoken Dutch conversation and from recordings of radio and television discussions and interviews. No detailed information is given on the provenance of these examples, since it is the phenomenology of the construction types, not their sociolinguistic or stylistic distribution, which is concentrated upon in this chapter.

5.1   Theme, Predication constructions in main clauses

Compare the following two Dutch sentences:

(1)   Dat nieuwe boek van jou is veel te   duur
       that new   book of   you is much too expensive
       "That new book of yours is much too expensive"

(2)   Dat nieuwe boek van jou, dat is veel   te   duur
       that new   book of you, that is much too expensive
       "That new book of yours, that is much too expensive"

In (1), *dat nieuwe boek van jou* is the Subject of the sentence and takes the P1 position in the functional pattern of the main clause. (2) is a common variant of (1), often found especially in spoken Dutch. In terms of FG (cf. Dik, 1978, 6.2.1; Section 1.2 above) we would say that this construction exemplifies Theme,Predication organization in which *dat nieuwe boek van jou* functions as Theme, providing a universe of discourse for the following Predication to bear upon, and is taken up by the demonstrative *dat* within the Predication. This demonstrative is coreferential with the Theme, and it functions as Subject and Topic within the Predication. It normally takes clause-initial P1 position, except in questions and imperatives:

(3)   Dat nieuwe boek van jou, is dat al   te krijgen?
       that new   book of you, is that already to obtain?
       "That new book of yours, is it already available?"

(4)   Dat nieuwe boek van jou, laat dat maar niet aan je   moeder zien!
       that new   book of you, let that but not to your mother see
       "That new book of yours, better not show it to your mother!"

Note that it is the demonstrative rather than the personal pronoun which fulfills the resumptive function in a Theme,Predication construction. Use of personal pronouns in this function leads to constructions of very doubtful acceptability:

(5)   ?Dat nieuwe boek van jou, het is veel te duur
      that new   book of you, it is much too expensive

The Theme may correspond to the Subject of the Predication, as in (2) and (3), to the Object of the Predication, as in (4), but also to other functions of the resumptive element within the Predication. Thus, the Theme can correspond to Recipient:

(6)   Die vriend van jou, daar leen ik geen boeken meer aan
      that friend of you, there lend I no   books more to
      "That friend of yours, I won't lend any more books to him"

to Instrument:

(7)   Die bijl, daar hak ik houtjes mee
      that axe, there chop I woods with
      "That axe, I use it to chop wood"

or to Direction:

(8)   Dat huisje op Texel, gaan jullie daar vaak heen?
      that house on Texel, go   you   there often to
      "That house on Texel, do you go there often?"

In fact, so it seems, the Theme can correspond to any term within the Predication proper, whatever its functional status. In every case, the Theme is resumed within the Predication by the appropriate demonstrative. The Predication is always a construction which could also be used on its own as a complete utterance. The Theme is set off from the Predication by a characteristic break in the intonation pattern.

In the examples given so far, the Theme appears in "absolute" form: there is no marking on the constituent functioning as Theme to express its functional relationship with the Predication. As in many other languages (Dik, 1978, 6.2.1), there is an alternative possibility in which the Theme is prepositionally marked for the function of its corresponding position within the Predication. Thus, we have:

(9) Aan die vriend van jou, daar leen ik geen boeken meer aan
     to   that friend of   you, there lend I no   books   more to

(10) Naar dat huisje op Texel, gaan jullie daar vaak heen?
     to   that house on Texel, go   you   there often to

(11) In Amsterdam, daar kan je   lekkere   haring eten
     in Amsterdam, there can you delicious herring eat
     "In Amsterdam, there one can eat delicious herring"

In general, the Theme,Predication construction is an optional alternative
to the corresponding "straight" construction. That is, by the side of any
sentence with Theme,Predication organization, there is a corresponding
sentence without such organization (compare (2) with (1)). In the "straight"
construction, however, the relevant constituent *must* be marked for its
proper function within the Predication and cannot appear in absolute form.
Compare:

(12) Aan die vriend van jou leen ik geen boeken meer
     to   that friend of you lend I no   books   more

(13) *Die vriend van jou   leen ik geen boeken meer aan
      that friend of   yours lend I no   books   more to

In (12) the Recipient is an integral part of the Predication, brought to P1
position on account of its Topic or Focus function, and necessarily marked
for its function within the Predication. In our analysis of the Theme,
Predication construction, however, we assume that the Theme is produced
outside the Predication as a scene-setter for the Predication to adjust to.
The Theme may either appear in absolute form (giving no information on
how the Predication is going to relate to it), or it may anticipate, through
its prepositional marking, the functional status of the position with which
it correlates within the Predication.

Although Theme,Predication organization is in general optional, there
may be circumstances in which it tends to become the favoured construction
type. This is the case (in Dutch and many other languages), when the
initial constituent is rather long and complex. In such a case the Theme,
Predication organization can be chosen to re-establish the proper relationships within the Predication, so that the processing load on the interpreter
is diminished. Thus, although the following two constructions are both
acceptable in Dutch, (15) would seem to be preferred to (14):

(14) Dat boek waar   jij   een paar maanden geleden over   vertelde en
      that book where you a   few   months   ago   about talked   and

      waar.van je   zei dat ik het beslist   moest lezen heb ik nog
      where-of you said that I it   definitely must read have I yet

      steeds niet kunnen vinden
      always not can   find

      "That book about which you told me a few months ago and of which
      you said that I definitely had to read it, I have still not been able to
      find so far"

(15) Dat boek waar jij een paar maanden geleden over vertelde en
      waarvan je zei dat ik het beslist moest lezen, *dat* heb ik nog steeds
      niet kunnen vinden

Theme,Predication organization is also a common phenomenon in constructions which start off with a subordinate clause, especially in the cases
of conditional/temporal clauses with *als* "if" or "when". Thus, although
(16) and (17) are both acceptable in Dutch, (17) would again seem to be
preferred to (16):

(16) Als   we alle relevante faktoren in beschouwing nemen, moeten
      when we all relevant factors in consideration take,   must

      we konkluderen dat . . .
      we conclude   that . . .

      "When we take all relevant factors into consideration we must con-
      clude that . . ."

(17) Als   we alle relevante faktoren in beschouwing nemen, *dan*
      when we all relevant factors in consideration take,   then

      moeten we konkluderen dat . . .
      must   we conclude   that . . .

Thus, although I know of no cases in which Theme,Predication organization is obligatory in Dutch, there are situations in which such organization
is strongly preferred. This concerns cases in which the initial constituent
in the clause is especially long or complex. Theme,Predication organization
seems to be used in such cases as a means of "chopping up" the information
to facilitate processing.

5.2   Theme, Predication constructions in subordinate clauses

For a better understanding of the behaviour of Theme,Predication constructions with respect to subordinate clauses it is useful to mention briefly some properties of subordinate clauses in Dutch. Dutch is like German and unlike English in that constituent order is determined by two distinct functional patterns, one for main clauses and one for subordinate clauses. The difference lies in the position of the finite verb: in the main clause, it is strongly tied to the second position in the clause, immediately after P1; in the subordinate clause, the finite verb is placed together with the non-finite verb (if any) at or towards the end of the clause. As far as the most important positions are concerned, the two patterns can be represented as:

(18)   Main clause: P1   Vf   S   O   Vi
      Subordinate clause: P1   S   O $\begin{pmatrix} \text{Vi} & \text{Vf} \\ \text{Vf} & \text{Vi} \end{pmatrix}$

    The main clause pattern is exemplified by:

(19)   Jan   heeft gisteren   een boek gekocht
      John has   yesterday a   book bought
      "John has bought a book yesterday"

(20)   Gisteren   heeft Jan   een boek gekocht
      yesterday has   John a   book bought
      "Yesterday John has bought a book"

(19) gives the most frequent main clause ordering, with the Subject in P1 position on account of its Topic or Focus function. Whenever some other constituent is placed in P1, however, as in (20), the Subject appears in postverbal position. This justifies the assumption that the actual pattern position of the Subject is after Vf, as indicated in (18), even though there is a strong preference for the Subject to go to P1 position.

    The subordinate clause pattern is exemplified in:

(21)   Ik geloof dat Jan   gisteren   een boek gekocht heeft
      I   believe that John yesterday a   book bought has

(22)   Ik geloof dat Jan   gisteren   een boek heeft gekocht
      I   believe that John yesterday a   book has   bought
      "I believe that John has bought a book yesterday"

(same reading for (21) and (22)).

Note that in subordinate clauses there is almost always some P1-constituent in P1 position (in this case the subordinator *dat* "that"), so that it is impossible, within the domain of the subordinate clause, to bring Topic or Focus constituents to P1.

In most cases, then, there is a clear difference of constituent ordering between main and subordinate clauses. Main clause ordering in subordinate clauses leads to ungrammatical results:

(23)   *Ik geloof dat Jan   heeft gisteren   een boek gekocht
         I   believe that John has   yesterday a   book bought

Now, if we take a Theme,Predication such as (24) and try to embed it according to the usual rules of subordinate clause formation, the result turns out to be unacceptable:

(24)   Die vriend van jou, die drinkt teveel
         that friend of   you, that drinks too much
         "That friend of yours, he drinks too much"

(25)   a   *Ik geloof dat die vriend van jou, die teveel   drinkt
             I   believe that that friend of   you, that too much drinks

         b   *Ik geloof die vriend van jou, dat die teveel   drinkt
             I   believe that friend of   you, that that too much drinks

Thus, whether we put the subordinator *dat* "that" before the Theme, as in (25a), or after the Theme, as in (25b), the result is equally bad. Even in informal spoken Dutch I have found no cases of constructions of the form (25a) or (25b).[1] In a functional grammar of Dutch these facts could be accounted for by assuming that the initial Theme position (Section 1.2) is available only at the main clause level. This implies that normally, Themes can occur only at the very beginning of any type of sentence.

Inspection of spoken Dutch shows, however, that speakers use two strategies for circumventing the problem that Theme,Predication organization cannot be straightforwardly applied within the domain of a subordinate clause. The first strategy is to use the main clause ordering pattern within the subordinate domain. The second strategy is to repeat the subordinator, so that the Theme gets insulated in between two identical subordinating elements.

5.2.1   Main clause ordering in subordinate clauses

We saw in (23) that using main clause ordering in subordinate clauses leads to ungrammatical results. Nevertheless, such ordering is commonly encountered in spoken Dutch, even apart from the problem constituted by Theme,Predication constructions. One might say that, in forming subordinate clauses, speakers of Dutch tend to "slip into" the main clause ordering pattern. Consider some actual examples:

(a)   Maar nu   hoorde ik toevallig   laatst, dat eh aan de overkant
      but   now heard   I incidentally lately, that eh on the over-side

      bij ons zijn ze   nu   gewone flats aan het bouwen
      near us are they now normal flats at   the build

      "But now I happened to hear some time ago that eh across the street
      near us they are now building normal flats"

(b)   Nee, ik heb   dus mijn vader nooit gekend, omdat   ik was eh vijf
      No, I have thus my   father never known, because I was eh five

      maanden dat ie overleed
      months   that he died

      "No, I have never known my father, because I was eh five months
      when he died"

In each of these cases, the subordinate clause has main clause ordering, contrary to the general rule of Dutch grammar. Whether this must be considered as a case of anacolouthon, or can be interpreted in terms of a growing tendency to assimilate the subordinate clause pattern to that of the main clause, cannot be decided without further research. It is clear, however, that when main clause organization is used within the domain of the subordinate clause, the road is free also for using Theme,Predication organization within that domain. This is what we actually find in examples such as the following:

(c)   . . . de katholieken in Nederland, die   die   dachten dat het
      . . . the catholics   in Holland,   those those thought that the

      Genesis-verhaal, dat is   werkelijk zo gebeurd, hè
      Genesis-story,   that has really   so happened, uh?

      ". . . Dutch catholics thought that the Genesis-story really happened
      like that, didn't they?"

Note that in this case the main Theme is *de katholieken in Nederland*, resumed by *die* "those" in the Predication. Within the domain of the subordinate clause with *dat*, however, we again have Theme,Predication organization with *het Genesis-verhaal* as Theme, resumed by *dat* in the Predication. The subordinate clause has main clause organization, witness the fact that (26) would be a well-formed main clause in Dutch:

(26)   Het Genesis-verhaal, dat is werkelijk zo gebeurd, hè?

For two further examples parallel to (c), consider:

(d)   En ik denk dat iedere opvolger die ooit nog na   mij zal
      and I think that every successor who ever yet after me will

      komen, die krijgt hetzelfde probleem
      come, that gets   the same problem

      "And I think that every successor who will ever come after me, he
      will have the same problem"

(e)   . . . hebben zij   gehoord dat in Delfzijl, daar konden ze   een
      . . . have   they heard   that in Delfzijl, there could they a

      vrije woning krijgen
      free house get

      ". . . they heard that in Delfzijl they could get a free home"

At the risk of over-emphasizing the degree of consciousness with which such constructions as (c) to (e) are formed, we could describe the speaker's strategy as follows:

The speaker
   (a)   starting the construction of a subordinate clause,
   (b)   wishing to effect Theme,Predication organization,
   (c)   knowing this to be impossible in the subordinate domain,
   (d)   slips into the main clause pattern as a means to overcome the
         contradiction between (b) and (c).

5.2.2   *Reduplication of the subordinator*

The second strategy for getting a Theme,Predication organization into the subordinate clause is to reduplicate the subordinating conjunction, so that the resulting construction comes out as indicated in the following schema:

(27)   subordinator₁ *Theme*, subordinator₂ Predication

This organization is exemplified in the following cases:

(f)   . . . waar juist in naar voren   kwam dat *die   aartsvaders en zo,*
       . . . where just in to   forward came that those patriarchs and so,

       dat dat   ook niet zo'n brave   mensen waren
       that those also not such innocent people were

       ". . . from which it actually appeared that those patriarchs were not
       such innocent people either"

Here, the first *dat* introduces the subordinate clause, *die aartsvaders en zo* constitutes the Theme, then comes a second instance of the subordinator *dat*, immediately followed by the demonstrative *dat* which resumes the Theme within the Predication (note that the subordinator *dat* and the demonstrative *dat* happen to be homophonous).

(g)   . . . ik denk dat *de mensen die bijvoorbeeld bij het braakfestijn*[2]
       . . . I think that the people who for example at the breaking-feast

       in het Sarphatipark eh zitten, nou dat die   nou hiernaartoe
       in the Sarphati park eh sit,   well that those now here-to

       komen . . .
       come . . .

       ". . . I think that the people for instance who are at the breaking-
       festivity in Sarphati park, well that they now come this way . . ."

Again, the Theme (italicized) is insulated in between two occurrences of the subordinator *dat*. In this case the second subordinator is preceded by the pragmatic element *nou* which in Dutch is a very common clause-introducing particle similar to English *well,* . . .

(h)   Ik vind wel dat *voor het opschrijven   van gedichten* dat je
       I think pos.[3] that for the writing-down of   poems,   that you

       daar een bepaalde koppigheid   voor moet hebben
       there a   certain   stubbornness for must have

       "I do think that for writing down poems, one must have a certain
       stubbornness"

Here we have a case in which the Theme does not appear in absolute form, but in the form (with the purposive preposition *voor* "for") corresponding

to the function of its resumptive element *daar . . . voor* within the Predication.

A similar organization with repeated subordinating element is also found
with infinitival constructions as in the following case:

(i)   . . . die kwam dus op het idee om *X dus van de VU, van vroe-*
      . . . that came thus on the idea for X thus of   the FU, of   for-

      vroeger   van de VU, om die op te bellen
      formerly of   the FU, for him up-to-call

      ". . . this person thus got the idea to call X of the Free University,
      formerly of the Free University".

With respect to these cases, then, we can describe the speaker's strategy
as follows:

The speaker

(a)   having started the construction of a subordinate clause,

(b)   having produced a Theme,

(c)   realizing that Theme,Predication organization is impossible
      within the subordinate domain,

(d)   starts again on the construction of a subordinate clause, so as to
      overcome the contradiction between (b) and (c) by producing the
      Predication, after all, in its proper subordinate form.

5.3   Conclusion

We saw in this chapter that Theme,Predication organization which is quite
common in Dutch main clauses cannot, without further measures being
taken, be implemented within the domain of the subordinate clause in
Dutch. Nevertheless, Dutch speakers seem to feel a need for effecting such
organization in certain conditions. It has been shown that they use two
escape strategies in order to overcome the problem. The first can be described as an "avoidance" strategy: by slipping into main clause organization, speakers avoid the problem posed by the subordinate clause pattern.
The second is rather a "repair" strategy: having produced a Theme within
the subordinate clause domain, speakers again start constructing a subordinate clause so that (i) the Predication gets its appropriate subordinate
form, and (ii) the Theme is outside the scope of that Predication, although
it is within the scope of the first subordinator.

These facts raise several questions which I shall not try to answer in the present context:

(i)   Why should a language grammatically disallow a type of organization for which speakers apparently may have a communicative need?

(ii) What implications might these escape strategies have for the historical development of a language? Should they be regarded as incidental aberrations from the constraints imposed by the rules of grammar, or might they—in the long run—have some impact on these rules themselves?

(iii) Or should these two strategies be regarded as an integral part of the communicative competence of speakers of Dutch, so that in this respect the distinction between rules of grammar and communicative strategies is only a pseudo-distinction, induced by a lack of attention to the organizing principles of informal spoken Dutch?

Notes

1   Note that (25b) comes very close to a construction with pure displacement which we found to be grammatical in Serbo-Croatian (Chapter 2; Gvozdanović, Chapter 6) Modern Greek (Chapter 2) and Hungarian (De Groot, Chapter 3).

2   *braakfestijn* "breaking feast" is a neologism from the jargon of the Dutch squatters' movement. Notice that *braak-* is ambiguous between "breaking" and "vomiting".

3   *wel* is a particle marking positive counter-assertions in Dutch. The closest English equivalent is emphatic *do* as given in the translation.

Reference

DIK Simon C.
   1978   "Functional Grammar". North-Holland Linguistic Series 37. Amsterdam, North-Holland.

6 Word Order and Displacement in Serbo-Croatian

JADRANKA GVOZDANOVIĆ

Department of Slavic Languages
University of Amsterdam

6.0 Introduction

Serbo-Croatian, a South Slavic language, is one of the languages which are traditionally referred to as having relatively free word order. In this chapter I shall try to show that word order is directly connected with pragmatic functions and that it interacts with intonational phenomena. Attention will focus on the possibility that constituents occur outside the predication to which they originally belong. For example, the Serbo-Croatian sentence *mislio sam da je dečko vidio most* "I thought that the boy had seen a/the bridge" (Section 6.3.1) can also occur in the form *dečko sam mislio da je vidio most*, where *dečko* can be seen as displaced in view of the unacceptability of **dečko sam mislio*. This phenomenon will be analysed against the background of the meaningful correlates of word order in general.

6.1 Word order and contrastive accent

6.1.1 Word order in Serbo-Croatian

Traditionally, the following restrictions of the Serbo-Croatian word order have been noted: interrogative pronouns or adverbs and conjunctions are placed in the initial position of a clause, whereas enclitics cannot occur in the initial position but follow the first constituent in a clause. The enclitics are short forms of personal pronouns, the reflexive *se* and *si* ("-self", gen, acc v. dat), the question particle *li*, and short forms of the auxiliary verbs *biti* "be" and *htjeti* "shall/will". The order in which the enclitics occur is: *li*, verbal enclitics except *je* (3rd p sg pres of *biti*), pronominal enclitics in the dative, genitive, accusative case, *se*, *je*.

Tomić (1977) examined translations of the English definite article into Serbo-Croatian and concluded that definiteness is translated by placing a noun phrase preceding the corresponding verb in Serbo-Croatian only in the case of the subject of a given clause. According to Tomić, it is contextual boundness rather than definiteness that determines the placement of a noun phrase preceding the verb.

Contextual boundness, referring to that which is given for the speaker and the addressee, played a role in the "functional sentence perspective" as viewed by the Prague school (see also Lyons 1977, 509). The latter can be defined as connecting the content of a message to the frame of reference, i.e. to the projection of the world as it is shared by the speaker and the addressee immediately before the time of the speech act (Ebeling, 1980). It was pointed out by various authors (e.g. Halliday, 1967; Ebeling, 1980) that the speaker has the possibility of disregarding that which is given, i.e. present in the frame of reference, in this sense that he can present as given also that which is not given for the addressee. This Chapter will investigate the possibilities of expressing information as present in the frame of reference and the possibilities of disregarding the frame of reference in Serbo-Croatian. These phenomena will be investigated in connection with word order and sentence accent, as their formal correlates.

6.1.2   *Contrastive accent*

With respect to Serbo-Croatian it can be stated that, apart from the difference between assertive and interrogative intonation and the marking of sentence or clause boundaries by means of a break in the intonation contour, the only phenomenon that interacts with word order in a relevant way is the so-called contrastive accent (called "focus" by Ivić and Lehiste, 1978), the presence of which is always opposed to its absence.[1] There is no other sort of independently functioning sentence accent. The function of contrastive accent is to indicate that the information X expressed by a non-enclitical word or words is opposed to other information in the frame of reference (i.e. -X), which could possibly fulfil the same function. Interaction between word order and contrastive accent occurs in so far as some cases of word order are possible only if there is contrastive accent on one of the words. In discussing alternative possibilities of word order, I shall indicate contrastive accent by italics.

An answer to (1) can be (2)–(9), (2) being the most neutral one.

(1)   Što čita Petar?   ("What reads Peter?" = "What does Peter read?")

(2)   Petar čita knjigu ("Peter reads a/the book")

(3)   Petar čita *knjigu*

(4)   Petar *knjigu* čita

(5)   Čita Petar knjigu

(6)   Čita Petar *knjigu*

(7)   Čita *knjigu* Petar

(8)   *Knjigu* čita Petar

(9)   *Knjigu* Petar čita

It can be seen from examples (2) and (5) that the information which is present in the frame of reference (in this case: "Petar" and "čita") neutrally precedes the information which is not present in the frame of reference (in this case: "knjigu"). The information which is not present in the frame of reference can precede the information which is present in the frame of reference only if having contrastive accent (cf. (4), (7), (8) and (9)). In the latter case, the information which is not present in the frame of reference is opposed to the information which is present there and could possibly fulfil the same function.

The difference between (2) and (3), with the contrastive accent on the new information (which is not present in the frame of reference) in the latter example and without it in the former, is due to the same regularity, by which the contrastive accent is used to mark the information which is in opposition with some other information in the frame of reference which could possibly occupy the same position. For example, sentence (3) can be used in order to indicate that Peter is reading a book, and not a newspaper. A similar regularity has been signalled for Dutch by Nooteboom, Kruyt and Terken (1980, 21), where so-called pitch accent (comparable with the contrastive accent of Serbo-Croatian) is governed by the following rules:

> "pitch accent": "look out; the referent (or concept) I am referring to is not the single most probable one that might have been referred to at this point";

"no pitch accent": "take it easy; the referent (or concept) I am referring to here is indeed the single most probable one that might have been referred to at this point".

Dutch differs from Serbo-Croatian in that "verbal expressions with referents that have not been referred to earlier in the same or in the preceding sentence, must be accented" in Dutch (Nooteboom *et al.*, 1980, 16), but not in Serbo-Croatian. In the latter language, there is no accent on information which is new simply because there is no comparable information in the frame of reference (and also not on that which is already present in the frame of reference). Only the information which is opposed to comparable information in the frame of reference is accented. This occurs when the information at the speaker's disposal differs from that which is present in the frame of reference shared by himself and the addressee. The information which is present in the frame of reference can occur in any position in the sentence, whereas new information can only occur in certain positions. It can be concluded from the examples given above that an argument following the corresponding verb can express either the information which is present in the frame of reference or new information. Placement of an argument preceding the verb expresses that the information conveyed by it is present in the frame of reference. If this is true of the speaker's frame of reference but not of that shared by himself and the addressee, there is opposition expressed by means of contrastive accent.

6.1.3   Pragmatic functions

Let us look for correlations between the notions described above and the pragmatic functions as defined by Dik (1978). In Dik's definition, the pragmatic functions Topic and Focus occur inside a given predication, and Theme and Tail occur outside it. A constituent with Theme function presents a domain or universe of discourse with respect to which it is relevant to pronounce the predication that follows; a constituent with Tail function presents, as an "afterthought" to the predication, information meant to clarify or modify (some constituent contained in) the predication. A constituent with Topic function presents an entity "about" which the predication predicates something in the given setting; Focus characterizes constituents which present the relatively most important or salient information with respect to the pragmatic information of the Speaker and the Addressee. Dik does not identify Focus with the "constituent receiving or containing main stress, although elements with Focus function will often be realized by such constituents" (1978, 131f.).

In the terminology used in this chapter, "the pragmatic information of the Speaker and the Addressee" is referred to as "the information which is present in the frame of reference".

With respect to Serbo-Croatian, the pragmatic function Focus as defined by Dik (1978) can be said to refer to the information which is distinctively absent from the frame of reference due to the presence of other comparable information there (i.e. contrastive Focus), and to the information for which there is no indication of its presence in the frame of reference. The former is expressed by means of contrastive accent; the latter by means of word order in the sense of placing an argument following the verb, or a Head following a Modifier.

The pragmatic functions occurring outside a predication (Theme and Tail) and those occurring inside it (Topic and Focus) are distinguished on the basis of the following formal means: intonation, enclitic placement and case marking. Theme is indicated by means of an intonational rise which is not directly followed by a fall. Tail is preceded by a fall. The enclitics can follow Topic but not Theme. Theme which is coreferential with an argument occurs either in the nominative or the vocative case (6.2.1 and 6.3.1), whereas no restrictions hold for other cases.[2]

6.2 Constituent placement and pragmatic functions

6.2.1 Simple sentences

In connection with simple sentences, the following phenomena can be observed:

(10) Vidio je   dečko most
     seen be$_{encl-3sg}$ boy bridge
     "A/the boy saw/has seen a/the bridge"

(11) Vidio je dečko *most*

(12) Vidio je *dečko* most

(13) *Vidio* je dečko most

(14) Vidio je *most* dečko

(15) Vidio je most *dečko*

(16)   Dečko je vidio most

(17)   Dečko je vidio *most*

(18)   Dečko je *vidio* most

(19)   *Dečko* je vidio most

(20)   Most je vidio dečko

(21)   Most je vidio *dečko*

(22)   Most je *vidio* dečko

(23)   *Most* je vidio dečko

(24)   Dečko je most vidio

(25)   Dečko je most *vidio*

(26)   Dečko je *most* vidio

(27)   *Dečko* je most vidio

(28)   *Most* je dečko vidio

(29)   Most je *dečko* vidio

(30)   Dečko, vidio je most

(31)   Dečko, most je vidio

(32)   Most, vidio ga je dečko ("ga" is a pronominal enclitic referring to "most")

(33)   Most, dečko ga je vidio

(34)   Vidio, dečko je most

(35)   Vidio, most je dečko

(36)   Vidio je most, *dečko*

(37)   Most je vidio, *dečko*

(38)   Vidio ga je dečko, *most*

(40)   Dečko most, *vidio* ga je

These are the only possibilities of word order and contrastive accent.

   The constituent preceding the predication (indicated by means of intonation and the enclitic placement) fits into the definition of Theme.

Note that any non-enclitical constituent can function as Theme. If it refers to the term filling the first argument of the subsequent predication, it is not referred to by means of a pronoun but is expressed in the verbal form. If it refers to any other argument of the subsequent predication, it must be referred to by means of a corresponding pronoun. Enclitical forms of auxiliary verbs are bound to occur within the predication. The same restrictions with respect to pronouns and enclitical verbs hold for predications which are followed by Tail. As far as I know, Tail is always characterized by contrastive accent. If this regularity is generally valid for Serbo-Croatian, it can be seen as a case of defective distribution, because Tail in that case contains information which is not present in the frame of reference.

We can see that within the predication which consists of the verb "vidio je" and two arguments, the first being "dečko" and the second "most", either argument can precede if there is a verb between them. If they occur next to each other, then either the only argument which is specified as animate or the first argument (which in the given examples coincide, but can possibly differ in other cases) neutrally precedes the remaining argument(s). It can be seen from the examples given above that this neutral order can be violated if there is contrastive accent on the non-enclitical word expressing either one of the arguments.

The meaningful correlates of word order which have been described above can be made explicit by means of the following sentences:

(41) Dečko bi   prešao most, ali nema mostova
      boy   would$_{encl-3sg}$ cross bridge but is not bridges
      "The boy would cross a/the bridge, but there are no bridges"

(42) Dečko bi   prešao most, ali ga   ne moze naći
      boy   would$_{encl-3sg}$ cross bridge but it $_{encl}$ not can$_{3sg}$ find$_{inf}$
      "The boy would cross a/the bridge, but cannot find it"

(43) a Dečko bi most prešao, ali *nema* mostova
      b *Dečko bi most prešao, ali nema mostova

(44) Dečko bi most prešao, ali ga ne može naći

(45) a Most bi dečko prešao, ali *nema* mostova
      b *Most bi dečko prešao, ali nema mostova

(46) Most bi dečko prešao, ali ga ne može naći

We can conclude that placement of an argument following the verb does not indicate anything about its presence in the frame of reference (as it can either be present or absent), whereas its placement preceding the verb indicates that either this or comparable opposed information is present in the frame of reference. In the latter case, contrastive accent occurs. In sentences (43) and (45), the first clause creates the frame of reference in which the bridge is present. The second clause, denying the presence of any bridge(s), is possible only if "there are no" is pronounced with contrastive accent, thus contradicting the information "there are" in the frame of reference. These sentences are unacceptable without contrastive accent.

6.2.2 Complex sentences

Some interesting phenomena connected with word order have been noted by M. Ivić (1973), who discussed sentences of the type:

(i)   Hoću   da   vidim Olgu
      $want_{1sg}$ that see_{1sg} $Olga_{acc}$
      "I want to see Olga"

(ii) Hoću *Olgu* da vidim

(iii) *Olgu* hoću da vidim

(iv) a   Olgu hoću da vidim

      b *Hoću da Olgu vidim

In the sentences above, "Olga" is the second argument of the predication (in the terminology used in this article). If "Olga" is the first argument of the predication, different possibilities seem to occur: i.e.

(v)   Hoću   da   vidi   Olga
      $want_{1sg}$ that see_{3sg} $Olga_{nom}$
      "I want that Olga sees"

(vi) Hoću da Olga vidi

(vii) Hoću *Olga* da vidi

The important point is that Ivić considers these sentences to have the same structural analysis, which means that "Olga" and "Olgu" are analysed as displaced into the main clause.

Ivić points to severe restrictions with respect to the distribution of the constituents. In her opinion, the "object" (which I call the second argument of a predication, predicting Object in Serbo-Croatian as defined by Dik (1978)) cannot precede the verb within a predication, whereas the first argument of a predication, predicting subject, can either precede or follow the verb. On the other hand, the "object" can be displaced either to the position directly preceding the conjunction or to the initial position, but the "subject" can only be displaced to the position directly preceding the conjunction. It is in the latter position that displaced constituents always have contrastive accent; the same restriction does not hold for the initial position.

Ivić's statement that (ivb) is unacceptable, in my opinion, has its origin in the fact that the contrastive accent placement in the embedded clause was not discussed. As far as I know, sentences (viii) and (ix), with the contrastive accent either on *Olgu* or on *ja* (which is a contrastively used personal pronoun) are acceptable whereas (ivb) is not.

(viii) Hoću da *Olgu* vidim

(ix) Hoću da Olgu *ja* vidim

This corresponds with my statement that "most je dečko vidio" can occur only if there is contrastive accent either on *most* or *dečko*.

As far as the displacement of the first argument is concerned, to my knowledge it is not restricted to the position directly preceding the conjunction, but the same possibilities exist as with respect to the second argument. Perhaps Ivić represents the Serbian system and I the Croatian one, but possibly there are individual (or analytical) differences.

6.3 Displacement

6.3.1 *Real displacement*

Consider the Serbo-Croatian sentence (47):

(47) Mislio   sam   da je   vidio dečko most
      thought$_{1sg}$ be$_{encl-1sg}$ that be$_{-encl3sg}$ seen boy bridge
      "I thought that a/the boy had seen a/the bridge"

The words that occur in this sentence can occupy several positions. Their pragmatic difference in meaning will be shown below. In the embedded clause "da je vidio dečko most", word order can be varied in the same way as in the simple sentence "vidio je dečko most" (cf. 6.2.1), on the understanding that "da" remains in the initial position in view of the enclitic placement and the intonational phenomena. The embedded clause can either precede or follow the main clause "mislio sam".[3] In addition to that, one or more constituents from the embedded clause can occur in the main clause either at its very beginning or at its very end, on the understanding that enclitics cannot be displaced (whereas the corresponding full, non-enclitical, forms can). This can be seen as an argument for treating pragmatic functions as operative on a level different from the semantic and syntactic ones, because enclitics serve to preserve the original structure of a clause as expressing a predication in cases of displacement caused by pragmatic functions (as will be shown below).

Displacement of the constituents from the embedded clause into the main clause can be of the following type, on the understanding that more than one constituent can be displaced, that the constituent added at the end of the main clause has the contrastive accent, and that word order within a clause can be varied in the same way as in a simple sentence (6.2.1):

(48) Mislio sam *vidio* da je dečko most

(49) Mislio sam *dečko* da je vidio most

(50) Mislio sam *most* da je vidio dečko

(51) Dečko sam mislio da je vidio most

(52) Most sam mislio da je vidio dečko

(53) *Dečko* sam mislio da je vidio most

(54) *Most* sam mislio da je vidio dečko

In addition, "vidio", "dečko" and "most" can precede the subsequent predication(s), thus functioning as Theme.

Next to the intonational marking and the enclitic placement (note that "da" cannot be considered an enclitic in view of its possible occurrence in the sentence-initial position), it can be showed that in the sentences (48)–(54) we have examples of constituents which are displaced from the predication they structurally belong to on the basis of unacceptability of the following examples, in any possible order:

(55) a   *Mislio sam dečko

      b   *Mislio sam most

      c   *Mislio sam vidio[4]

What is the pragmatic function fulfilled by the displaced constituents? We have seen that when there is a Theme constituent preceding a predication, it must be referred to by means of a pronoun if it is coreferential with an argument of the subsequent predication which is not the first one. In sentences (50), (52) and (54), however, there is no such coreferential pronoun. This means that the displaced constituent cannot be equated with Theme as established for simple sentences, or in connection with complex sentences when preceding the entire remaining predication(s). Furthermore, such Theme occurs in the nominative or the vocative case, whereas displaced constituents keep their original case marking (in "most", the nominative and the accusative have the same form, but the difference can be made explicit by means of the pronoun referring to it). The left-displaced constituent without contrastive accent can be said to contain the information which is presented by the speaker as present in the frame of reference of the sentence as a whole, as distinguished from the information following it in the corresponding clause, for which no similar assumption holds.

A left-displaced constituent which occurs at the beginning of the main clause preceding the embedded one can either have the contrastive accent or not. It expresses the information which is either present in the frame of reference of the sentence as a whole, or opposed to comparable information in the frame of reference of the sentence as a whole. There is contrastive accent in the latter case but not in the former. A left-displaced constituent which occurs at the end of the main clause, i.e. directly preceding the conjunction, expresses the information which is either present in the frame of reference of the subsequent embedded clause, or opposed to comparable information in this frame of reference. The obligatory contrastive accent on such left displaced constituents occurring at the end of the main clause (6.2.2) is presumably due to the opposition with comparable information present in the frame of reference created by the clause in which the left-displaced constituent occurs.

Theme of a subordinate clause can occur at the end of the main clause if described by means of the construction "što se tiče+genitive" = "what concerns .../ concerning ...". A coreferential enclitical pronoun does occur in such cases in the subsequent predication:

(56)   a   Mislio sam, što se tiče dečka, da je vidio most

   b   Mislio sam, što se tiče mosta, da ga je vidio dečko

Case marking in the left-displaced constituents, as distinguished from Themes, can be further illustrated by the following examples:

(57) Vjerovao sam   da   se   svira   sonata
    believed be$_{encl-1sg}$ that Refl$_{encl}$ play$_{3sg}$ sonata

    "I believed that a/the sonata was played"
   = "I believed a/the sonata to be played"

(58) Vjerovao sam da se sonata svira

(59) Vjerovao sam *sonata* da se svira

(60) *Sonata* sam vjerovao da se svira

(61) Vjerovao sam   da   sviraju sonatu
    believed be$_{encl-1sg}$ that play$_{3pl}$ sonata$_{acc}$

    "I believed that they were playing a/the sonata"
   = "I believed them to be playing a/the sonata"

(62) Vjerovao sam da sonatu sviraju

(63) Vjerovao sam *sonatu* da sviraju

(64) a   *Sonatu* sam vjerovao da sviraju

    b   *Vjerovao sam sonatu

    c   *Sonatu sam vjerovao

(65) Vjerovao sam   da   se   ponose   sonatom
    believed be$_{encl-1sg}$ that Refl$_{encl}$ be proud of$_{3pl}$ sonata$_{Inst}$
    "I believed that they were proud of a/the sonata"
   = "I believed them to be proud of a/the sonata"

(66) Vjerovao sam da se sonatom ponose

(67) Vjerovao sam *sonatom* da se ponose

(68) a   *Sonatom* sam vjerovao da se ponose

    b   *Vjerovao sam sonatom

    c   *Sonatom sam vjerovao

Displacement which has been described above occurs in connection with embedded predications, if the predication expressed by the main clause contains a verb of the following type: *htjeti* "want", *morati* "must", *željeti* "wish", *reći* "say", *pitati* "ask", *misliti* "think", *vjerovati* "believe", *nadati se* "hope", *čekati* "wait (for)", *očekivati* "expect", *vidjeti* "see", *gledati* "look", *čuti* "hear", *slušati* "listen", etc. Comparable phenomena occur in other languages in the same geographical area (see for example De Groot (Chapter 3); Sandfeld (1930)).

6.3.2 Seeming displacement

In connection with the verbs of perception (*vidjeti, gledati, čuti* and *slušati*), displacement occurs only when an embedded predication functions as the second argument of the main predication. This is clearly distinguished from the cases when an embedded predication functions as a satellite, whereas the second argument of the main predication is filled by some constituent, as can be illustrated by the following examples:

(69) a   Ivan   vidi *Petar*   da   svira sonatu
          John$_{nom}$ see Peter$_{nom}$ that play sonata$_{acc}$
          "John sees Peter to be playing a/the sonata"

      b   *Ivan vidi Petar

(70) Ivan   vidi Petra   da   svira sonatu
      John$_{nom}$ see Peter$_{acc}$ that play sonata$_{acc}$
      "John sees Peter that he is playing a/the sonata"

(71) Ivan vidi Petra
      "John sees Peter"

(72) Ivan   vidi da nema   Petra
      John$_{nom}$ see that there is no Peter$_{gen=acc}$
      "John sees that there is no Peter"

(73) a   Ivan vidi *Petra* da nema

      b   *Ivan vidi Petra da ga nema

In (69), "Petar" is displaced from the embedded predication, whereas "Petra" in (70) is the second argument of the main predication, within which it occurs. This can be shown by the fact that (71) is acceptable. Similar to (69), "Petra" in (73a) can be seen as left-displaced from the subsequent embedded predication (cf. 72). In (73b), however, "Petra" is coreferential with the enclitical pronoun "ga" in the embedded predication, which means that the former cannot be analysed as left-displaced. It can only be the second argument of the main predication, but then the sentence is self-contradictory, meaning "John sees Peter that he is not there".

"Petra" in (73), as a displaced constituent, has the contrastive accent (cf. 6.2.2), whereas "Petra" in (70), as an argument of the predication within which it occurs, need not have one.

Needless to say that no right-displacement occurs, but only Tail.[5]

6.4 Summary and conclusions

I have tried to show that the pragmatic functions in Serbo-Croatian are determined by the frame of reference shared by the speaker and the addressee, and the information at the speaker's disposal.

The frame of reference existing before the presentation of a given sentence undergoes additional replenishment in the course of the presentation of the sentence. This replenishment of the information in the frame of reference is not purely linear, but partly hierarchically structured. Hierarchy can be defined as asymmetrical implication, e.g. a verb implies its arguments but not vice versa, and a Modifier its Head but not vice versa. Such a hierarchical structure functions as a single information unit at a higher level and as a combination of information (sub)units at the lower level. I hope to return to this question on another occasion. The initial position in a sentence is reserved either for the information which is present in the frame of reference, or information which is in opposition with comparable information in the frame of reference. In the latter case, contrastive accent is used.

I have investigated the positions that can be occupied by the arguments of a verb and concluded that an argument can precede the verb only if it expresses information which is present in the frame of reference or which is in opposition with comparable information in the frame of reference. An argument following the verb can express information which either is present or absent in the frame of reference. These two possibilities are not distinguished by any formal means. An argument following the verb can also express information which is in opposition with comparable information in the frame of reference, in which case, contrastive accent is used. This means that information which is not present in the frame of reference, and also not in opposition with comparable information in the frame of reference, cannot be expressed by placing an argument preceding the verb, but can following it.

The constrastive accent, expressing opposition with comparable information in the frame of reference (i.e. that which could possibly fulfil the same function and occur in the same position), can be used in any position.

Each hierarchical structure such as those mentioned above is characterized by some neutral word order (e.g. a verb is neutrally followed by its
arguments), which is not meaningful. Any violation of the neutral word
order is meaningful, governed by the principle by which new information,
adding specification, follows the information which is present in the frame
of reference.

Acknowledgements

I should like to thank my colleagues, both in the Functional Grammar discussion
group and on the linguistic staff of the Slavic Studies Institute, University of
Amsterdam, for discussions about this and related topics.

Notes

1 The prosodic system of Serbo-Croatian (at least of the standard language)
differs from that of, for example, Dutch in that in the former, accent is
predictable from prosodic boundaries. In word phonology, accent is predictable from tone and prosodic word boundaries—on the understanding
that enclitics always form one prosodic word with the directly preceding
morphological word (Gvozdanović, 1980, 39). In addition, there are larger
prosodic units, coinciding with syntactic units unless pragmatic factors
necessitate a different division. All prosodic units are characterized by a
unifying fundamental frequency line, whereas a break in the fundamental
frequency line (from low to high, or from high to low) is characteristic of
prosodic boundaries. A prosodic unit corresponds with a unit of information.
A falling fundamental frequency signals termination; a rising fundamental
frequency signals continuation. A rising fundamental frequency at the end
of a prosodic unit signals that it will be followed by another prosodic unit
which will form with it a single unit at the next higher level (both in the
sense of its phonetic manifestation and informational content).
    There are two main types of sentence intonation, the assertive and the
interrogative. The assertive intonation is characterized by a fundamental
frequency which is relatively falling after the tone in the last prosodic word
(for a definition of prosodic words see Gvozdanović (1980, 12)) or the one
with the contrastive accent, and the interrogative intonation is characterized
by a rise which starts on the prosodic word with the contrastive accent (or,
in cases of its optional usage, on the last prosodic word in a given sentence).
The beginning of a sentence or clause is characterized by a relatively non-
falling fundamental frequency.
    The more or less continuous fundamental frequency line within a prosodic
unit at the phrase and sentence levels is in certain cases, which will be
defined below, broken by the occurrence of the contrastive accent. In

combination with the assertive intonation, the contrastive accent is indicated by means of a relatively high fundamental frequency which may be said to exhibit a convex line. In combination with the interrogative intonation, it is indicated by means of a concave fundamental frequency line. The contrastive accent indicates that the information X expressed by a given prosodic word or larger unit is opposed to comparable information (i.e. -X), which is present in the frame of reference shared by the speaker and the addressee. It is thus used whenever the information at the speaker's disposal contradicts comparable information shared by himself and the addressee.

Further investigation of both production and perception of the Serbo-Croatian intonation and other prosodic phenomena is necessary. An important step in this direction has been made by Lehiste and Ivić (1978). The prosodic marking of phrase boundaries which I have tried to describe above shows some similarity with the marking of syntactic boundaries in Dutch as established by Collier and 't Hart (1978, 22f.). The difference consists in the fact that next to the contrastive accent there are no "prominence-lending rises and falls" in Serbo-Croatian, only prosodic boundaries as described above, which mark the boundaries of information units and can coincide with any of the syntactic boundaries.

2   Cases in Serbo-Croatian are: nominative, genitive, dative, accusative, vocative, locative and instrumental.

3   Either clause can be inserted as well, which is then indicated by means of the intonation characteristic of indicating clause boundaries (see note 1).

4   Note, however, that these examples become acceptable if there is contrastive accent on *dečko*, *most* or *vidio*, which presupposes the presence of expectation in the frame of reference such that it can be interpreted as a predication within which the given constituent can indeed occur.

5   Note that the first sentence is acceptable and the second is not:

Da je vidio dečko, *most*, mislio sam
*Da je vidio dečko, *most* sam mislio

References

BROWNE WAYLES, E.
   1968   Srpskohrvatske enklitike i teorija transformacione gramatike. *Zbornik za filologiju i lingvistiku* **XI**, 25–30.
COLLIER, R. and J. 't Hart
   1978   "Cursus Nederlandse intonatie". Instituut voor Perceptie Onderzoek, Eindhoven, Manuscript no. 333.
DIK, S. C.
   1978   "Functional Grammar". Amsterdam, North-Holland.
EBELING, C. L.
   1980   "On the Demarcation of Linguistic Meaning". Studies presented to Coseriu (in press).

GVOZDANOVIĆ, J.
1980 "Tone and Accent in Standard Serbo-Croatian, with a Synopsis of Serbo-Croatian Phonology". Vienna.
HALLIDAY, M. A. K.
1967 Notes on transitivity and theme in English, *Journal of Linguistics* III, Part I: 37–81, Part II: 199–244.
IVIĆ, M.
1973 "Neka pitanja reda reči u srpskohrvatskoj zavisnoj rečenici s veznikom 'da' ". *Zbornik za filologiju i lingvistiku* **XVI/I**, 187–196.
LEHISTE, I. and P. Ivić
1978 "Interrelationship between Word Tone and Sentence Intonation in Serbo-Croatian. Elements of Tone, Stress and Intonation". Donna Jo Napoli (ed.). Washington, 100–128.
LYONS, J.
1977 "Semantics". Vol. 2. Cambridge, Cambridge University Press.
NOOTEBOOM S., T. Kruyt and J. Terken
1980 "What Speakers and Listeners Do with Pitch Accents: Some Explorations". Instituut voor Perceptie Onderzoek, Eindhoven, Manuscript no. 397.
SANDFELD, Chr.
1930 Linguistique balcanique, Paris.
TOMIĆ MIŠESKA, O.
1978 "Definiteness and Word Order". Proceedings of the Twelfth International Congress of Linguists. Wolfgang U. Dressler and Wolfgang Meid (ed.). Vienna, 720–723.

7 Subject Assignment in the Impersonal Constructions of French

CO VET

Department of French
University of Groningen

7.0 Introduction

This chapter deals with the so-called impersonal constructions in French. The different forms in which they occur are illustrated by examples (1a)–(5a) and by (1b). Examples (1c) and (2b)–(5b) form the corresponding personal variants:

(1) a   Il pleut
         "It rains"

     b   Il pleuvait des pierres dans son jardin
         Lit.: "It rained stones in his garden"

     c   Des pierres pleuvaient dans son jardin
         "Stones rained in his garden"

(2) a   Il arrive deux trains
         "It arrives two trains"

     b   Deux trains arrivent
         "Two trains arrive"

(3) a   Il est regrettable que Jeanne ne soit pas venue
         "It is regrettable that Jean has not come"

     b   Que Jeanne ne soit pas venue est regrettable
         "That Jean has not come is regrettable"

(4) a   Il est difficile de corrompre la concierge
         "It is difficult to bribe the concierge"

   b   La concierge est difficile à corrompre
        "The concierge is difficult to bribe"

(5) a   Il semble que Jeanne embrasse son mari
         "It seems that Jean kisses her husband"

   b   Jeanne semble embrasser son mari
        "Jean seems to kiss her husband"

The impersonal constructions are characterized by the fact that the main verb is preceded by the pronoun *il* which does not refer to any person or object in the (non-linguistic) situation; nor does it have an anaphoric function. There is agreement between this *il* and the verb and not, as in English, between the verb and the noun phrase which follows the verb (cf. (2a)). With certain verbs the *séquence* (the noun or embedded sentence following the verb in impersonal constructions) may be absent as is shown by (1a).

   In this chapter I shall briefly survey some traditional and transformational descriptions of the impersonal expressions in French and discuss the points which, from a theoretical point of view, seem the most interesting to me. I shall then propose a description in the framework of Functional Grammar. More specifically, I shall formulate two hypotheses about the ways impersonal constructions can be handled in FG: the first is that the syntactic function of Subject must be assigned to the *séquence*. In the second any Subject assignment to the *séquence* has been omitted. The consequences of these hypotheses are examined in the light of the actual data. It will be shown that the second hypothesis has the greater explanatory power and at the same time confirms some of the intuitions of traditional grammarians.

7.1   Some traditional and transformational approaches

One of the main problems with which traditional approaches have dealt is a classificatory one:[1] what is the function of the pronoun *il* and what is the function of the *séquence*? In the most current view (see e.g. Grevisse, 1970) *il* is regarded as an "apparent subject", the *séquence* being the "real subject" of the sentence. This analysis is criticized by Pieltain (1964). The "real subject" does not possess what may be considered the most characteristic feature of this function; the fact that the verb agrees with it in number (and gender). Example (2a) clearly shows that there is no agreement between the verb (*arrive*) and the *séquence* (*deux trains*). This is different from comparable constructions in, for example, English and Dutch (*there arrive/*arrives two trains*; *er komen/*komt twee treinen aan*). The solution put forward by Pieltain himself is, however, rather metaphysical; following in this respect Bally and Spitzer, he does not regard *il* as an empty word but as a kind of anonymous agent ("Nature") which is the cause of the event referred to by the impersonal sentences. Though in example (1a) and in the following:

(6)   Il te pousse des boutons
      "You get pimples"

this view seems plausible, for other examples (see (2a)) it is totally untenable.

   The *séquence* is sometimes regarded as a kind of direct object because of the position it occupies.[2] There are, however, strong arguments against this view. First, most of the verbs are one-place (intransitive) verbs which never take a direct object. Further, for the same reasons as given for Serbo-Croatian by Dik and Gvozdanović (1981), it is not necessary to assume for French the existence of Object-assignment, so that the position occupied by, for example, *deux trains* in (2a) cannot be explained by the fact that it has been assigned the function of Object. Finally the behaviour of *séquences* in impersonal constructions is quite different from that of direct objects: there is no passivization, pronominalization, etc. Compare:

(7)   a   Pierre voit des trains. Il les voit.
          "Peter sees trains. He sees them"

      b   Il arrive des trains. *Il les arrive.
          Lit.: "It arrives trains. It arrives them"

   A more interesting view is put forward by Séchehaye (1926, 148–149), who holds that in sentences such as (2a) the element which was the subject has ceased to be a subject without becoming a *"complément"* (object). A comparable view has been put forward by Eskénazi (1968, 113); according to him *il* is not an apparent subject but a kind of *"indice introducteur"*. The *séquence* (*deux trains*) is a "desyntacticized" element. I shall return to this point later.

   Martin (1970) gives a transformational description of the impersonal constructions. Roughly speaking he proposes to derive a sentence such as (2a) from a "personal" deep structure (by means of a kind of extraposition transformation):

(8)   NP VP → *il* VP NP

where NP may be a clause. Martin discusses several constraints on the application of this transformation; one of the most important is that if NP is a "normal" noun phrase (i.e. if it is not a sentence), it must be indefinite:

(9)   a   Il arrive des trains/beaucoup de trains/deux trains/etc.
          Lit.: "It arrives trains/many trains/two trains/etc."

      b   *Il arrive les trains/ces trains/Jeanne/etc.
          "It arrives the trains/these trains/Jean/etc."

The same type of constraints are also formulated by Eskénazi who gives examples with definite *séquences*:

(10)   Si vous le faites, il vous arrivera le même malheur qu'à moi
       "If you do so you will suffer the same misfortune as I do"

Martin explains the difference between (9b) and (10) by the fact that the definiteness of *les trains*, etc. in (9b) is caused by its anaphoric function or its direct reference to an object in the non-linguistic context. In (10) the definiteness of *malheur* is caused by postmodification. In the latter case the impersonal construction is possible, for Martin regards as the main function of this kind of expressions that it places the subject in the comment part of the sentence. This is possible only if the subject is not yet known. This is not the case if the definiteness of the NP is caused by premodification, but is possible in the case of postmodification. For the same reason the *séquence* cannot be generic. For further details see Martin (1970): the other points he mentions are not important for our argument, but what is relevant is that in Martin's analysis the NP which becomes the *séquence* of the sentence is in fact regarded as the real subject of the sentence (in its deep structure). Note that agreement must take place after the application of the transformation of (8).

In Ruwet (1972) the notion of subject also plays an important role. In particular he analyses examples such as (5a, b), which for convenience are repeated here:

(5)   a   Il semble que Jeanne embrasse son mari
          "It seems that Jean kisses her husband"

      b   Jeanne semble embrasser son mari
          "Jean seems to kiss her husband"

Ruwet argues that *Jeanne* in (5b) is not the subject of *sembler* but of *embrasser*, because there are no selection restrictions between *sembler* and *Jeanne*, but between *Jeanne* and the embedded verb (*embrasser*). This is for Ruwet a strong argument to derive sentences such as (5) from a deep structure which has the following general form:

(11) Δ sembler $_S$[NP – VP]

where Δ is an empty element which is replaced by *il* later in the derivation. In the derivation of (5b) a transformation ("Subject Raising") moves the embedded NP to the Δ-position. It becomes then a kind of pseudo-subject of *sembler*. The subject raising transformation is formulated as follows (Ruwet, 1972, 60):

(12) Δ – sembler $_S$[NP – X – Y]
　　　 1　　2　　 3　　4　 5
　　 $\Rightarrow$3 –　2　$\emptyset$ –　4 – 5

Note that this transformation is the opposite of Martin's. The main difference is that Ruwet assumes the existence of an empty subject in deep structure. *Sembler* is regarded as a two-place verb which is essentially impersonal. Note, too, that in (2b) there are selection restrictions between *arriver* and the *trains*, so there is no reason to adopt for this kind of construction the solution put forward by Ruwet for sentence (5b).[3]

In what follows I shall try to give a description which is valid for all the impersonal constructions mentioned in (1)–(5). In FG there is an elaborate theory about the function of the Subject, so we may expect that this theory offers the possibility to solve at least part of the problems discussed in this section. There is another reason why FG may be preferred to the transformational approach: it does not encounter the theoretical difficulty of the too powerful transformations.

7.2   Two hypotheses about Subject assignment

In Sections 7.2 and 7.3 I shall examine the plausibility of two hypotheses (A and B) concerning Subject assignment in the impersonal constructions of French. Hypothesis A is that in these constructions Subject assignment takes place in the usual way. The personal variants result from the fact that Subject has been placed in Subject-position. The impersonal variants can be explained by the influence of the general principle of language-independent preferred order of constituents (LIPOC) put forward by Dik

(1978, 189ff.). Hypothesis B is that, in contrast with what happens in the personal constructions, Subject assignment has not taken place in the derivation of impersonal sentences, which is possible only if the argument which is potentially a candidate for Subject assignment is indefinite. I shall first illustrate these hypotheses by the derivation of the sentences (3a, b):

(3)   a   Il est regrettable que Jeanne ne soit pas venue
          "It is regrettable that Jean has not come"

      b   Que Jeanne ne soit pas venue est regrettable
          "That Jean has not come is regrettable"

After this I will discuss the other types of impersonal expressions. In the framework of FG *regrettable* as used in (3a, b) is a one-place predicate of the class of adjectives (A); it indicates a property of a state of affairs. This is represented in the following predicate frame:

(13)   regrettable$_A$ (x$_1$: [predication] (x$_1$))$_\theta$

that is to say, *regrettable* has one argument (x$_1$) and this argument is itself a predication; for (3a, b) it is the embedded clause *Jeanne est venue*. $\emptyset$ means that the argument has an unmarked semantic function; sentences derived from (13) refer to states. For (3a, b) the complete predication has the following form:

(14)   regrettable (x$_1$: [NEG venir$_V$ (d1x$_j$: Jeanne (x$_j$)$_{Ag}$] (x$_1$))$_\theta$

where d means "definite" and 1 "singular". The semantic function of x$_j$ in the embedded predication is that of Agent. According to hypothesis A the assignment of the syntactic function of Subject to (14) gives for (3a, b) the following result:

(15)   regrettable$_A$ (x$_1$: [NEG venir$_V$ (d1x$_j$: Jeanne (x$_j$)$_{AgSubj}$] (x$_1$))$_{\theta Subj}$

Note that the order of the elements of (15) is not specified. In FG the elements of a predication are given a place according to general principles. I shall now show how these work in the derivation of (3a, b) (see Dik, Chapter 1 for a more general discussion).

First we have to look more closely at the function and the form of LIPOC. For us the principal point is that this principle says that there is a strong tendency to place complex constituents in a position to the right of the one occupied by non-complex constituents having the same function. Starting from the assumption that French is a real SVO-language (or, rather, a "SVX-language", since French probably has no Object-assignment) we adopt the following basic constituent order for the sentences of French (see also Dik, 1978, 198):

(16) P1 S Vf Vi NP PP

where S marks the Subject position, Vf that of the finite verb, Vi that of the non-finite verb. P1 indicates a specific universal initial position which in French serves for constituents having the pragmatic function of Topic or Focus. With the exception of P1 the pattern of (16) is illustrated by the following sentence:

(17) Jean (S) a (Vf) donné (Vi) le livre (NP) à Pierre (PP)
      "John has given the book to Peter"

If the order of NP–PP is inverted this results in an unacceptable sentence:

(18) *Jean a donné à Pierre le livre
      "John has given to Peter the book"

However, if the NP is more complex, e.g. if it is a clause or if it contains a relative clause, its grade of complexity becomes higher, in which case LIPOC stipulates that such a NP may or must be placed in a position which is at the right of the "normal" position for NPs:

(19) a Jean a dit à Pierre (PP) qu'il est malade (NP)
         "John has said to Peter that he is ill"

      b *Jean a dit qu'il est malade à Pierre
         "John has said that he is ill to Peter"

(20) a Jean a donné à Pierre le livre que je lui avais conseillé
         "John has given to Peter the book which I had recommended to him"

      b *Jean a donné le livre que je lui avais conseillé à Pierre
         "John has given the book which I had recommended to him to Peter"

It should be noticed that the P1-position of (16) is outside the sphere of influence of LIPOC.

According to hypothesis A the difference between (3a) and (3b) can now be explained as follows: in (3a) the Subject clause (*Que Jeanne ne soit pas venue*) is placed by LIPOC to the right of the verb because of the complexity of this constituent. Since the P1-position is not influenced by LIPOC, the embedded clause may also be placed in that position if it receives the pragmatic function of Topic. This results in (3b). The introduction of the pronoun *il* can take place (just as for English *it*) by means of the following convention (Dik, 1978, 205):

(21)   If a clausal Subject is placed after the pattern position for the Subject, this position is marked by *il*.

Hypothesis B says that in sentence (3a) the syntactic function of Subject has not been assigned at all to the embedded clause. This is why it cannot be placed in the S-position of (16) so that the constituent order is "V-*Séquence*" as in (3a). However, if the function of Subject is assigned to the embedded clause, it is placed in the S-position. The predications underlying (3a) and (3b) differ in that x_i in (3a) has not been assigned the function of Subject (nor that of Topic), while the x_i in the underlying predication of (3b) has the function of Subject (which, by the way, seems conditional on the assignment of the pragmatic function of Topic in this case).[4] Finally the convention of (21) must be accommodated to hypothesis B:

(22)   If Subject assignment has not taken place the pattern position for Subject is marked by *il*.

7.3   The genuinely impersonal verbs

The simplest form of the impersonal construction is that of sentences containing what is sometimes called a "genuinely impersonal verb" ("verbe impersonnel proprement dit"). Most of the verbs of this class refer to atmospheric conditions: *neiger* ("snow"), *pleuvoir* ("rain"), *geler* ("freeze") etc. For these verbs the predicate frame has the following form:

(23)   neiger $(x_1 : \emptyset)_\theta$

This means that *neiger* etc. are necessarily accompanied by an empty argument to which, evidently, no syntactic or pragmatic function can be assigned.

Hypothesis B provides a solution for this case in the form of convention (22); *il* precedes the verb if Subject assignment has not taken place. For hypothesis A, which can only use the influence of LIPOC, the following condition must be added to (21): "or if the verb has one empty argument".

Examples (1b, c) show, however, that the emptiness of the argument of this group of verbs is not always absolute (see also Grevisse, 1970, § 604). In these examples we are concerned with a relatively marginal case: the metaphorical use of the verb *pleuvoir* in (1b, c) has apparently given rise to a modification of the selection restrictions so that it has become a "normal" one-place verb. It then meets with the same constraints mentioned by Martin and Eskénazi for this construction (see Section 7.1):

(24) *Il pleuvait les grosses pierres dans son jardin
      Lit.: "It rained the big stones in his garden"

7.4 Impersonal constructions with intransitive, pronominal and passive verbs

In French there is a category of verbs, roughly characterized as intransitive, pronominal and passive verbs, which may be used in constructions of the type illustrated by (2a, b) (for a more detailed description see Martin, 1970). Other examples of this construction are:

(25) a   Il meurt un grand nombre d'enfants
          Lit.: "It dies a great number of children"

      b   Un grand nombre d'enfants meurt
          "A great number of children die"

(26) a   Il en a été vendu des centaines
          Lit.: "It has been sold hundreds of them"

      b   Des centaines en ont été vendues
          "Hundreds of them have been sold"

(27) a   Il s'est présenté plusieurs candidats
          Lit.: "It has gone in several candidates (for the examination)"

      b   Plusieurs candidats se sont présentés
          "Several candidates have gone in (for the examination)"

(These examples are from Corbeau 1951, 82.) As we have already seen, the *séquence* of the a-sentences may not refer to a specific (known) person or object. Note further that the impersonal variant is possible only if the surface verb presents itself as a one-place predicate. With a so-called *verbe pronominal impropre* which is accompanied by a reflexive pronoun having a syntactic function the impersonal variant is not possible:

(28) a   Plusieurs enfants se sont lavés
          "Several children have washed (themselves)"

      b   *Il s'est lavé plusieurs enfants
          "It has washed itself several children"

A more important point for us is the fact that, unlike the variation between (3a) and (3b), the difference between the a- and b-sentences of (2a, b) and (25a, b)–(27a, b) cannot be explained very easily by hypothesis A, which can use only LIPOC for the explanation of these phenomena. The fact is that the NP-arguments of these sentences are not at all complex, so that nothing can explain their position after the verb.

According to hypothesis B the a-sentences are characterized by the fact that no Subject assignment has taken place to *deux trains, des centaines* etc., which is a rather natural explanation of the positions they occupy. Hypothesis B is more suited to the description of this construction type than hypothesis A. For the sake of clarity I shall give here the generation of (26a, b); for *vendre* ("sell") I start from the predicate-frame represented in (29a). For (26a, b) the underlying predication of (29b) will be assumed.

(29) a   vendre$_V$ $(x_1)_{Ag}$ $(x_2)_{Go}$ $(x_3)_{Rec}$

      b   vendre$_V$ $(x_1:\emptyset)_{Ag}$ $(imx_j:$ centaines de x_k $(x_j))_{Go}$ $(x_1:\emptyset)_{Rec}$

Where in the configuration imx_j the term operator i means "indefinite" and m means "plural". We do not deal here with the pronominalization of de x_k. In the predication underlying (26a, b) the first and the third argument have remained empty so that *vendre* may present itself as a predicate with one argument, which is a constraint on the derivation of the a-sentence.

According to hypothesis A, given the fact that Subject assignment to x_1 is blocked because it has remained empty, the syntactic function. Subject will be assigned to the Goal (x_j) of the predication. The constituent order for French, given in (16), stipulates that, now that it has the funtcion of Subject, *des centaines* must be placed in the Subject-position, before the verb. This leads to the structure of (26b). It is, as said before, much more difficult to find an explanation for the structure of (26a), at least in hypothesis A. There is no reason to place *des centaines* after the verb. In hypothesis A it is possible to explain why in sentences such as (26a, b) the verb takes the passive morphology. There is a general principle according to which in French the verb takes the passive morphology if the syntactic function of Subject has not been assigned to the Agent, but to the Goal (there are no other possibilities for Subject assignment in French).

In hypothesis B this last point does not give rise to difficulties either. Here the rule for the passivization of the verb can be formulated as follows: if in a predication containing an Agent and a Goal there is no Subject assignment to the Agent the verb takes the passive morphology. The difference with hypothesis A is that here Goal has not been assigned the function of Subject. In (26b) this function has been assigned to *des centaines* which is therefore placed in the S-position. In (26a) the S-place remains empty because *des centaines* does not have the function of Subject. Instead the form *il* is placed in the S-position by convention (22).

7.5   Constructions with *sembler*

In the light of the preceding discussion I shall examine in this section the more complicated constructions illustrated by examples (5a, b):

(5) a Il semble que Jeanne embrasse son mari
        "It seems that Jean kisses her husband"

     b Jeanne semble embrasser son mari
        "Jean seems to kiss her husband"

The difference between (5a, b) and (3a, b) consists in the fact that there does not exist any sentence corresponding to (5a) in which the embedded sentence occupies the Subject position:

(30) *Que Jeanne embrasse son mari (me) semble
       "That Jean kisses her husband seems (to me)"

while *regrettable* does not allow the construction of (5b):

(31) *Jeanne est regrettable de ne pas être venue
       "Jean is regrettable not to have come"

In my view a grammar will fail to make a generalization if it does not relate the phenomena of (3) and (5). It seems plausible to assume for the sentences of (5a, b) an identical predication of the following form:

(32) $sembler_V$ (x_i: [$embrasser_V$ ($d1x_j$: Jeanne (x_j)$_{Ag}$ ($d1x_k$: son mari (x_k)$_{Go}$] (x_i))$_\theta$

I shall examine what may be the different results of the application of hypotheses A and B for the description of the sentences containing *sembler*.

Of course hypothesis A explains easily why sentence (5a) is possible because LIPOC allows the placement of the embedded clause in a position to the right of the "normal" Subject position. In hypothesis B the derivation of (5a) is no problem either, for here the embedded clause has not been assigned the function Subject.

The exclusion of sentences such as (30), however, does form a difficulty in either hypothesis. Note that *sembler* is not the only verb which behaves in this way. There is a small group of (impersonal) verbs which do not allow arguments in S (or P1) position. Compare for example:

(33)   a   Il fait bon vivre dans ce pays
           "It is good to live in this country"

       b   *Vivre dans ce pays fait bon

(34)   a   Il faut que vous partiez
           Lit.: "It must that you leave"

       b   *Que vous partiez faut

Another member of this group is *paraître* ("appear").[5] I think that this behaviour can be regarded as a lexical property of these verbs. Their meaning provides so little semantic information that the verb cannot function on its own as the comment of a sentence. Thus, the lexical entries of *sembler*, *paraître* etc. must contain the constraint that the argument x_1 can never be placed into P1-position (hypothesis A) or that these verbs do not allow Subject assignment to x_1 (hypothesis B). I prefer the second, more syntactic solution.

As far as sentence (5b) is concerned, our two hypotheses do not differ very much; neither offers a solution or an explanation for the possibility to generate such kind of sentences. I shall therefore propose a description which makes use of the notion of "pseudo-argument" and then examine whether this leads to an analysis compatible with one (or both) of my hypotheses.

The first point to be considered is whether there is any reason to adopt for (5b) a predicate-frame which is different from that given in (32), in other words whether there exist two different verbs *sembler*. There are, however, no semantic reasons for such an assumption because (5a) and (5b) are synonymous (see also 7.0). We have seen already that the absence of selection restrictions between the subject in sentences such as (5a) and *sembler* leads to the idea that we have to do in these cases with a pseudo-argument (Ruwet, 1972).

To form a sentence of the type (5b), we have to assume that in (32) the function of Subject is assigned to the embedded Agent x_j (*Jeanne*). As we have seen, this is in hypothesis B the only possibility for Subject assignment. It must be assumed that in the derivation of sentences such as (30) the placement into the S-position of an embedded Subject is possible but only under very special conditions: any Subject assignment to an argument of the main verb must be blocked. In hypothesis A, Subject assignment in the main clause is possible, so it is very difficult to explain why placement in the Subject position is blocked for the Subject of the main clause and possible for the Subject of the embedded clause. For this reason hypothesis B must be preferred here.[6] Note finally that in the *sembler*-constructions the function of Subject can also be assigned to the Goal of the predication (which is normal in French). This leads to sentences such as:

(35)   Pierre semble avoir été embrassé par Jeanne
       "Peter seems to have been kissed by Jean"

This confirms the idea that the subject of this kind of sentences is a pseudo-subject because it is not the verb *sembler*, but *embrasser* which takes the passive morphology.[7]

Sentences (4a, b):

(4)   a   Il est difficile de corrompre la concierge
          "It is difficult to bribe the concierge"

      b   La concierge est difficile à corrompre
          "The concierge is difficult to bribe"

might be formed in the same way as (5a, b). Since *difficile* is a one-place predicate, one may assume for both (4a) and (4b) the underlying predication of (36):

(36)   difficile$_A$ (x_i: [corrompre$_V$ (x_j: $\emptyset$)$_{Ag}$ (d1x_k: la concierge)$_{Go}$] (x_i))$_\theta$

However, an important difference with respect to the *sembler*-sentences is that the adjective *difficile* allows also constructions of the following type:

(37)   Corrompre la concierge est difficile
       "Bribing the concierge is difficult"

This would destroy the argument that for the appearance of a pseudo-subject it is necessary that Subject assignment to an argument of the main clause is entirely blocked. To find a solution I shall give a more detailed analysis of (4a, b) and (37). I shall first give a brief survey of the possibilities which both hypotheses offer for the formation of these sentences from (36). For hypothesis A these are as follows. In (4a) the function of Subject has been assigned to x_i, which is not placed in the normal Subject position but in a position after the verb because of the influence of LIPOC. As to (4b) the function of Subject must have been assigned to both x_i and the embedded argument x_k (*la concierge*) (but see note 6). Here *la concierge* is placed in the Subject position. In (37) x_i, which has also the function Subject, has been placed in the P1-position which is outside the influence of LIPOC. According to hypothesis B, Subject assignment does not take place at all in the derivation of (4a); (4b) is derived in the same way as in hypothesis A with the exception that x_i has not become Subject, but only x_k. In (37) the function of Subject has been assigned to x_i.

A point which merits closer inspection is that on the basis of general rules for passivization in French and of what we have seen in the derivation of (35) one might expect that Subject assignment to the Goal which is postulated for (4b) would give rise to the passivization of the verb. Not only is this not the case in (4b), but it would lead to totally unacceptable sentences:

(38)   *La concierge est difficile à être corrompue
        "The concierge is difficult to be bribed"

Further there is a contrast with what was possible in the sentences of (5) and (35): in (4b) and (37) the Agent must always remain unspecified. These differences make it very unlikely that both (4a, b) and (37) go back to the predication of (36). It seems much more plausible that both (4a) and (37), but not (4b), have (36) as underlying predication. The adjectives *regrettable* and *difficile* would then allow exactly the same type of constructions (3a: 3b = 4a : 37). The sentence (4b), on the contrary, possesses a quite different syntactic structure, which gives indeed a slightly different semantic interpretation: in (4a) and (37) the predication involves the reference to a state of affairs, while in (4b) it concerns the person of the concierge. This is why (4b) entails (4a) or (37), but not the other way round. Sentence (4b) is synonymous with:

(39)   La concierge est difficilement corruptible
        "The concierge is not easily corruptible"

That is why I prefer to adopt for (4b) the following predication:

(40)   difficile à corrompre$_A$ (d1x$_1$: la concierge (x$_1$)$_\theta$

where the predicate *difficile à corrompre* is the result of a predicate formation rule which forms complex adjectives from simpler ones.[8]

7.6   The verb category of *menacer, pouvoir, devoir* etc.

In this last section I want to examine some verbs which do not allow an
impersonal variant but for which two different predicate-frames must be
assumed, one of which has some resemblance to the construction of (5b).
The category of these verbs comprises among other things *pouvoir* ("can"),
devoir ("must", "have to"), *risquer* ("risk"), *menacer* ("threaten") and
promettre ("promise"), for example:[9]

(41)   a   Jeanne doit travailler pour vivre
            "Jean has to work in order to live"

       b   Jeanne doit avoir trente ans
            "Jean must be thirty years old"

(42)   a   Jeanne a promis de venir
            "Jean has promised to come"

       b   Jeanne promet de devenir une bonne actrice
            Lit.: "Jean promises to become a good actress" (she is very
            promising)

(43)   a   Le patron l'a menacé de son couteau
            "The boss threatened him with his knife"

       b   Le discours menace d'être long
            Lit.: "The speech threatens to be long"

The correspondence between the *sembler*-sentences and the b-sentences of
(41)–(43) is that the selection restrictions are not between the subjects of
these sentences and the finite verb but between the subjects and the infini-
tives. Unlike the *sembler*-constructions, however, the impersonal variant is
never possible:

(44)   a   *Il doit que Jeanne ait trente ans
            "It must (be) that Jeanne is thirty years old"

b *Il promet que Jeanne devienne une bonne actrice
"It promises that Jeanne becomes a good actress"

c *Il menace que le discours soit long
"It threatens that the speech will be long"

The only verb which can be used in an impersonal expression is *pouvoir*:

(45) Il se peut que Jeanne ait trente ans
"It may be that Jean is thirty years old"

but this expression is idiomatic (because of the presence of the reflexive pronoun *se*).

In spite of the ungrammaticality of sentences such as (44a–c) Ruwet (1972) proposes to derive the b-sentences from a deep structure which is analogous to that put forward for the *sembler*-sentences (see (11)). This means that for e.g. (43b) he postulates the following deep structure:

(46) Δ menacer s[le discours être long]

That is to say, he regards the verbs of this group as a kind of two-place predicates. In the derivation of sentences containing a verb of this category the transformation of subject raising is always obligatory. I think an objection can be made against Ruwet's analysis of the verb *menacer* in (43b): it seems more plausible to regard this verb essentially as a one-place predicate. A strong argument in favour of this idea is that the a-sentences allow pronominalization while the b-sentences do not:

(47) a Jeanne doit travailler pour vivre; elle le doit
"Jean has to work in order to live; (Lit.:) she must it"

b Jeanne doit avoir trente ans; *elle le doit
"Jean must be thirty years old; she must it"

This syntactic difference gives rise to the assumption that in (47a) *travailler pour vivre* is a direct object which can be pronominalized, while the constituent *avoir trente ans* in (47b) is not, so that pronominalization is blocked.

The question whether a description of the phenomena of (41b)–(43b) is satisfactory depends in my opinion largely on the place accorded to the semantic interpretation. It is clear that the syntactic proposal made by Ruwet (1972) (see also Ross 1969) constitute an anticipation of the semantic interpretation and makes this interpretation easier in that it relates a semantically untransparent surface structure to a semantically (more) transparent deep structure. This kind of "concession" is, however, rather costly because the discrepancy between deep structure and surface structure necessitates a great number of transformations, or other kinds of rules. Moreover, for the sentences (41b)–(43b) there is no variation in the surface structure which can support the idea that there is a discrepancy between surface structure and deep structure. I shall now examine the possibilities of dealing with this kind of phenomena in FG.

There are roughly two possibilities of generating (41b)–(43b) in the framework of FG; the first makes use of the notion of pseudo-subject in the same way as in the derivation of (5b); the second consists in the formation of complex predicates by means of predicate formation rules (see Dik, 1979). In the first approach the underlying predication of (43b), for example, is as follows:

(48)   menacer$_V$ (x_i: [long$_A$ (d1x_j: discours (x_j)$_\theta$] (x_i))$_\theta$

According to hypothesis A the function of Subject is assigned to x_i. Placement of this argument into the S-position must be blocked because this would lead to the ungrammatical sentence:

(49)   *Que le discours soit long menace
       "That the speech is long threatens"

As I noted already, it is also impossible to place the embedded clause after the verb which could have been expected on the basis of LIPOC (see (44c)). The only possibility is to place the embedded Subject (*le discours*) into the S-position, which in hypothesis A is less plausible because x_i is Subject, too. In hypothesis B there is no Subject assignment to x_i (as in the sentences with *sembler*). Thus LIPOC does not have any effect. As we have seen, the absence of Subject assignment to arguments of the main verb was regarded as a condition on the possibility to place an embedded argument into the S-position (here *le discours*).

The second possibility, which is also compatible with the framework of FG, offers a more syntactic, or rather, lexico-syntactic solution. It consists in the application of predicate formation rules. This would mean that in the derivation of (43b) the following rule has been applied:

(50)   φ (x_1) . . . (x_n)→[menacer$_V$] (x_1) . . . (x_n)

where n $\geq$ 1 and where φ indicates some predicate. Rules such as (50) operate on the lexicon and combine *menacer* etc. with other predicates to form new, more complex predicates. This explains very well both the fact that there are no selection restrictions between *menacer* and the argument(s) of (50), but only between φ and its argument(s), and also the fact that pronominalization is not possible (47b).

It is clear that a predicate formation rule can also be adopted for the generation of the sentences with *sembler*. This would offer the advantage that the notion of pseudo-subject could be dropped from our description. However, the reason why I do not choose this solution for the *sembler* sentences is that I think that the impersonal constructions of French may be regarded as forming a kind of hierarchy of increasing complexity: the *pleuvoir*-type of sentences are the simplest, followed by the type illustrated by (2a) (*il arrive deux trains*), then the sentences containing adjectives such as *regrettable* and *difficile* and finally the constructions with *sembler* etc. which are the most complex. All the constructions of this hierarchy have the typical form of the impersonal construction in French (i.e. they begin with the empty pronoun *il*). The reason why the construction with *menacer*, etc. does not fit into this hierarchy is that it does not possess this character- istic: if a verb of this group appears in an impersonal construction it does so in an idiomatic way (*il se peut que* . . .). That is why I think the cut-off point of the hierarchy (see Dik, 1978, 9) must be placed between *sembler* and *menacer*, etc., this in spite of the fact that the construction of sentences such as (43b) has a certain resemblance to that of (5b). If, however, one tries to derive both the *sembler*-sentences and sentences such as (43b) in the same way, one suggests a regularity which in fact does not exist. In the solution which makes use of predicate formation rules, *menacer*, etc. (in (41b)–(43b)) is regarded as a kind of auxiliary verb, which explains very well the behaviour of this category of verbs.

7.7 Conclusion

Although in some cases my two hypotheses lead to the same results, I prefer B to A, because B allows a more uniform characterization of the impersonal constructions in French. The most important argument in favour of B is that the absence of Subject assignment which it claims, gives a better explanation for the possibility of sentences such as (2a) and (25a)– (27a). Moreover B was found to be able to establish a relationship between the absence of Subject assignment and the appearance of a pseudo-subject.

Another result of my analysis is that it provides arguments for the differentiation of semantically very closely related constructions with *difficile* etc. (as in (4a, b)). Further, the notion of hierarchy has been useful in our discussion of constructions as illustrated by (43b), which in my opinion do not belong to the class of impersonal constructions of French. This category of verbs does not allow the formation of impersonal constructions in a systematic way. Finally, it is interesting to see that hypothesis B reflects the intuitions of linguists like Séchehaye, who regarded the impersonal constructions of French as constructions without a subject.

Acknowledgement

I wish to thank Ans de Kok and Dolf Hartveldt for their valuable suggestions which have improved the form and the content of this paper.

Notes

1 This section has profited greatly from the excellent survey given in Pieltain (1964).
2 The *séquence* of the impersonal expression *il y a* ("there is"):

(i) Il y a deux bouteilles dans cette boîte
"There are two bottles in that box"

which contains the verb *avoir* ("have") may be a direct object from a diachronic point of view. In a synchronic description there is no reason to adopt this view, let alone to generalize it to the other impersonal constructions.
3 Ruwet (1972) does not deal with sentences such as (2a–b). It seems to me that both in (2) and (3) the same kind of mechanism is at work and that Ruwet's description would miss a generalization, since it is impossible to derive (2) by means of the subject raising transformation which Ruwet uses for (3). The same remark can be made with respect to (3a–b); (3a) is derived by means of Extraposition (Ruwet, 1972, 67).
4 To be complete a rule has to be formulated which forms a verbal predicate from an adjective and a copula, but this does not play any role in my argumentation.
5 It may be doubted whether impersonal expressions such as *il y a* ("there is") and *il fait* . . . (Lit.: "it makes") belong to this category. Compare:

(i)a Il y a beaucoup de livres ici
"There are many books here"
  b *Beaucoup de livres y ont ici

    (ii)a Il fait du vent/ du verglas
        "There is (some) wind/ there is a frost"

      b *Du vent/ du verglas fait

Rather these expressions are related to constructions of the type illustrated by (2a) with which they have in common that the *séquence* must be indefinite (see 7.1). The predicate frames of these verbs must contain the same constraint as that formulated for the verb *sembler* (arguments cannot be placed into the S-position).

6 In fact, there is in FG a third possibility, introduced for English by Dik (1979). He assumes, for embedded clauses, an alternative hierarchy of Functions in which the Subject of the embedded clause (Subj$_e$) becomes one of the candidates to which the Subject assignment of the matrix clause can apply:

    (i)   Ag Go Rec Ben Subj$_e$
                                     Subj$_m$

For (32) this repeated Subject assignment can yield the structure represented in (ii):

    (ii)   sembler$_V$ (x$_1$: [embrasser$_V$ (d1x$_j$: Jeanne)$_{Ag}$ $_{Subj_e}$ (d1x$_k$:
          son mari)$_{Go}$] (x$_1$))$_\emptyset$ $_{Subj_m}$

In the same way Subj$_e$ and Subj$_m$ can be assigned to the Goal of (32). The argument which has the function of Subj$_m$ is placed in the S-position of the matrix clause; for (ii) this results correctly in (5b).

    I am not sure, however, whether this complicated Subject assignment must be adopted for French since, unlike English, this language has a rather poor system of syntactic functions. It is, for example, highly probable that the grammar of French can do without Object assignment. Moreover, as I have shown in Section 7.1, there are strong arguments in favour of the absence of Subject assignment in sentences such as (2a), because of the fact that there is no agreement between the argument (*deux trains*) and the verb. For these reasons I prefer to maintain for French the solution of hypothesis B put forward in this paper.

7 Note that *sembler* and *paraître* are the only verbs which allow this kind of pseudo-argument. Since expressions such as *faire bon* does not take *que*-clauses it does not offer this possibility (the argument of *vivre* in (33a) is always empty). Sentence (34a) however has a variant of the following form:

    (i) Il vous faut partir
       Lit.: "It must for/to you to leave"

Here the embedded argument seems to have become a dative—a not totally unknown, but very restricted phenomenon in French. Compare:

    (ii) Je trouve qu'*il* a bonne mine
        "I think he looks well"

(iii)   Je *lui* trouve bonne mine

I shall not deal with this kind of construction here.

8   On the basis of this analysis I do not believe that a subject raising transformation can be used in the derivation of (4b) as suggested by Ruwet (1972).

9   Some of these examples are taken from Ruwet (1972).

References

COMRIE, Bernard
1974   Impersonal subjects in Russian. *Foundations of Language* **12**, 103–115.
CORBEAU, L. J.
1951   "Grammaire du Français Contemporain". Zutphen, Thieme.
DIK, Simon C.
1978   "Functional Grammar". Amsterdam, North Holland.
1979   Raising in a Functional Grammar. *Lingua* **47**, 119–140.
DIK, SIMON C. and Jadranka Gvozdanović
1981   Subject and Object in Serbo-Croatian. *In* T. Hoekstra, H. van der Hulst and M. Moortgat (ed.). "Perspectives on Functional Grammar". Dordrecht, Foris.
ESKÉNAZI, André
1968   Note sur les constructions impersonnelles du français contemporain. *Revue Romane* **3**, 97–115.
GREVISSE, Maurice
1970   "Le Bon Usage. Grammaire Française". Gembloux, Duculot.
MARTIN, Robert
1970   La transformation impersonnelle. *Revue de Linguistique Romane* **34**, 375–394.
1979   La tournure impersonnelle: essai d'une interprétation sémanticologique. "Festschrift Kurt Baldinger" Vol. I, Tübingen, Niemeyer, 208–219.
PIELTAIN, Paul
1964   La construction impersonnelle en français moderne. "Mélanges de Linguistique Romane et de Philologie Médiévale Offerts à M. Maurice Delbouille. I: Linguistique Romane". Gembloux, Duculot.
ROSS, John Robert
1969   Auxiliaries as main verbs. *In* W. Todd (ed.). "Studies in Philosophical Linguistics I". Evanston, Ill.: The Great Expectation Press.
RUWET, Nicolas
1972   La syntaxe du pronom "en" et la transformation "montée de sujet". *In* "Théorie syntaxique et syntaxe du français". Paris, Seuil, 48–86.
SÉCHEHAYE, Albert
1926   "Essai sur la structure logique de la phrase". Paris, Champion.

8   The Interaction of Subject and Topic in Portuguese

SIMON C. DIK

Institute for General Linguistics
University of Amsterdam

8.0   Introduction

This chapter discusses a number of properties of Portuguese grammar relevant to the general theme of this volume and consists of two main parts. Part 1 considers the fact that Subjects in Portuguese may occur either preverbally or postverbally. Two ways of accounting for this fact are discussed critically. According to the first approach (Perlmutter, 1976), postverbal Subjects are not "real" Subjects, i.e. are thought to have lost their Subject properties through a rule of Subject Downgrading. According to the second approach (Brito and Duarte, 1980a, b), postverbal Subjects are regarded as "real" Subjects, but the preverbal Subject position is taken as basic, so that some rule of Subject postposing must be postulated. After discussion of the advantages and drawbacks of these two proposals, a third approach is formulated within the framework of FG. According to this approach, postverbal Subjects are regarded as "real" Subjects, but the postverbal Subject position is also seen as the (or: a) pattern position of the Subject in Portuguese.

In Part 2, the various possible constructions with the Portuguese verb *parecer* "to seem" are studied. *Parecer* is a one-place verb which can take a predication for its argument and accordingly can be expressed with a sentential Subject. It is also possible, however, for the Subject of the embedded predication to be displaced out of its proper clause, and/or to start behaving "as if" it were the Subject of *parecer*. These different possibilities result in various types of agreement within the relevant constructions. Two different ways of accounting for these agreement patterns are suggested and evaluated with respect to each other.

8.1   Status and position of the Subject

8.1.1   Preverbal and postverbal Subjects

The normal order for a predication with a definite Subject in Portuguese is SV . . .:

(1)   O   jardineiro cortou a   árvore
      the gardener   cut   the tree

In quite a few circumstances, however, it is possible for the Subject to also appear after the Verb. Compare:

(2)   a   O   João chegou ontem
          the John arrived yesterday
          "John arrived yesterday"

      b   Ontem   chegou o   João
          yesterday arrived the John
          "Yesterday John arrived"

In certain cases the Subject strongly prefers the postverbal position. This is especially so in the case of indefinite Subjects of existential verbs or "presentative" verbs (or verbs of "appearance on the scene", such as *arrive, arise, appear*, etc.).[1] Compare:

(3)   a   Sempre acontecem coisas interessantes em Nova Iorque
          always happen$_{3pl}$ things interesting   in New York
          "There always happen interesting things in New York"

      b   Coisas interessantes sempre acontecem em Nova Iorque
          things interesting   always happen$_{3pl}$ in New York
          "Interesting things always happen in New York"

In such a case (3b) will automatically be interpreted in such a way that the Subj is not taken as indefinite but as generic. In that case (3b) is taken as a general statement about where "interesting things" happen. Such an interpretation is impossible in the case of (3a). Thus, although (3b) is in itself a grammatical Portuguese sentence, it seems correct to say that an indefinite Subject, such as *coisas interessantes* in (3a), cannot be placed in preverbal position.

In certain cases, preposing the Subject to the Verb even leads to ungrammaticality (Brito and Durante, 1980b):

(4) a   Veio gente afecta   ao   antigo patrão
        came people devoted to-the old   boss
        "There came people devoted to the old boss"

     b   *Gente afecta ao antigo patrão veio

It is clear then that any grammar of Portuguese will have to account for
the relationship between preverbal and postverbal Subjects and for the
factors which influence whether a given Subject will be placed in the one
position or the other.

We shall now look at some solutions which have been suggested in the
literature.

8.1.2   Subject downgrading

It is usually assumed that the most unmarked constituent order, SVO, (at
least in the case of sentences with definite Subject terms) is also the most
basic or underlying order. Starting from this assumption Perlmutter (1976)
has suggested that there is a rule of Subject downgrading in Portuguese
which brings the Subject to postverbal position under certain conditions
and at the same time deprives it of a number of its Subject properties: the
postverbal Subject, according to this approach, is not a "real" Subject any
more in surface structure, although it originates as a real Subject in
underlying structure.

This idea of Perlmutter's is based on the fact that it can be shown that
there are a number of rules in Portuguese grammar which apply to preverbal NPs but not to postverbal NPs. If these rules are formulated in
terms of the notion Subject, it is expedient to assume that preverbal NPs
do have Subject function but postverbal NPs do not have this function.

As an example of the relevant type of rules, consider the following facts
about so-called Floating quantifiers:

(5) a   Os escoceses chegaram ontem
        the Scots   arrived   yesterday

     b   Todos os escoceses chegaram ontem
        all   the Scots   arrived   yesterday

     c   Os escoceses chegaram ontem   todos
        the Scots   arrived   yesterday all

(6) a   Chegaram os   escoceses ontem
         arrived   the Scots   yesterday

     b   Chegaram todos os   escoceses ontem
         arrived   all   the Scots   yesterday

     c   *Chegaram os   escoceses ontem   todos
         arrived   the Scots   yesterday all

Assuming that the universal quantifier *todos* "all" originates within the NP
which it quantifies (i.e. in the position in which it appears in (5b) and (6b)),
one must postulate some rule of Quantifier Floating to derive constructions
such as (5c), in which the quantifier is separated from the NP which it
quantifies. This rule can be shown to be applicable only to preverbal
Subject NPs, as in (5). All other NPs, including postverbal NPs as in (6),
cannot launch floating quantifiers. This argument establishes, then, that
there is some essential difference between *os escoceses* in (5) and *os escoceses*
in (6) and that the rule of Quantifier Floating is sensitive to just this difference. Perlmutter adduces a number of rules which similarly discriminate
between preverbal and postverbal NPs, and assumes that the required
difference is that preverbal NPs are Subjects, whereas postverbal NPs have
lost their Subject function through the rule of Subject downgrading. The
relevant rules can then be formulated in terms of Subject function, and
will automatically leave unaffected all non-Subject NPs, including down-
graded ones.

   Even apart from the question whether something equivalent to Perlmutter's rule of Subject downgrading could be formulated within the
framework of FG, this rule raises a number of problems, as is demonstrated
at length by Brito and Duarte (1980a, b). The most important problems
are the following:

(i) Postverbal NPs have two properties which are usually considered as
    criterial for Subjects:
    (a) the finite Verb agrees with postverbal NPs just as it does with
        preverbal NPs. Brito and Duarte show that it is very difficult, if
        not impossible, to formulate the agreement rule correctly if it is
        assumed that postverbal NPs are not Subjects.
    (b) if the relevant postverbal NP is expressed in pronominal form or
        if it is referred to anaphorically in later discourse, the pronoun
        invariably appears in the nominative, just as it does in the case of
        preverbal Subjects.

(ii) There is evidence that the difference between preverbal and postverbal NPs is not so much a matter of syntactic function but rather reflects a difference in pragmatic function.

That a pragmatic difference is involved is in fact mentioned in passing by Perlmutter (1976, 97), in his discussion of the following pair:

(7) a Sempre surgem controvérsias como essas em Nova Iorque
        always arise   controversies like these in New York
        "There always arise controversies like these in New York"

     b Controvérsias como essas sempre surgem em Nova Iorque
        "Controversies like these always arise in New York"

Perlmutter describes the difference between (7a) and (7b) as follows:

> (7a) is a neutral description of a certain state of affairs. (7b), on the other hand, is a sentence in which *controvérsias como essas* is the theme or topic of the sentence—that is, a sentence about the subject *controvérsias como essas*.

This suggests that, in a model which distinguishes syntactic functions such as Subject and pragmatic functions such as Topic as independent functional relations, there is another possibility to account for the difference between preverbal and postverbal NPs. This is to assume that both preverbal and postverbal NPs have Subject function, but that the former also have Topic function, whereas the latter are just Subjects. This line is taken by Brito and Duarte (1980a, b), whose position I shall now summarize.

8.1.3   Subject postposing

Brito and Duarte's position is basically that in Portuguese declarative sentences, non-Topic Subjects go to postverbal position, and Subject–Topic constituents to preverbal position. This explains why indefinite Subject terms which normally cannot receive Topic function cannot normally be placed in preverbal position: preverbal position is normally reserved for definite or generic Subjects.

  Taking Topic, and not Subject, function as the factor differentiating preverbal and postverbal NPs entails that those rules which Perlmutter demonstrated could only be applied to preverbal NPs must be made sensitive to Topic rather than to Subject function. Thus, the rule of Quantifier Floating (or whatever other rule accounts for the differences between (5b) and (5c) above) must be formulated in such a way that only Topics can launch quantifiers. This accounts for the fact that only preverbal Subjects (which, according to this view, must have Topic function) are affected by this rule. According to Brito and Durate, this view is reinforced by the fact that non-Subject constituents, too, may launch floating quantifiers, if they have Topic function. Consider:

(8) a   Todos esses livros, o   João leu
         all   these books, the John read

     b   Esses livros, o   João leu   todos
         these books, the John read all
         "These books, John read them all"

In a similar way, the other rules discussed by Perlmutter can be made sensitive to Topic rather than Subject function. I shall return to this in Section 2.

Sentences of type (8a) exemplify another interesting property of Portuguese, which provides some problems for the distinction between Theme and Topic function. In terms of FG we can formulate this phenomenon as follows. As we saw above, Subject–Topic constituents must take the P1 position in the clause. Non-Subject Topic, however, cannot in the same way be brought into P1 position. Consider the following facts:

(9) a   O   João viu esse filme ontem
         the John saw this film   yesterday
         "John saw this film yesterday"

     b   *Esse filme viu o João ontem

     c   Esse filme, viu o João ontem

     d   Esse filme, o João viu ontem

     e   Esse filme, o   João viu-o ontem
         this film, the John saw-it yesterday

From (9b) it is clear that the Object–Topic cannot simply be placed in clause-initial, P1 position. If it is preposed, it must be followed by an intonation break characteristic for constituents in P2 position, as in (9c–d). One might assume, then, that *esse filme* in (9c–d) has Theme rather than Topic function. However, this is countenanced by the fact that there is no resumptive pronoun in the constructions to reaffirm the Theme within the predication: *o João viu ontem* (9d), without any further indication of the Object, does not form a complete clause in Portuguese. The true Theme,

Predication construction is given in (9e) in which there is a resumptive pronoun, and in which *o João viu-o ontem,* by itself, could form a complete clause. It seems necessary, then, to follow Brito and Duarte in their assumption that non-Subject Topics are placed in P2 rather than in P1 position, so that P2 position in Portuguese can be used both for Themes and for non-Subject Topics (notice that Brito and Duarte do not make the distinction between Theme and Topic: they treat all constituents in P2 as "marked Topics").

Although I believe that Brito and Duarte's idea of differentiating preverbal and postverbal Subjects in terms of presence and absence of Topic function is basically correct, there is one aspect in their approach which provides some problems, both in general, and especially within the framework of FG. Their use of the term Subject Postposing suggests that they take the SVO pattern as basic, and wish to generate postverbal Subjects by means of some movement operation applied to this pattern. This poses a general problem in that, on this approach, the application of the rule of Subject Postposing is in certain cases (e.g. in the case of (4a)) obligatory. This means that certain Subjects are generated, in the basic structure, in a position in which they can never occur in the final structure of the sentences involved. The special problem for FG is that this model does not allow for movement rules of the required type: constituents must be placed in their proper position in one go. Let us see, therefore, how the relevant facts could be accounted for in a way compatible with the principles of FG.

8.1.4 *A postverbal pattern position for the Subject*

The FG theory of constituent ordering has been briefly summarized in Chapter 1, Section 1.2. More detailed information on this theory can be found in Dik (1978, ch. 8–9; 1980, ch. 6–7). This theory holds that each language has one or more functional patterns, conforming to the general schema:

(10) P2, P1 (V) S (V) O (V), P3

and that placement rules bring the constituents of the as yet unordered underlying predication to the positions of these patterns. Placement must be carried out in one go: no subsequent movements are allowed, once a constituent has obtained a position in the pattern. P2 and P3 are the positions for Theme and Tail constituents, respectively; the commas indicate intonation breaks. In between the commas we find the possible patterns for the clause proper, where a clause constitutes the expression of a complete predication. The rules for placement of constituents within the domain of the clause operate in such a way that it is first decided which constituents must or may go to P1 position. First it is checked whether there are any P1-constituents in the predication: constituents which must go to P1 if they are present (in many languages, the class of P1-constituents includes question words, relative pronouns, and subordinating conjunctions). If none of these is present, then constituents with Topic or Focus function may be placed in P1. When the P1 rules have been applied, all other constituents of the predication go to their respective "pattern positions", indicated by S, O, V, and other possible symbols in the functional pattern.

Given these principles, it is possible to postulate the following functional pattern for constituent ordering in Dutch main clauses:

(11)   P1 Vf S O Vi

in which Vf indicates the position for the finite Verb, and Vi the position for infinite Verbs. Note that the pattern position for the Subject is specified as the position after the Vf, although the most frequent ordering in Dutch main clauses is SVO. This is because, whenever some constituent other than the Subject appears in P1 position, the Subject itself appears postverbally:

(12)   a   Jan   heeft gisteren   dit boek gekocht
           John has   yesterday this book bought
           "John has bought this book yesterday"

       b   Dit boek heeft Jan gisteren gekocht
           "This book John has bought yesterday"

       c   *Dit boek Jan heeft gisteren gekocht

       d   Gisteren heeft Jan dit boek gekocht
           "Yesterday John has bought this book"

       e   *Gisteren Jan heeft dit boek gekocht

Since we need a rule for placing Topic and Focus constituents in P1 anyway, we can now use this same rule for placing Subject–Topic or Subject–Focus constituents in clause-initial position. The fact that the Subject more often appears before than after the Verb (the ratio is about 7:3) is explained by the fact that the Subject is by its very nature the primary candidate for receiving Topic or Focus function.

Note that this theory has at least two advantages: (i) the initial position of the Subject is described as a special case of a more general rule placing Topic and Focus constituents in initial position; (ii) no rule of Subject Postposing or Subject–Verb inversion is needed: the principle is that the Subject ends up in its postverbal pattern position if it has not been placed in P1 on account of its pragmatic functionality.

The postverbal pattern position is strongly favoured by indefinite Subjects of existential and similar constructions. In fact, there are close parallels between the Portuguese constructions (3) and (4) above and the following Dutch sentences:[2]

(13) a   Er   gebeuren altijd   interessante dingen in New York
        There happen   always interesting   things in New York

     b   Interessante dingen gebeuren altijd   in New York
        interesting   things   happen   always in New York

(14) a   Er   kwamen mensen die   verknocht waren aan de   oude baas
        there came   people who devoted   were   to   the old   boss

     b   *Mensen die verknocht waren aan de oude baas kwamen

Thus, (13a) is the normal expression form for predications with indefinite non-Topic Subjects. Indefinite Subjects in P1 position are difficult to get: (13b) can only be interpreted as a generic statement. (14b), too, would be grammatical in a construction which could be given a generic or habitual interpretation:

(15)   Mensen die   verknocht waren aan de   oude baas kwamen hem
       people   who devoted   were   to   the old   boss came   him

       elke   dag een bezoekje brengen
       every day a   visit   bring

       "People devoted to the old boss came to pay him a visit every day"

Given these close parallels, it seems interesting to see to what extent the analysis devloped for Dutch can also be applied to Portuguese constituent ordering. Thus, we would assume that Portuguese has a functional pattern of the form:

(16)   P2, P1 V S O, P3

This pattern can now be used to account for all those cases with VS . . . ordering by assuming that these are cases in which there was no pragmatic reason to place the Subject in P1, so that P1 is left empty. SV . . . constructions are now seen as cases in which the Subject has been placed in P1 on account of its having Topic function. As to initial non-Subject constituents, matters are a bit more complicated than in Dutch, since it appears from the facts given in (9) that non-Subject Topics cannot be placed in P1 position, but must be placed in P2, followed by an intonation break. This fact, however, can be used to explain that in such cases the Subject may be placed in postverbal pattern position, as in (9c), or in preverbal P1 position, as in (9d). Pattern (16) also works well in accounting for Q-word questions: if, in such questions, a non-Subject is questioned and thus placed in P1, the Subject cannot appear in preverbal position:

(17) a Quantos   bolos tiveram os meninos ao   chá?
         how-many cakes had$_{3pl}$ the boys   at-the tea?
         "How many cakes did the boys have at tea?"

      b *Quantos bolos os meninos tiveram ao chá?

Pattern (16), however, is not sufficient for accounting for all clause types. Consider relative clauses: these can have the Subject in postverbal position, as predicted by pattern (16), as in:

(18)   Dom Bento, com quem se   entendia   bem Camões, era um
       Don Bento, with whom refl. understood well Camoes, was a

       santo
       saint

       "Don Bento, with whom Camoes got on well, was a saint"

but this order is a bit archaic. More usual would be:

(19)   Dom Bento, com quem Camões se entendia bem, era um santo

If we assume that *com quem* in (19) is in P1 position, then it follows that *Camões* cannot be in that position. Therefore, at least for relative clauses, there must be an alternative pattern position for the Subject in front of the Verb. In order to account for this, we can modify pattern (16) as follows:

(20)   P2, P1 S$_a$ V S$_b$ O, P3

and we must add rules to the effect that at least within the domain of relative clauses, the S_a position may be chosen for the Subject, and is even preferred in certain styles. Those same rules can then be used to account for the differences between normal Q-word questions on the one hand, and Cleft questions on the other, as in:

(21)   a   Que comprou Alberto?
           what bought   Alberto
           "What did Alberto buy?"

       b   *Que Alberto comprou?

(22)   a   Que foi que Alberto comprou?
           what was what Alberto bought
           "What was it that Alberto bought?"

       b   ?Que foi que comprou Alberto?

In Dik (1980, ch. 10) it has been argued that questions of the form (22) can be analysed in terms of an underlying predication of the general form:

(23)   What was the thing that Alberto bought?

which contains the underlying structure of a relative clause. If this is done, then it is immediately explained why the Subject in (22a) prefers the pre-verbal position, whereas in questions of the form (21) the Subject cannot possibly occur in that position: in (22a) P1 of the embedded clause is occupied by the relative pronoun. The extra pattern position S_a is not only available in the case of relative clauses, but more generally for all subordinate clauses. Thus, we can come a long way in accounting for constituent ordering in Portuguese by adopting pattern (20), stipulating that in main clauses only S_b is available and in subordinate clauses both S_b and S_a (where the latter position is even preferred in certain conditions), and specifying the appropriate rules for the uses which can be made of the special positions P1 and P2.

The main point to remember in the next section is that in declarative main clauses preverbal Subjects normally have Topic function and have been placed in P1 position on account of that fact.

8.2   Some displacement and Raising phenomena

In his argumentation for a rule of Subject Downgrading, Perlmutter (1976) discusses the following different construction types with the verb *parecer* "to seem":

(24) Parece que as crianças estão cansadas
      seem$_{3sg}$ that the children are   tired
      "It seems that the children are tired"

(25) As crianças parece que estão cansadas
      the children seem$_{3sg}$ that are   tired
      "The children it seems that are tired"

(26) As crianças parece estarem cansadas
      the children seem$_{3sg}$ be-inf$_{3pl}$ tired
      "The children it seems to be tired"

(27) As crianças parecem estar cansadas
      the children seem$_{3pl}$ to-be tired
      "The children seem to be tired"

In (24) *parece* "it seems" appears with a subordinate, fully finite clause as Subject. In (25) the Subject of the embedded clause appears before the main verb *parece*, but without triggering agreement on that verb. The remainder of the subordinate clause is just as finite as in (24). In (26) the Subject is similarly placed before the main verb, but now the embedded predication is given non-finite expression in an infinitival construction which has a property peculiar to Portuguese: the infinitive agrees in number and person with the Subject *as crianças*. Portuguese uses this inflected infinitive in a number of circumstances in which the Subject of the embedded predication is not identical to the Subject of the higher verb. Compare:

(28) Passei   sem   os   ver
      passed-I without them see
      "I passed without seeing them"

(29) Passei   sem   me verem
      passed-I without me see-they
      "I passed without them seeing me"

In (28) we have the "bare" infinitive, signalling that the one who saw is the same as the one who passed; in (29) we find the 3rd person plural infinitive, signalling that the seeing and the passing was done by different people. A sentence such as (26) can thus be more or less literally paraphrased as: "The children it seems for them to be tired".

In (27), finally, the Subject of the embedded predication acts as if it is the Subject of the higher verb, which now agrees with it in number and person. The complement is expressed by a "bare" infinitive construction which shows *no* agreement with the Subject.

Perlmutter describes the constructions (24)–(27) in terms of two rules, which provide further evidence for the difference between preverbal and postverbal Subjects:

(a) *Subject Raising*. The assumption is that (27) is derived from the structure underlying (24) through a rule of Subject Raising. Perlmutter then demonstrates that only preverbal Subjects can be raised in this way. Thus, starting from a construction such as (30), it is impossible to arrive at a construction such as (31):

(30)   Parece que existem muitos candidatos nesta   eleição
       seem$_{3sg}$ that exist$_{3pl}$ many   candidates in-this election
       "It seems that there are many candidates in this election"

(31)   *Muitos candidatos parecem existir   nesta   eleição
       many   candidates seem$_{3pl}$ to-exist in-this election

Given our analysis of pre- and postverbal Subjects, we shall have to assume that the relevant rule can only apply to Subjects which are also Topics and so we shall leave unaffected postverbal, non-Topic Subjects.[3]

(b) *Head Start*. Constructions such as (25) and (26) are described by Perlmutter through a rule of Head Start, which takes out the Subject NP from the embedded sentence and preposes it to the main verb *parece*, without, however, causing agreement on this main verb. Perlmutter's argument in this case is similar to that concerning Subject Raising. He shows that this rule only affects preverbal, that is, in his view, "real" Subjects. Thus, given a construction such as (30), neither (32) nor (33) can be derived:

(32)   *Muitos candidatos parece que existem nesta eleição

(33)   *Muitos candidatos parece existirem nesta eleição

From our point of view, again, we shall have to say that the relevant rule can apply only to those Subjects that are also Topics.

Let us now see how the different constructions (24)–(27) can be handled within the general framework of FG, and the specific framework sketched in Chapter 2. Quicoli (1976) demonstrates convincingly that *parecer* must be considered as a one-place verb taking a sentential Subject. Within our framework the underlying predicate-frame of *parecer* would thus have the following form:

(34)   parecer$_V$ (sub x$_1$: [PREDICATION] (x$_1$))$_\theta$

The predication underlying (24) could then be specified as follows:

(35)   parecer$_V$
(sub x$_1$: [estar$_V$ cansad- (dmx$_j$: criança$_N$(x$_j$))$_\theta$Subj Top] (x$_1$))$_\theta$Subj

Thus, the verb *parecer* is applied to an argument x$_1$ (= the something which seems to be the case), where x$_1$ is specified by a predication which, independently, would be expressed as:

(36)   As crianças estão cansadas

The element sub stands for the subordinating device which, in the case of (24), will be expressed by *que* (cf. Chapter 2, Section 2.1, above). The embedded predication consists of a one-place predicate, consisting of *estar* plus a participle applied to a term to be realized as *as crianças* "the children". This term has Zero semantic function (the predication designates a state), Subject function, and Topic function. Being a Subject–Topic, it is entitled to appear in preverbal position.[4] (24) is the most faithful mapping of (35): the domain structure of the subordinate clause corresponds to the domain structure of the underlying predication.

Now note that (25) differs from (24) only in the position of the embedded Subject. In theory, there are two possible interpretations of constructions of this type. The first would be to regard (25) as an example of a Theme, Predication construction. There are arguments for and against such an analysis. One argument for is that *parece que estão cansadas* "it seems that they are tired" in itself constitutes a complete predication. Another argument for this analysis lies in the fact, adduced by Quicoli (1976, 84), that constructions of this form cannot be embedded, although those resulting from Subject Raising can:

(37)   *O João crê   que as crianças parece que estão cansadas
the John believes that the children seems that are   tired

(38)   O   João   crê   que as   crianças parecem estar cansadas
       the   John believes that the children seem   to-be tired

As discussed in Chapter 5 on embedded Themes in Dutch, it is difficult in many languages to get a Theme,Predication within the domain of a subordinate clause. Thus, interpreting (25) as a Theme,Predication construction might provide an explanation for the difference between (37) and (38). Against this interpretation, however, is the fact that in (25) there is no intonation break between the Subject and the rest of the construction. Thus, it appears that *as crianças* is in P1 rather than in P2 position.

For this reason, a second possible interpretation of (25) is in terms of pure displacement of the embedded Subject–Topic (see (35)) to the P1 position of the main clause. Since, on this assumption, all the syntactic and pragmatic relations remain the same, agreement will not be affected, although the syntactic Subject of *parece* (cf. (35)) is in this case pragmatically split up into *as crianças . . .* and *. . . que estão cansadas*.

Note that the displacement resulting in (25) is explicable in terms of a general predilection of Topics to take the initial position in the sentence. To explain (26) as derivable from the same underlying predication (35) we may assume that if displacement is applied, the remainder of the embedded predication may get non-finite expression (cf. Chapter 2, Section 2.3.3). This involves the following adjustments:

(39)   (i)   the subordinating element sub is left unexpressed;

       (ii)   the embedded verb is expressed in the infinitive;

       (iii)   this infinitive agrees with the Subject in person and number.

In (27), finally, it appears that the embedded Subject-Topic *as crianças* effectively functions as a pseudo-argument to the main verb *parecer*. In this case, the complement *must* occur in the form of an infinitival construction, i.e. the following is ungrammatical:

(40)   *As crianças parecem que estão cansadas

However, in (27) it is not the infinitive, but the main verb *parecer* which agrees with the Subject–Topic in person and number.

Assuming that (27), too, has to be derived from the underlying structure (35), there would in principle seem to be two possible ways of doing so (cf. Chapter 2, Section 2.4). Let us call these Solution I and Solution II, and consider their merits one by one:

Solution I: Agreement after Placement. If it is assumed that agreement rules can apply after placement rules, then one might think that, after *as crianças* has been brought to the initial position just before *parecer*, the agreement rule might "mistakenly" take *parecer* rather than *estar* as the verb with which the displaced Subject is to agree. According to this Solution, then, (27) would come out as the result of a low-level morphological operation which is sensitive to the linear position in which the constituents have been placed.

It is not difficult to demonstrate, however, that Solution I cannot be correct. The problems are the following. First, on this view it would not be clear why mistaken agreement could not apply in the case of finite expression of the complement, as in (40). Second, it would be difficult to explain why mistaken agreement would have to be obligatory in subordinate clauses (compare the difference between (37) and (38)). Third, there are higher predicates such as *consta* "it is certain" which allow for displacement, but never show agreement with the displaced constituent:[5]

(41) a   Consta que os pilotos morreram do coração
          certain that the pilots died   of heart
          "It is certain that the pilots died of a heart-attack"

      b   Os pilotos consta que morreram do coração

      c   *Os pilotos constam que morreram do coração

Finally, and most decisively, there are cases in which the higher verb agrees with the embedded Subject, although this Subject has not been placed in initial position immediately before the verb. Brito and Duarte (1980b) give the following example:

(42) Parecem acontecer coisas como essas só   nos   Balcãs
      seem3pl happen   things like   those only in-the Balcans
      "Things like that only seem to happen in the Balcans"

Note that this example is also very difficult to account for on Perlmutter's theory. For discussion of the problems involved, see Brito and Duarte (1980b). I briefly return to this construction type below. It seems, then, that agreement of the higher verb with the embedded Subject is independent of the position of this embedded Subject with respect to the higher verb. Therefore, Solution I cannot be correct.

Solution II : Penetrating Subject Assignment. This solution would be similar to that developed for English *believe*-constructions in Dik (1979), and summarized in Chapter 2, Section 2.4. According to Solution II one could assume that the Subject function pertaining to *parecer*, which in (35) is assigned to the embedded predication as a whole, may alternatively be assigned to the Subject of the embedded predication, thus "penetrating" into this predication. This would lead to an underlying predication of the form:

(43)   parecer$_V$
    (sub x$_i$: [estar$_V$ cansad- (dmx$_j$: criança$_N$(x$_j$))$_{\theta SubjTopSubj}$] (x$_i$))$_\theta$

To this it would have to be added that in the case of this form of Subject assignment, non-finite realization of the complement is obligatory (the same is the case in English *believe*-constructions). This would then account for the ungrammaticality of constructions such as (40).

Solution II requires a number of special stipulations in the grammar: it involves an exceptional form of Subject assignment, to be lexically governed in such a way that it is triggered (optionally) by verbs like *parecer*, but not by verbs like *constar*; it results in a term having two distinct Subject functions, one pertaining to its own embedded verb, and the other pertaining to the higher verb; and it requires non-finite expression of the complement to be made obligatory. However, Solution II does not encounter the problems raised by Solution I and therefore seems to be the more adequate analysis for this type of construction. From this it follows that the agreement pattern exemplified by (27) reflects a deeper difference connected with Subject assignment and cannot be accounted for in terms of a superficial morphological operation.

Finally let us return to the problems posed by constructions of the form (42). Consider the following paradigm:

(44)   a   Acontecem coisas interessantes em Nova Iorque
        happen$_{3pl}$ things interesting   in New York
        "There happen interesting things in New York"

     b   Parece que acontecem coisas interessantes em Nova Iorque
        "It seems that there happen interesting things in New York"

     c   Parece acontecerem coisas interessantes em Nova Iorque

     d   Parecem acontecer coisas interessantes em Nova Iorque

We have analysed the postverbal Subject *coisas interessantes* as a non-Topic Subject which has ended up in its pattern position S$_b$ after the verb. It would therefore seem natural to assign the same status to the postverbal Subjects in (44b–d). However, on that assumption, (44c) and (44d) have some interesting implications.

(44c) shows that there can be non-finite expression of the embedded predication without either displacement or "penetrating" Subject assignment having been applied to the embedded Subject. From this it is clear that non-finite expression of the embedded predication cannot be described as a consequence of some sort of "removal" of the Subject from that predication. Further, this sort of non-finite expression would seem to involve no morphological adjustment of any kind of the Subject constituent *coisas interessantes*: the Subject has the same morphological form as in the finite complement in (44b). This is relevant to the claim embodied in schema (46) of Chapter 2, to the effect that non-finite expression would necessarily involve some sort of morphological adjustment. It is not, however, a straightforward counterexample to that claim. For notice that the inflected infinitive which we find in (44c) constitutes in a sense an intermediate case in between finite and non-finite expression: it has infinitival properties with respect to constraints on the expression of Mode, Tense, and Aspect, but is shares with the finite verb the expression of person and number categories.

The implications of (44d) are different but no less interesting. This construction shows that postverbal Subjects may trigger agreement on the higher verb. From this it follows that our equivalent to "Raising", i.e. "penetrating" Subject assignment, is not restricted to Subject–Topic targets, but can also be applied to non-Topic Subjects within embedded predications. Thus, it is an advantage that we can generalize over both preverbal and postverbal Subjects in terms of the notion Subject, whereas we can differentiate between them in terms of the notion Topic. The ungrammaticality of examples such as (31) therefore does not seem to lie in the fact that Raising has been applied to a non-Topic Subject, but in the fact that such a non-Topic Subject, with or without Raising, is not entitled to preverbal position.

8.3 Conclusion

I believe that it has been demonstrated in this chapter that a number of crucial phenomena in the grammar of Portuguese can be profitably interpreted within the framework of FG when the following assumptions are adopted:

(i) the grammar of Portuguese requires a functional pattern of the form P1 S_a V S_b O, in which S_b is the pattern position of the Subject in declarative and interrogative main clauses;

(ii) Subjects go to P1 when they also have the pragmatic function Topic;

(iii) Subject-Topics embedded under verbs like *parecer* may be displaced to the P1 position of the main clause; in that case the remaining complement may be realized in finite or in non-finite form, but in both cases the embedded verb will agree with the Subject-Topic;

(iv) the Subject function pertaining to verbs like *parecer* may optionally be assigned to the Subject of a predication embedded under *parecer*; in that case the remaining complement must be expressed in non-finite form, and *parecer* rather than the embedded verb agrees with the embedded Subject. If, in such a case, the embedded Subject also has Topic function, it must be placed in the P1 position of the main clause.

Acknowledgements

I am grateful to Ana Maria Brito, Inês Silva Duarte, and Reineke Bok for discussion about the facts and problems treated in this chapter. Of course, I alone am responsible for the views defended here.

Notes

1   See Perlmutter (1976) and the papers by Brito and Duarte for discussion of these verb types.

2   Note that Dutch, unlike Portuguese, requires a dummy element *er* "there" in constructions of this type with postverbal Subjects. That is connected with the fact that Dutch is a "strong V2" language, i.e. a language in which the finite verb is strongly tied to the second position in the clause. For discussion, see Dik (1980, ch. 7).

3   We shall see below that this statement will probably have to be qualified.

4   There is a problem involved in this statement which I shall not try to solve here. If we assume that in the subordinate clause embedded in (24) the subordinator *que* is in P1 position, then the Subject *as crianças* must be in the S_a position of pattern (20). The problem is that it is not clear whether the same conditions hold for placing Subjects in P1 position in main clauses

and in S_a position in subordinate clauses. Should this be the case, it might be more appropriate to assume that the S_a position in subordinate clauses is in fact an *extra* special position P0, for which similar rules hold as for P1 in main clauses. For the status of such an extra special position in Hungarian see De Groot (Chapter 3).

5   See Quicoli (1976) for discussion of the similarities and differences between the verb classes to which *parecer* and *constar* belong.

References

BRITO, Ana Maria, and Inês Silva Duarte
   1980a Condiçoes sobre posposição do sujeito em Português. Paper, University of Oporto.
   1980b Conditions on SU Postposition in Portuguese declarative sentences (abridged English version of 1980a). Paper, University of Oporto.
DIK, Simon C.
   1978   "Functional Grammar". North-Holland Linguistic Series 37. Amsterdam, North-Holland.
   1979   Raising in a Functional Grammar. *Lingua* 47, 119–140.
   1980   "Studies in Functional Grammar". London and New York, Academic Press.
PERLMUTTER, David M.
   1976   Evidence for Subject Downgrading in Portuguese. *In* Schmidt-Radefeldt (1976), 94–138.
QUICOLI, António C.
   1976   On Portuguese impersonal verbs. *In* Schmidt-Radefeldt (1976), 63–91.
SCHMIDT-RADEFELDT, Jürgen (ed.)
   1976   "Readings in Portuguese Linguistics". North-Holland Linguistic Series 22. Amsterdam, North-Holland.

9 Some Discrepancy Phenomena in Spanish

HENK A. COMBÉ

Department of Spanish
University of Amsterdam

9.0 Introduction

In this chapter I shall discuss some phenomena involving discrepancy between certain expressions in Spanish and their corresponding underlying predications.

The first section is dedicated to so-called impersonal constructions, especially those with the two-place verbs *parecer* "seem", and *resultar* "turn out", and the one-place verb *poder* with inferential meaning: "can" = "be possible".[1] Various sentence types will be considered and special attention given to the above-mentioned discrepancy between expression and predication in sentences such as *Los precios parecen subir* "Prices seem to be rising", which in Transformational Grammar (TG) are described as the result of an extracting and raising process. Secondly I will deal with a configuration such as *El método es fácil de comprender* "The method is easy to understand", sometimes described in terms of a "tough movement" operation in TG (see Section 9.1.4). In Section 9.2 I shall discuss a discrepancy in the construction of relative clauses with a preposition, e.g. *No sabes de lo que estás hablando* "You don't know what you are talking about". Finally I will treat a case of "intertwining": a restrictor with embedded clause, such as *Ahí viene el hombre que tú creías que estaba enfermo* "There comes the man who you thought that was ill", again a construction which in TG would be described by means of a movement rule (see Section 9.3).

In each of the three cases my principal aim is to consider whether the configuration under discussion must be viewed as a case of "conspicuous" placement or whether it is a case of an argument "slipping into" another predication. I shall try to present the proper formulas as instructions for syntactic function assignment and placement in FG. Hardly any expression rules will be formulated nor, consequently, any conditions on rules.

9.1 Impersonal constructions: *parecer, resultar, poder*

9.1.1 *Possible constructions*

9.1.1.1 Preliminary remarks.   In Dik (1978) chapters 8 and 9 are dedicated to the linear order of sentence constituents. It is argued that this order follows from the interaction between two principles:

(a)   A general functional patterning, as expressed in the following schema:

(1)   P2, P1 (V) S (V) O (V), P3

and

(b)   A language-independent preferred order of constituents (LIPOC).

In (1) P1 is a special sentence-initial position, used for "designated categories of constituents", such as Question-constituents, subordinators and relative pronouns. When these do not occur in the predication, P1 is open for constituents with the pragmatic functions of Topic or Focus. The effect of LIPOC is that "the preferred position of constituents is from left to right in increasing order of categorial complexity" (Dik, 1978, 192). This hypothesis predicts that a subordinate clause, being a complex constituent, will normally have final position in the sentence. As a matter of fact, this is the case in Spanish. I shall demonstrate this by the following sentences, restricting myself to constructions frequently designated as "impersonal", such as in (2)–(4):

(2)   Me extraña que no me previnieran
      "(It) amazes me that (they) did not give me a warning"

(3)   Es evidente que no ha leído el libro
      "(It) is obvious that (he) has not read the book"

(4)   Consta que la reunión tendrá lugar mañana
      "(It) is an established fact that the meeting will take place tomorrow"

The above sentences all have unmarked ("neutral") constituent order. On the assumption that Spanish is a P1 S V O language,[2] it must be noticed that in (2)–(4) on account of LIPOC the Subject-constituent does not occupy the Subject pattern position.

Now, there are two factors which may be of significance in influencing the above constructions to occur with a different order:

(a) In many languages, Spanish among them, Subjects show a high frequency in being Topic of the sentence. Since P1, if not already filled by another element, is available for Topic-placement, there is a high frequency of sentences that start with SubjTop.

(b) P1 is "in principle insensitive to LIPOC" (Dik, 1978, 204). This provides the possibility to form sentences with a preposed subordinate clause:

(2) a Que no me previnieran me extraña

(3) a Que no ha leído el libro es evidente

(4) a Que la reunión tendrá lugar mañana consta

In (2a)–(4a) the subordinate clauses are SubjTop; this sentence order is marked. It is indeed the case that (2)–(4) and (2a)–(4a) are pragmatically different arrangements of the same semantic content, i.e. with the same underlying predication.

There are, however, predicates, similar to the above mentioned, where SubjTop-assignment to the subordinate clause is not allowed, as will be shown in (ii).

9.1.1.2 Parecer, resultar, poder. If we add to the examples already given sentences with the verbs *parecer* "seem" and *resultar* "turn out" (as in (5a)–(6a)), we find again, in accordance with LIPOC, the subordinate clause in final position. But here, as opposed to (2a)–(4a), the inverted order (5b)–(6b) is not possible:

(5) a (Me) parece que los precios suben
        "(It) seems (to me) that prices are rising"

     b *Que los precios suben (me) parece

(6) a (Me) resulta que los precios suben
        "(It) appears (to me) to be the case that prices are rising"

     b *Que los precios suben (me) resulta

The same holds for the modal verb *poder* "can" = "be possible", cf.:

(7) a   Puede que los precios suban
         "(It) is possible that prices are rising"

     b *Que los precios suban puede

The ungrammaticality of (5b)–(7b) requires an explanation. One possible
suggestion is that *parece, resulta* and *puede* have too slight a semantic content to by themselves function comment constituents. (This is the explanation chosen by Vet (Chapter 7) for the French construction with *sembler*,
analogous to (5b). See also note 3.) This suggestion, however, is not completely convincing. Note that in the following stretches of speech the
reactions of the addressee, (8b)–(9b), are incorrect (apart from certain
conversational strategies), whereas in (8c)–(9c) they are grammatical:

(8) a   Las tropas extranjeras han dejado el país
         "The foreign troops have left the country"

     b *Parece

     c   Así parece

(9) a   Las tropas extranjeras han dejado el país

     b *Puede

     c   Es posible

Yet, at the same time, the difference between the semantic load of *Así
parece* and *Es posible* on the one hand, and of *Parece* and *Puede* on the
other, if any, must be a very small one. The former occur "independently".
It should be noted that this potential independency is normal for all verbs
with "impersonal" construction, such as: *Es evidente, Es deseable, Con-
viene*, etc.

    There do exist other alternative configurations for (5a)–(7a). These are
given in (5c)–(7c):

(5) c   Los precios parecen subir
         "Prices seem to be rising"

(6) c   Los precios resultan subir
         "Prices turn out to be rising"

(7) c   Los precios pueden subir
         "Prices may be rising"

In these examples the verb of the embedded verb in (5a)–(7a) appears as an Infinitive. I shall come back to sentences (5a)–(7c). First some remarks need to be made about the ungrammatical expressions of (5b)–(7b) and (8b)–(9b).

With regard to the non-independency of *parecer*, etc. we must perhaps simply stipulate that these verbs have an argument-position which

(i) cannot be left unfilled,

(ii) accepts as fillers an Infinitive-construction (as in (5c)–(7c)), or a subordinate clause (as in (5a)–(7a)), and

(iii) the fillers of which must follow the verb in surface-realization.[3]

Such a stipulation would exclude (5b)–(7b) and (8b)–(9b). (I here deliberately leave out those uses of *parecer* and *resultar* which share distributional properties with the copula *ser* "be", and which admit adjectives, nouns and adverbs as fillers as in (8c).)

9.1.2   Discrepancy

As we have seen in 9.1.1, a term which in (5a)–(7a) has Subject-function in the embedded clause, has that same function with *parecer*, etc. in (5c)–(7c), as is demonstrated by the morphological adjustment: the "subordinate" verb *subir* appears in non-finite form and the noun-phrase agrees with *parecer*, etc. The noun-phrase, in other words, is a pseudo-argument, because of the discrepancy between syntactic function assignment and underlying predication.

The fact that (5b)–(7b) are not possible in Spanish implies that an expression of alternative pragmatic function-arrangement, such as available for other "impersonal" sentences (see (2a)–(4a)) is lacking. This may have contributed to the existence of (5c)–(7c). Moreover, the hypothesis that (5c)–(7c) are an alternative function-arrangement for (*5b)–(*7b) is in agreement with the tendency signalized by Dik (Chapter 2, Section 3):

> Another possible explanation for displacement might lie in a presumed tendency of speakers to construe the world in terms of relations between persons and things rather than between persons and states of affairs, or between states of affairs.

This explanation can be expanded somewhat: . . . and between things and states of affairs rather than between states of affairs. The latter claim allows for (5c)–(7c). Accordingly, I propose in (10a) the type of underlying predication for sentences such as (5a)–(7a) and (5c)–(7c), exemplified by the predication underlying sentence (5) before Subject assignment. (10b) and (10c) show the predication after Subject assignment, resp. for the (a) and the (c) sentences.

(10)   a $parecer_V$ $(x_i: [subir_V (dmx_j: precio (x_j))_{Proc}] (x_i))_\theta$

       b $parecer_V$ $(sub\ x_i: [subir_V (dmx_j: precio (x_j))_{ProcSubj}] (x_i))_\theta$

       c $parecer_V$ $(x_i: [subir_V (dmx_j: precio (x_j))_{Proc}] (x_i))_{\theta Subj}$

9.1.3   Two more candidates for the same predication?

There remains a question about *parecer*, etc. constructions. Consider the following pairs of sentences:

(5)   d   Parece ser que los precios suben

      e   Los predios parece que suben

(6)   d   Resulta ser que los precios suben

      e   Los precios resulta que suben

(7)   d   Puede ser que los precios suban

      e   Los precios puede que suban

The question is whether (5d)–(7d) should be taken as a third, and (5e)–(7e) as a fourth realization of (10a). In my opinion the answer in both cases must be negative.

As far as (5d)–(7d) are concerned, these constructions have an added semantic value. They somehow reflect an emphatic, matter-of-fact or explanatory force:

"It seems to
"It turns out to ⎱ be the case . . ."
"It may

Compare the meaning of the finite *Es que* in:

(11)   No puedo devolverte el dinero. Es que no lo tengo
       "(I) cannot give you back the money. As a matter of fact . . .
       It happens to be the case that . . . / (I) don't have it"

As to the sentences (5e)–(7e), at first sight they could be viewed as alternative realization of the same underlying predication (10a). Observe, however, the following, ill-formed construction:

(5)   f   *Los precios parecen que suben

The fact that there can be no agreement between *los precios* and the verb *parecer* makes it clear that *los precios* is not a Subject of *parecer*. At the same time there seems to be no other candidate for Subject-assignment in the predication.

Now let us consider the following sentence:

(12)   Los precios parece que mi hermano los ignora
       "The prices (it) seems that my brother does not know them"

Sentence (12) is well-formed. In this sentence the anaphorical Object-pronoun *los* has the feature marking of its antecedent *precios*: masculine, plural.

Sentence (5e), too, can be paralleled by a sentence with an anaphorical pronoun:

(5)   g   Los precios parece que ellos suben

From (5g) is clear that (5e) does have a Subject in the embedded predicate. In Spanish it is normal for non-emphatical Subject-pronouns not to appear overtly in the sentence, so that the pattern position for Subject remains empty.

To show that (5e) is not an alternative arrangement of (10a), I shall propose an interpretation of (5e), (5g) and (12) within the framework of FG. These constructions are frequently referred to in TG as instances of left-dislocation. Recently M. L. Rivero (1980) treated left-dislocation and topicalization in Spanish. She follows the proposal of Chomsky (1977) (and some other authors) to eliminate left-dislocation as a movement operation, assigning the properties of left-dislocated structures to the base. On the assumption that structure-building transformations are to be rejected, her reason for rejecting a transformational solution lies in the fact that in many cases the TOP-elements (in Rivero's terminology) do not observe a number of constraints and, more essentially, show a wide variety of constructions, which "eliminate a transformational solution in principle".

Examples (13)–(14) illustrate the latter reason:

(13)   Hablando de libros, te enviaré el nuevo catálogo
       "Talking about books, (I) will send you the new catalogue"

(14)   En cuanto al verano, no le gustaba demasiado calor
       "As for summer, he didn't like too much heat"

Although Rivero's approach refutes a transformational solution, it remains fundamentally different from the FG-approach. In FG there is no "base"-component in the sense of a syntactically ordered DS. The central entity is the predication. Semantic structures (predications) are mapped on to syntactic structures, i.e. syntactic functions are assigned to the arguments of the predication. Secondly, so called left-dislocations are viewed as introductory elements to, rather than parts of, the predication. They are referred to as "Theme", which is a pragmatic notion, defined in Dik (1978: 130) thus: "A constituent with Theme function presents a domain or universe of discourse with respect to which it is relevant to pronounce the following predication." (Note that Chomsky recognizes the status of left-dislocation as a pragmatic function: "The proposition must be 'about' the item focussed in the left-dislocated phrase. How close the relation of 'aboutness' must be is unclear, some speakers seem to permit a rather loose connection." He compares it to certain speech situations, the rules of which "are not rules of sentence grammar at all" (Chomsky, 1977, 81). In a Functional framework Theme constituents occupy the P2-position in the general functional pattern (1). According to the definition of Theme we must analyse (5e) in the following way:

(a)   Theme: *Los precios*

(b)   The predication proper: *parece que suben*

The latter component is the expression of a predication which follows P2. The predication and its expression are the same as those of (5a), with the proviso that with non-emphatical Subject-pronoun the pattern position of the embedded predication is allowed to remain empty.

As a conclusion it can be stated that (5e) differs pragmatically from (5a) and (5c). The difference should not be described in the same terms as the difference between (5a) and (5c), namely as a difference in syntactic function assignment. Sentence introduction by means of Theme with a coreferential (anaphoric) element in the sentence proper is a general productive rule and not an operation limited to the sentence-types under discussion. Moreover, Theme-formation is, by definition, a pragmatic device of another level than Top and Foc assignment.

It is interesting to compare (5e) and its interpretation with the seemingly equivalent configuration in Portuguese, discussed by Dik (Chapter 8). The configuration is (cf. Dik's sentences (24–27)):

(15)   As crianças parece que estão cansadas (cf. (5e))
       "The girls seem$_{3sg}$ that are tired"

Together with (16) and (17):

(16)   Parece que as crianças estão cansadas (cf. (5a))

(16)   As crianças parecem estar cansadas (cf. (5c))

and still another configuration, (15) is one of four possible arrangements of Top and Foc of the same underlying predication. If this analysis and the one given for the Spanish "equivalent" (5e) are both correct, this is an example of very similar sentences in closely related languages, with completely diverging underlying structures.

9.1.4   Fácil+de+*Infinitive*

I now turn my attention to the following sentences:

(18)   a   Es fácil comprender el método
           "(It) is easy to understand the method"

       b   Comprender el método es fácil

       c   El método es fácil de comprender

(18a) and (18b) obviously have the same underlying predication, realized with different word orders. The difference between the two corresponds to that between (2)–(4) and (2a)–(4a). The two positions allowed for the subordinate clause are here filled by an infinitival clause. The Infinitive has no specified Agent. Quite a number of the (2)–(4) type of predicates have the same possibility. However, there is no parallel to (18c):

(19)   a   Es preferible leer el libro
           "(It) is preferable to read the book"

       b   Leer el libro es preferible

       c   *El libro es preferible de leer

Now the question arises whether (18c) has the same underlying predication as (18a–b); whether *el método*, which semantically is an argument of *comprender* in (18a–b), is a "displaced" Subject (of *fácil*) in (18c). The former two expressions are about the easiness of understanding the method, which can be classified as a "situation". The ease of understanding may be a logical implication of the method itself being easily understandable and yet semantically be different from the meaning of (18c). The meaning of (18a–b) leaves the question about the properties of the method undecided. If it can be shown that the expression (18c) is about a property of *el método* it can be argued that it is not a third syntactic function arrangement of (18a–b). Of course we can try to come to a decision by actually paraphrasing . . . *fácil de comprender* by the corresponding adjective:

(20)   . . . fácilmente comprensible
    ". . . easily understandable"

(20) seems to be semantically equivalent to (18c). However, the question is whether there is not too much risk in considering such an equivalence as a proof that constructions as (18a–b) and (18c) are semantically different. Any paraphrasing adjective that would, or, at least, could, evidently reflect a "situation", a "contingent property", would falsify the proof and confront us, again, with the question about the difference in meaning between (18a–b) and (18c). This risk can be easily understood if we realize that there are very few adjectives indeed that cannot express a "situational, contingent property" as well as an "inherent property". These different meanings are activated by the copulas *estar* and *ser*, respectively. At the same time this "mechanism" is the source which yields direct evidence. Cf. (21):

(21)   *El método *está* fácil de comprender

The obligatory use of the copula *ser* makes it clear that the adjective in (18c) denotes an inherent quality, a definitional property.

   This statement holds even when the interpretation of the context suggests the opposite:

(22)   Mario, que por lo general tiene la mente abierta para toda clase
    "Mario, who generally   has   an open mind   for   all   sorts

    de argumentos, aunque   sean   contrarios a su propia
    of arguments,   although (these) may be contrary   to his own

    opinión, en este caso *es* difícil de convencer
    opinion, in this case is hard   to convince"

Although in the foregoing argumentation I rejected the interpretation of *el método* as a displaced Subject of *fácil*, it is undeniably a Subject in its own right, as can be seen by the agreement with *ser* in (23):

(23)   Los métodos son fáciles de comprender

As to the underlying predication of (18c) and (23), it would be difficult to relate it to the one underlying (24):

(24)   El método es fácil
       "The method is easy"

In (24) *fácil* is semantically different from *fácil* in *fácil de comprender*, which gets its special meaning precisely in the combination with the Infinitive.

The only solution left seems to be the interpretation of *fácil de* . . . as a complex predicate with a variable Infinitive as complement of the adjective, *ser* being bearer of mood, tense and aspect:

(25)   a $\{\text{predicate}_A\ de\ \text{Predicate}_{V\text{Inf}}\}\ (x_i)_\theta$

After term insertion the predication of (18c) will be (25b):

(25)   b $\{\text{fácil}_A\ de\ \text{comprender}_{V\text{Inf}}\}\ (d1x_i\colon \text{método}\ (x_i))_{\theta \text{Subj}}$

The "A" of the complex predicate may be represented by the adjectives *agradable, confuso, desagradable, difícil, digno, duro, extraño* ("strange"), *fácil, imposible, interesante, largo* ("long") *malo*, which, of course, have all their specific selection restrictions for "predicate$_{V\text{Inf}}$". I assume that the copula *ser* will be introduced by a later expression rule.

9.2   "Degraded" antecedents in relative clauses

In this section I shall discuss a very different type of discrepancy, namely that of an antecedent being "captured" by a preposition.

Spanish has four relative pronouns: (a) *que*, (b) *quien*, and two compound forms: (c) *el que*, (d) *el cual* (only the masculine singular forms are given). The compound forms operate as "whole", inseparable forms. This has the effect that the two constituents are not allowed to be separated by a preposition. This can be demonstrated by some examples, in which the predicate frame of the verb in the relative clause takes a nuclear argument or satellite preceded by a preposition:

(26)   Al fin   consiguió   los resultados, por los que se   había
       "Finally (he) attained the results,   for which (he) had

       esforzado   tanto
       used so much effort"

(27) A lo lejos vimos   unas casas   en las   que vivían
      "Far away (we) saw some houses in which there lived

      campesinos
      peasants"

(28) Para su extraña conducta Rosa aducía   unas razones de las
      "For her strange behaviour Rosa advanced some reasons about

      cuales yo dudaba mucho
      which I   doubted strongly"

(29) A poca   distancia había   una colina desde la cual   se
      "At a short distance there was a   hill   from   which the

      veía   el pueblo
      village could be seen"

When the antecedent is a repetition of a noun which is already mentioned, the former can be substituted by the demonstrative pronoun *aquel* (*aquella*, *aquellos*, *aquellas*) or deictic *el* (*la*, *los*, *las*):

(30) a   Este caballo es el caballo que ha ganado la carrera
          "This horse is the horse that won the courses"

      b   Este caballo es aquél que ha ganado la carrera
          "This horse is 'that' (one) that won the courses"

      c   Este caballo es el que ha ganado la carrera
          "This horse is 'the' (one) that won the courses"

(31) a   Mi casa es más grande que la casa en que vive ella
          "My house is bigger than the house in which she lives"

      b   Mi casa es más grande que aquélla en que vive ella
          "My house is bigger than 'that' (one) in which she lives"

      c   Mi casa es más grande que la en que vive ella
          "My house is bigger than 'the' (one) in which she lives"

As can be seen in (31c), deictic *el* (here: *la*) has the function of antecedent and *que* is relative pronoun (a). The preposition takes its normal position before the relative pronoun. According to María Moliner (1966) sentences like (32)–(34):

(32) Iba en dirección contraria a la en que van los coches
"(He) went in the direction opposite to 'the' (one) in which the cars drive"

(33) Lo encontré en lugar distinto del en que lo dejé
"(I) met him in (a) place different from 'the' (one) in which (I) had left him"

(34) Me indicó un hotel distinto del a que él iba
"(He) showed me a hotel other than 'the' (one) to which he went"

are of dated literary style, and when they occur nowadays they make a rather artificial impression. Furthermore the construction seems to be admissible only or mainly with the prepositions *en* ("in, on") and (even less frequently) *a* ("to"). (It is not entirely clear to me why sentences as (32)–(34) are more artificial than, for example, sentences (30c)–(31c). Perhaps the reason is the less euphonic co-occurrence of the two prepositions.)

Now, the *Gramática de la Real Academia* accepts (marginally?) sentences like (35a), which is synonymous to (35b):

(35) a Horas como éstas no son en las que vienen   a
        Hours like   these are not in those   which (they) come to

        negociar
        negotiate

        "Hours like these are not those in which they come to negotiate"

     b Horas como éstas no son las en que vienen a negociar

In (35a) deictic *el* (here: *las*) and the pronoun *que* are treated as an un-separated cluster, like the compound relative pronoun (c): *el que*, although there is no "contiguous" antecedent. Notice, however, that in (35a) the pronominal antecedent does have a corresponding term (which need not be coreferent!) mentioned before in the sentence: *horas*. Informants, trying out sentences of the (35a)-type, but without such an afore-mentioned term, such as (36)–(37), judged them as "incorrect", "hardly acceptable," "acceptable on second or third look":

(36) ??Te prometo de las   que   me hablaste   ayer
        (I) promise you about those which(you) to me yesterday

"I promise you the ones about which you talked to me yesterday"
(Talking about magazines: *las revistas*)

(37) ??Mañana   te explicaré   sin   los   que
      Tomorrow (I) shall explain to you without those which

      nunca   comprenderás mi conducta
      (you) never will understand   my behaviour

      "Tomorrow I'll explain to you the ones without which you never
      will understand my behaviour" (Talking about motives: *los motivos*)

On the other hand, the construction exemplified by (36)–(37) is the normal,
grammatical expression when the deictic pronoun is the neuter *lo*. Cf.
(38)–(40):

(38) a Ya sabes a lo que vengo
         "(You) surely know with what purpose (I) come"

      b *Ya sabes lo a que vengo

(39) a Dime de lo que estáis hablando
         "Tell me what (you people) are talking about"

      b *Dime lo de que estáis hablando

(40) a Te aconsejo escribirle en lo que te ocupas[4]
         "(I) suggest you to write him on what (you) are engaged"

      b *Te aconsejo escribirle lo en que te ocupas

It might be supposed that the phenomenon illustrated by (38a)–(40a) is an
analogy with the compound relative pronoun (c) and that the introductory
function of prepositions tends to prepose them to a position preceding the
deictic pronoun, thus creating a "pseudo-cluster", against grammatical
logic. The question then is why the non-neuter deictic pronouns in (36)–
(37) are so reluctant to form a pseudo-cluster, and are not susceptible to
the same analogy. The reason might be that non-neuters, as soon as they
form a pseudo-cluster with *que*, become "difficult" without an antecedent,
because of their coinciding with the real compound pronouns (c). These
demand an antecedent, as in (30c)–(31c) and (32)–(34). Even in the case
of a pseudo-cluster at least a corresponding, before mentioned, term is
needed, as in (35a). Neuter *lo* does not meet this impediment, since
Spanish has no neuter nouns, and thus fits easily in a pseudo-cluster.

However, even when the above explanation for deictic pronouns is correct, there are other, even more striking examples in which the preposition "captures" a noun antecedent, argument of the higher clause, and attracts it to the domain of the embedded verb. Cf. (41)–(43), where the (a) sentences and the (b) sentences are all grammatical:

(41)   a   Cuando vio el ahinco con que la mujer trabajaba, . . .
           "When (he) saw the persistency with which the woman worked, . . ."

       b   Cuando vio con el ahinco que la mujer trabajaba, . . .

(42)   a   Faltá saber las condiciones en que está
           "It is necessary to know the circumstances in which (he) is.."

       b   Falta saber en las condiciones que está

(43)   a   Según el cine a que vayas
           "Depending on the movies to which (you) are going"

       b   Según al cine que vayas

If I maintain my interpretation that *el, la, los, las, lo* are pronoun antecedents, which seems to be a plausible assumption according to (30c)–(31c), the sentences (35a) and (38a)–(40a) on the one hand, and (41b)–(43b) on the other hand, can be described by the same predication formula (44):

(44) ver_V $(d1x_i: \text{Juan} (x_i))_{\emptyset\text{Subj}}$ $(d1x_j: \text{ahinco} (x_j))$:
        trabajar_V $(d1x_k: \text{mujer} (x_k))_{\text{AgSubj}}$ $(Rx_j)_{\text{Mann}})_{\emptyset\text{Obj}}$

Rule (45):

(45)   Art N Prep Rel $\rightarrow \begin{cases} \text{(a)   Art N Prep Rel} \\ \text{(b)   Prep Art N Rel} \end{cases}$

will allow for (41a) and (41b), respectively. It further will be stipulated that option (b) is obligatory when the antecedent is the deictic pronoun *lo*.

9.3   Intertwining

Finally I shall consider a construction which shows similarity with Wh-preposing, alluded to in Chapter 2. Let us consider the following sentence:

(46)   En la calle vi al hombre que$_1$ tú creías que$_2$ estaba enfermo
        "In the street (I) saw the man who you thought that was ill"

Here we find a relative pronoun (*que$_1$*), coreferent with a noun (*hombre*), about the referent of which somebody (*tú*) believed that something was the case (*estaba enfermo*); *que$_2$* is a subordinator. To express this in one complex sentence the expression takes the form of noun antecedent with a restrictor, the latter having an embedded predication. The underlying predication can be represented as follows:

(47)   ... (d1x$_j$: hombre (x$_j$): (creer$_V$ (d1x$_k$: tú (x$_k$))$_{PoSubj}$
        (sub x$_1$: [enfermo$_A$ (Rx$_j$)$_{\theta Subj}$] (x$_1$)))

In (47) the embedded predication has its subordinating element *que$_2$* in its normal P1-position. "R" triggers special expression rules to bring (x$_j$)$_{\theta Subj}$ to P1 of the complex restrictor-clause and give it the form of a relative pronoun. The notion "Subj" in (Rx$_j$)$_{\theta Subj}$ (or another syntactic function) is important, apart from its normal functional indication, for thus we can also apply, if necessary, morphological adjustment to the relative pronoun:

(48)   Este es el hombre a quien tú creías que estábamos buscando
        "This is the man whom you believed that (we) were looking for"

(49)   Estas son las niñas por las que tú creías que me estaba
        preocupando
        "These are the girls you believed that (I) was worrying about"

Here we see that, although the relative pronoun is separated from its proper domain (*buscar* with *a* as marker of Direct Object); *preocuparse por*), it remains an argument of its own predicate, so we cannot speak of discrepancy but rather of "conspicuous placement". In commenting on formula (47) I said that the relative pronoun was brought to P1 of the complex restrictor. This is, in fact, the only possible position for relative pronouns in Spanish. The effect of this placement, however, is that the relative pronoun, which originates in the embedded predication, is "displaced" to a position outside its proper domain.

I am aware that my discussion of the sentence-type illustrated in the last section touches upon only one instance of a whole field of similar displacements, such as:

(50)   Es una cosa que no cómo explicarla
       "(It) is a matter that (I) do not know how to explain it"

However, as mentioned in 9.0, my present aim has not been to map out all possible constructions with their pertaining rules and constraints but merely to give an account of a certain type of displacement in terms of FG. Nor did I try to list and characterize the verbs that may play the role of bridge function. For the latter type of investigation inspiring material is to be found in Milner (1979) and Chomsky and Lasnik (1977, where some remarks are also made on some related phenomena in Spanish).

9.4   Concluding remarks

This chapter consists of several parts. In the first part, I investigated a number of constructions in Spanish in which (on first view) one and the same predicate figures in different syntactic constructions. For different classes of predicates (verbal and adjectival) I considered the question whether we in fact are dealing with one and the same underlying predication. In Section 9.1 I discussed some "impersonal" constructions which have two, pragmatically different, orders, such as (i) *es evidente que ha leido el libro* and (ii) *que ha leido el libro es evidente*. Sentences with the verbs *parecer, resultar* and *poder*, such as (iii) *parece que los precios suben*, do not have the same possibility. The predicate *parecer* also figures in an alternative pattern (iv) *los precios parecen subir*. The latter, however, differs from (iii) only in syntactic function assignment, not in pragmatic function arrangement. In (iv) the Subject is a pseudo-argument of *parecer*. It is further demonstrated that configurations like *parece ser que los precios suben* and *los precios parece que suben* do not have the same underlying structure as (iii) and (iv), for semantic and pragmatic reasons, respectively. At the end of the section, I demonstrated that a sentence like *el método es fácil de comprender* has an underlying semantic structure which is different from that of *es fácil comprender el método*.

In the second part of the chapter, I discussed two different peculiarities which may occur in Spanish relative clauses (i.e. restrictor-clauses). In Section 9.2 I discussed the phenomenon of antecedents "slipping into" the predication of restrictor-clauses with a preposition. The result is a specific type of "discrepancy" between semantic structure and syntactic construction (cf. Dik, Chapter 1). Finally (Section 9.3) I considered a specific type of "intertwining" occurring in Spanish. This construction involves a relative clause which itself contains an embedded predication. The antecedent of the relative clause is coreferential to an argument of this embedded predication. The relative pronoun occupies in this case a position outside the embedded predication to which it semantically belongs.

Notes

1 *Parecer* and *resultar* are considered here as two-place verbs because of the possibility of adding an Experiencer-argument, realized syntactically as an Indirect Object. This is demonstrated only in the examples (5)–(6). Of course, this interpretation depends on the one given to "added" in the above sentence, i.e. on an all-round semantic interpretation of the verbs in question.

2 I assume that Spanish is a P1 S V O language. Perhaps also a P1 V S O pattern is needed. (See Dik, 1978, ch. 8, for further detail).

3 The constructions dealt with in Section 9.1 "coincide" partially with those treated by Vet in "Subject-assigment and Impersonal Constructions in French" (Chapter 7), i.e. part of the latter can be considered as analogues of the Spanish examples.

For French impersonal sentences, which have *Il* in the pattern position for Subject, such as (Vet's examples (3a) and (5a)):

(i)   Il est regrettable que Jeanne ne soit pas venue
      "It is regrettable that Jean has not come"

(ii) Il semble que Jeanne embrasse son mari
      "It seems that Jean kisses her husband"

Vet prefers as an explanation the hypothesis called "hypothesis B", which introduces the notion of non-assignment of Subject. Given the variety of specific impersonal constructions in French, this analysis seems to be rather convincing. However, Vet explains (Vet (30)):

(iii) *Que Jeanne embrasse son mari (me) semble
      "That Jean kisses her husband seems (to me)"

by the same hypothesis.

I wonder whether the stipulation suggested for Spanish *parecer* might not be preferable for (iii) too. Interpreting *sembler* as a verb which has, in its syntactic realization, a following slot which may not be left unfilled reduces the problem: once the condition of the proper slot-filling elements is not met, the question of assignment or non-assignment is not even relevant, because we then have to do with an ill-formed predicate. This solution will have hypothesis B applying to all French impersonal constructions and to these only, which seems to be a more consistent solution.

4 (38a)–(40a) have real relative constructions and should not be mistaken as examples of "dependent questions". Compare:

(i)   No sabes a qué vengo
      "(You) don't know what I'm coming for"

(ii) Dime de qué estáis hablando
      "Tell me what (you people) are talking about"

These sentences evidently do not have an antecedent. The pattern-position
P1 of the embedded clause is occupied by an interrogative pronoun.

References

CHOMSKY, N.
  1977   On Wh-movement. *In* P. W. Culicover *et al.* (ed.). "Formal Syntax".
         New York and London, Academic Press. 71–132.
CHOMSKY, N. and H. Lasnik
  1977   Filters and Control. *Linguistic Inquiry*, **8**, 425–504.
DIK, Simon C.
  1978   "Functional Grammar". Amsterdam, North-Holland.
GILI GAYA, S.
  1976   "Curso Superior de Sintaxis Española". Barcelona, Ediciones "Spes".
HADLICH, Rodger L.
  1971   A Transformational Grammar of Spanish. Englewood Cliffs, NJ,
         Prentice Hall.
MILNER, Jean-Claude
  1979   La Redondance Fonctionnelle. *Linguisticae Investigationes,* **3**, 87–145.
MOLINER, María
  1966   "Diccionario de Uso del Español". Madrid, Editorial Gredos.
RIVERO, María Luisa
  1980   On Left-dislocation and Topicalization in Spanish. *Linguistic Inquiry*,
         11, 363–393.
SKYDSGAARD, Sven
  1977   "La Combinatoria Sintáctica del Infinitivo Español". Madrid, Editorial
         Castalia.

10 Factivity as a Condition for an Optional Expression Rule in Latin: the "Ab Urbe Condita" Construction and its Underlying Representation

A. MACHTELT BOLKESTEIN

Department of Latin
University of Amsterdam

10.0 Introduction

In this chapter I shall discuss certain aspects of a construction occurring in Latin which in view of its characteristics offers a problem for description because—as in most other constructions discussed in this volume—there is an incongruence between the predication underlying it and its syntactic realization. Furthermore the construction seems to be the output of an expression rule which is conditioned by the presence of specific semantic and perhaps also pragmatic factors, which, in some way or other, must be accounted for in the predication underlying the sentence as a whole as well. The construction involved is known as the "dominant participle" or "ab urbe condita" construction (AUC).

First I shall briefly indicate the main properties of the construction, notably its difference in behaviour from other constructions with similar syntactic characteristics, the criteria for differentiating the two types from each other, and the ways in which the observed differences may be represented within the framework of Functional Grammar by means of different internal structures to be attributed to the two types of nominal phrase involved (Section 10.1). Subsequently, I shall show that the construction under consideration is in fact the output of an optional rule which produces a syntactic realization for certain types of embedded predication in the form of an NP (Section 10.2). I shall discuss the nature of the rule involved in more detail in Section 10.3. I shall then investigate the conditions which trigger the application of the rule (Section 10.4). Possible conditions are semantic factors (10.4.1) and pragmatic function arrangement (10.4.2). In Section 10.5 I shall formulate a proposal as to how the relevant conditions may be represented in a Functional Grammar framework in the predication underlying sentences containing an AUC.

10.1   The main properties of the AUC

The formation of the AUC-construction is optional: it may always be replaced by certain other ways of expression which are semantically equivalent, i.e. without noticable difference in meaning (see Section 10.2). The AUC is exemplified by the italicized NPs in the following two sentences:

(1) a   laete   ferunt milites   *consulem   occisum*
        gladly take$_{3pl}$ soldiers$_{nom}$ consul$_{acc}$ killed$_{participle\ acc}$
        "the soldiers are glad about the fact that the consul has been killed"

    b   *consul   moriens*   milites   movebat
        consul$_{nom}$ dying$_{part\ nom}$ soldiers$_{acc}$ moved$_{3sg}$
        "the dying of the consul moved the soldiers"

Sentences (1a–b) contain a complex nominal phrase. This NP consists of a noun plus a perfect tense (1a) or a present tense (1b) participle; the NP as a whole functions as Obj (1a), respectively Subj (1b), of the main predicate.[1] The construction may also consist of a noun plus an adjective or substantive. It may occur in all other caseforms available in Latin and, moreover, on various syntactic levels: it occurs as an argument of the main predicate, as in (1a–b); as a satellite (for a definition of these terms see Dik, 1978a, 17); as a "complement" of a noun (in which case it often carries the genitive caseform); it may also be governed by a preposition, carrying whatever caseform is required by the preposition involved. Instances of all these uses are given in Bolkestein (1980a, b).[2]

In translating AUC-NPs such as those in (1a–b), they must be paraphrased in a way different from that possible for other complex NPs which syntactically look similar, such as the one exemplified by the italicized NP in (2):

(2) *consul*   *occisus*   in foro   iacebat
consul$_{nom}$ killed$_{part\ nom}$ on forum was-lying$_{3sg}$
"the killed consul after being killed the consul was lying on the
forum"

By means of various tests—e.g. by the effect of substitution and omission
(Bolkestein, 1980a, b)—the semantic difference intuitively felt to exist
between the two types of NP, and well-recognized in Latin grammars[3]
may indeed be made visible. The conclusion to be drawn from this is, that
the structure underlying AUCs (cf. 1a–b)) cannot adequately be captured
by the pattern which in Functional Grammar is attributed to NPs with a
Head Modifier structure such as the one in (2) (see Dik, 1978a, 65–66; see
also Rijksbaron, Chapter 11).
The structure underlying the NP of (2) is (3):[4]

(3) $(x_1: consul_N (x_i)_\theta: occidere_V (x_j)_{Ag} (x_i)_{GoSubj})$

In (3) it is indicated that the term x_i designates an entity such that this
entity is specified by the nominal predicate *consul*; the class of possible
referents of x_i is further restricted to "consuls" specified as being involved
(as Goal) in a state of affairs of killing. The restrictor in (3) is a predication,
in which Subject function is assigned to the Goal argument (I shall return
to the reasons for treating participles as non-basic predicates in Section
10.2). Note that the restrictor in (3) could also be expressed as a relative
clause. I shall not consider the problem, touched upon in Dik (1978a, 65–
66), of whether the two syntactic realizations possible for (3) must in fact
be distinguished by different underlying predications as well (see Rijksbaron, Chapter 11; Kwee, 1981).
In this description of the internal structure of the NP in (2) the fact that
the participle *occisus* is treated as having the status of a restrictor implies
that it could be omitted from the sentence without leading to illformedness.[5]
This, however, is an essential difference between the NP in (2) and the
AUC in (1a–b). In (2), the Modifier may indeed be omitted, as implied by
(3). The semantic properties of the Head of the NP are such that they
agree with the semantic constraints imposed by the governing predicate
(i.e. *iacere* "to lie"). In (1a–b), on the other hand, omission of the participle
always leads to a change in interpretation and often even to illformedness:
the Head of the NP may, by itself, violate the semantic constraints imposed
by the governing predicate, as it would in (1a). The NP involved is as a
whole required for satisfying the restrictions imposed by it. In (1a), for

example, *laete ferre* "to take gladly" requires that its second argument designates a "state of affairs". Such a state of affairs is indeed designated by the AUC-NP as a whole, but not by its Head-noun by itself.

Formulated differently, I claim that in (2) the Head-noun by itself designates the class of possible referents to which the argument required by the predicate *iacere* belongs; in (1a–b) on the other hand, the Head-noun does not designate the class of possible referents to which the argument of the predicate involved belongs. This class of possible referents is designated by the NP as a whole. In (1a–b), in other words, the Head-noun of the NP is not an argument of the predicate *laete ferre*.

The way in which this observation may be incorporated in the underlying predicational structure assigned to (1a) is given in (4) (for the moment I treat the participle as a basic predicate; see Section 10.2).[6]

(4)   laete ferre$_V$ (milites)$_{ExpSubj}$ (x_i: [occisus$_{part}$ (consul)$_\theta$] (x_i))$_{Phen}$

In (4) it is indicated that the second argument of *laete ferre* is an entity x_i such that x_i is specified by the predication "occisus$_{part}$ (consul)$_\theta$". This entity has the semantic function of Phenomenon (and might be claimed to have, in sentence (1a), the syntactic function Obj) in relation to *laete ferre*. The essential difference in status between *consul* in (3) and *consul* in (4) becomes clear when the term x_i in (4) is specified in more detail (cf. 10.2) as (5):

(5)   (x_i: [occidere$_V$ (x_j)$_{Ag}$ (x_k: consul$_N$ (x_k)$_\theta$)$_{Go}$] (x_i))

Pattern (5) shows clearly that the term x_k which is specified by the nominal predicate *consul* does not itself function as an argument on the level of *laete ferre*.

By describing x_i as having the structure of (4) or (5) in the case of AUC-NPs such as those in (1a–b), and attributing an internal structure such as (3) to NPs such as (2), the AUC is treated as a term specified by a predication and other complex NPs as containing an (omittable) restrictor. In this way it is indeed possible to differentiate the two types of NP in a satisfying way (whether (4) or (5) is assumed to be the right underlying structure is irrelevant in this respect).

I shall now explain why I prefer (5) rather than (4) as the structure underlying AUC-NPs and try to formulate how the relation between (5) on the one hand and (4), which is closer to the actual sentence (1a), on the other must be viewed.

10.2 The formation of the term

Whatever analysis will be adopted with respect to the relation between a term of the form of x_i in (4) and x_i in (5), it must agree with at least three properties of the AUC-construction. (*a*) It must be compatible with the fact that the construction is optional. (*b*) It must take into account that the participle system in Latin is defective—three participles are available instead of the theoretically possible six: active voice, present tense and future tense; and passive voice, perfect tense. (*c*) It must agree with the fact that AUC-NPs are not limited to a Head plus a participle but may contain more constituents than the minimally required number, whether nominal, adverbial or otherwise. Property (*a*) is illustrated by the existence of the semantically equivalent constructions given in (6a–d). These constructions may always replace the AUC (at least when it is an argument of the main predicate).[7] In (7) I give an example of an AUC which contains more constituents than just a Head and a Modifier (cf. also the attested instances (14a–b) below):

(6) a laete ferunt consulem occisum   esse
gladly take$_{3pl}$ consul$_{acc}$ killed$_{part\ acc}$ to-be (AcI-construction)
"they are glad that the consul has been killed"

b laete ferunt quod consul   occisus   est
gladly take$_{3pl}$ that consul$_{nom}$ killed$_{part\ nom}$ is$_{3sg}$
"they are glad that the consul is killed"

c laete ferunt caedem   consulis
gladly take$_{3pl}$ killing$_{acc}$ consul$_{gen}$
"they are glad about the killing of the consul"

(7) consul   heri   subito   in foro   moriens milites   movebat
consul$_{nom}$ yesterday suddenly on forum dying$_{nom}$ soldiers$_{acc}$ moved$_{3sg}$
"the fact that the consul yesterday suddenly died on the forum moved the soldiers"

Now, there are in principle two solutions to the question concerning the origin of the predication specifying x_i in (4).

(i) The first possibility is that the predication specifying x_i in (4) is the output of a so-called predicate formation rule. (See Dik (1978a, 16; 1979b, 88) on these rules.) In this view, the predication specifying x_i in (4) is as such present in the fund of predicates of Latin from which terms are formed for insertion into predicate frames in underlying predications. Such rules are assumed to apply before and independently of the formation of predications. This view is to be rejected on several grounds. It is incompatible with property (*c*) of the AUC demonstrated in (7) above, namely the fact that an AUC may in addition to its minimal number of constituents contain a theoretically unlimited number of other elements, arguments as well as satellites. Furthermore, it also does not agree with a property of the AUC not mentioned above, namely the fact that AUC-NPs always refer to an identifiable state of affairs in which identifiable entities are involved (I shall return to this phenomenon in 10.4.2). In other words, elements within the predication specifying x_i may have their own reference to extra-linguistic entities. This phenomenon is in disagreement with the notion held in Functional Grammar concerning the nature of predicates and predicate formation rules (see Dik, 1979b, 89). Consequently, the view that the predication specifying x_i in (4) is a basic predicate must be rejected.

   (ii) If x_i in (4) is not a derived predicate (i.e. the output of some predicate formation rule which takes place before and independently of predications), the alternative is that x_i in (4) is the output of some rule which operates in sentences which have the underlying structure (8):

(8)   laete ferre$_V$ (milites)$_{Exp}$ (x_i: [occidere$_V$ (x_j)$_{Ag}$ (consul)$_{Go}$] (x_i))$_{Phen}$

In (8), the second argument of the predicate *laete ferre* has the form suggested above, cf. (5); the term x_i is characterized by a predication of the form "occiderе$_V$ (x_j)$_{Ag}$ (consul)$_{Go}$". This embedded predication is, like predications which are not embedded, liable to the rule of Subj assignment. This leads to the structure "occiderе$_V$ pass (x_j)$_{Ag}$ (consul)$_{GoSubj}$". After Subj assignment in the whole predication given in (8), the underlying structure will look like (9):[8]

(9)   laete ferre$_V$ act (milites)$_{ExpSubj}$
                    (x_i: [occiderе$_V$ pass (x_j)$_{Ag}$ (consul)$_{GoSubj}$] (x_i))$_{Phen}$

The assumption that sentence (1a) has an underlying structure such as (9) and that the second argument of *laete ferre* has the form of x_i in (9) has a number of advantages. It explains why an AUC-NP may contain more material than the minimal number of constituents: if its underlying structure is that of a predication it may contain all elements which a predication may contain. It also agrees well with the fact that some of the semantically equivalent expressions illustrated in (6) which may always replace the AUC are clauses: non-finite clauses, such as the AcI in (6a), or finite clauses as in (6b). This phenomonen can simply be explained by assuming that two or three alternative expression rules may operate upon (9), leading to different syntactic realizations. Only one of these rules leads to a structure such as (4), and a realization (1a).

I shall now consider the exact nature of the rule which converts the predication (9), in which the embedded predication contains a verbal predicate into a structure such as (4), which is closer to the syntactic construction exemplified in (1a): in (4) the embedded predicate has different properties from in (9). Note that in both cases there will be agreement between it and the noun *consul*: in (1a) the predicate *occisus* does not agree in person and number, as a verbal predicate to its Subj, but in gender, number and case-form, as an adjectival Modifier to its Head. Consequently, the Head-noun *consul* is not recognizable as an argument of the predicate *occidere*: it looks as if it is an argument of the governing predicate *laete ferre*, since it carries the accusative caseform required by that predicate for its second argument when Subj function is not assigned to it.

10.3 The nature of the rule of AUC-formation

In the previous section I argued that there must be a rule of AUC-formation. This rule operates optionally upon predications such as those in (9) and leads to a structure such as (4). The rule involved may have a different status, depending on the stage in the formation of the sentence at which it applies and on what precisely it affects.

10.3.1 Function assignment

One way in which a rule converting (9) into (4) could conceivably be described is to assume that in a structure such as (9) the governing predicate "looks for" a nominal constituent to which it can attach the caseform which it normally requires for its second argument, if this is a nominal one. Which caseform this is in each individual case is presumably specified in the lexical entry for the predicate concerned. It must then be assumed that the governing predicate may "dip into" embedded predications for this purpose in a way not dissimilar to what in Dik (1979b; Chapter 8) is argued to happen in the case of so-called Raising-verbs, such as Engl. *to believe*. It is also to a certain extent reminiscent of the Latin patterns discussed by Bolkestein in Chapter 4 where certain cases of so-called pseudo-argument formation, i.e. of displacement of a nominal constituent out of embedded predications plus morphological adjustment of this NP to the governing predicate, are considered. The types of pseudo-argument formation involved occur under certain specific conditions.

However, the rule of AUC-formation differs from these two phenomena in two points. First (see Section 10.1) AUC-NPs occur not only as Subj or Obj of a predicate or as argument in some other caseform, but also in other syntactic positions such as that of satellite (in the ablative caseform), as complement to a noun (in the genitive caseform) and governed by a pre-position. In other words, if this approach is followed, we shall not be dealing with some form of syntactic function assignment as defined in Dik (1978a, 72–79) but with a much wider process of caseform-assignment "dipping into" embedded predications. Case-marking, however, is taken to apply at a later stage in the formation of sentences than syntactic function assignment.[9] Furthermore, the output of the rule is different as well, since although it triggers a second rule by which the "remaining" predicate is realized as "non-finite", in the case of AUC-formation, the predicate does not become an infinitive (whereas this frequently is a result when syntactic function assignment "dips into" embedded predications (see Kiparsky and Kiparsky, 1970, 356–357; Dik 1979a, Chapter 8)). In the case of AUC-formation, the "remaining" predicate becomes a participle, i.e. an adjec-tival form with the distributional properties of adjectives. Apart from this, such a rule of caseform assignment by the governing predicate apparently can only apply if the embedded predication carries the right constellation of tense and voice of the embedded predicate; otherwise the presumed rule is blocked (cf. my remark on the defectiveness of the Latin participle system). In view of this constraint it is unlikely that there is a rule of case-form assignment into embedded predications in Latin. Instead we may be dealing with a rule of "participialization" which takes place *before* caseform assignment and forms the input for it rather than being triggered by it.

10.3.2   *The rule of AUC-formation: a peculiar type of nominalization*

From the above observations I conclude—unlike Bolkestein (1980b)—that the rule which turns (9) into a structure such as (4) is not at all comparable to the rule assumed to apply in the case of "Raising" phenomena. The rule needed to account for AUC-formation must apply *after* syntactic func-tion assignment (because of the choice of passive v. active voice for the embedded predicate) and *before* the expression rule which is responsible for case-marking. The effect of the rule is that a syntactic category is selected for the embedded predication in (9), namely that of an NP; the embedded predication is, in other words, "nominalized". This categorial status is attained by means of a categorial change in the embedded predicate, which is expressed as a participle instead of a finite verb. This type of nominalization differs from the most common way in which, in many languages, embedded predications are "nominalized", i.e. by expressing the predicate as a noun. Note that in the latter type of nominalization all agreement between the predicate and its argument is lost, whereas in the case of AUC-formation one type of agreement is replaced by another type of agreement. As may be seen from (4), the argument-status of *consul* in relation to *occidere* remains clearly recognizable in the underlying structure. Naturally the rule involved only applies when the right constellation of tense of the embedded predicate and syntactic function assignment within the embedded predication is present. If this condition is not satisfied, the embedded predication will have to be syntactically expressed in a different construction, e.g. in one of the ways demonstrated in (6) above.

Once the embedded predication has received the categorial status of an NP, it is liable to the general expression rule valid in Latin which distributes caseforms over nominal constituents. In (1a), for example, the argument represented by x_1 in (4) does not carry the syntactic function Subj in relation to the governing predicate; therefore the caseform required for it is the accusative. The participle will have to agree with its nominal Head, in accordance with the general rule concerning Head Modifier agreement in Latin. Thus there are three stages to be distinguished in the formation of a term with the properties of x_1 in (4)–(5), all three *after* syntactic function assignment within the embedded predication. Notice, that they have to apply in a specific order as well:

(a) a rule of selection of category which turns an embedded predication into NP by means of participializing the embedded predicate;

(b) the general rule by which each individual predicate distributes its normal case pattern over its nominal constituents, if available;

(c) the general rule of caseform agreement between Heads and Modifiers (if adjectival or participial) in Latin.

Only the first of these three rules is exclusively relevant for the process of AUC-formation: the other two rules have a wider relevance and apply obligatorily in every Latin sentence.

The three stages in the formation of an AUC subsequent to (9) are explicitated in (10)–(12):[10]

(10) laete ferre$_{V\ act}$ (milites)$_{ExpSubj}$
$$(x_i: [occisus_{part\ pass} (x_j)_{Ag} (consul)_{GoSubj}]_{NP} (x_i))_{Phen}$$

(11) laete ferre$_{V\ act}$ (milites)$_{ExpSubj\ nom}$
$$(x_i: [occisus_{part\ pass} (x_j)_{Ag} (consul)_{GoSubj}]_{NP\ acc} (x_i))_{Phen}$$

(12) laete ferre$_{V\ act}$ (milites)$_{ExpSubj\ nom}$
$$(x_i: [occisus_{part\ pass\ acc} (consul)_{GoSubj\ acc}]_{NP} (x_i))_{Phen}$$

structure (12) will finally end up as sentence (1a).

It now remains to determine to what types of embedded predications the above rule of AUC-formation applies. As demonstrated in Bolkestein (1980b), it is not an optional rule which may apply arbitrarily to any embedded predication: many predicates which govern embedded predications, that is, to which the underlying structure given in (9) may be attributed, cannot govern AUC-NPs. An example is the class of predicates designating the production of speech and thought, i.e. the class alluded to by means of the labels "expositive" and "cognitive" or "propositional" (covering both subclasses). They may not govern an AUC, even if the right conditions (of tense and syntactic function assignment) are satisfied.

10.4 Conditions triggering the rule of AUC-formation

When we look for those factors which condition AUC-formation as formulated in the previous section, basically two different types of condition may be relevant: semantic factors or pragmatic factors. As we have seen above, syntactic function assignment must have taken place before AUC-formation. What particular syntactic function assignment has taken place is relevant only in so far as it prohibits AUC-formation in certain cases; it does not, however, trigger AUC-formation, as is shown by the observation made in Section 10.3, that not all embedded predications which satisfy the right constellation of syntactic function and verbal tense may be realized as an AUC-NP.

I shall briefly discuss both semantic factors (10.4.1) and pragmatic function possibilities (10.4.2). Subsequently, I shall formulate a proposal as to how the relevant conditions may be accounted for in the underlying predicational structure (Section 10.5).

10.4.1   Semantic conditions for AUC-formation: factivity

AUC formation on sentence level[11] may apply only when the embedded predication is "factive" in the sense defined by Kiparsky and Kiparsky (1970). Predications are said to be factive, when the state of affairs designated is implied by the speaker to have actually taken place (to be taking place, or to be going to take place in the future, respectively). Thus, the AUC-construction is regularly found with many predicates which have been distinguished as "factive" verbs, such as predicates designating emotional or evaluative reaction of some human being to a state of affairs (i.e. the "verba affectuum" in Latin grammars), often labelled "emotive" verbs. In Case Grammar terms one might speak of predicates having an Experiencer argument and a Phenomenon argument in their frame.[12] An example of such a predicate is given in (1a) above. In fact one of the possible syntactically different but semantically equivalent alternative ways of expression, namely the paraphrase with a finite subordinate clause introduced by *quod* (cf. example (6b)), is in Latin almost exclusively reserved for factive embedded predications as well.[13]

A second group of predicates which in Latin frequently occurs governing embedded predication realized as an AUC, and which on closer look in that case similarly govern a factive embedded predication, is formed by predicates which designate "causation", i.e. the bringing about of a change in state of affairs by some state of affairs (for these predicates see also Kiefer, 1978, 181), Causation predicates in Latin may either have a two-place frame in which the two arguments are a Cause and an (affected) Goal (cf. 1b), or a frame in which the second argument is an (effected) Goal as in (10a):

(10)   a   consul   moriens   suspicionem movet
           consul$_{nom}$ dying$_{nom}$ suspicion$_{acc}$ moves$_{3sg}$
           "that the consul was dying causes suspicion"

In both frames the Cause argument is usually factive. Thus there seems to be a connection between the property of being factive and the semantic function fulfilled by the embedded predication involved: in a frame with an Experiencer both Cause arguments and Phenomenon arguments are *usually* factive. I do not say *necessarily*: it has been demonstrated (e.g. Kempson, 1975, 68–69, 80; Kiefer, 1978, 181) that the claim that factivity is required by such predicates is too strong: even with emotive predicates, factivity is a "cancellable implication" (Kempson), i.e. it may be absent in certain contexts and is normal but not necessary.

A third group of predicates with which the AUC occurs as a syntactic realization of factive embedded predications is formed by one-place predicates which designate evaluation of some state of affairs from the part of the speaker. An example is (11a). With such predicates I have only encountered the AUC when the predicate consists of a noun plus copula (e.g. *esse* "to be"), perhaps because in case of an adjective the agreement would have to be the Head noun of the AUC-NP, thereby resulting in an expression which is difficult to interpret as in (11b):

(11) a   consul   occisus   facinus   est
          consul$_{nom\ masc}$ killed$_{nom\ masc}$ crime$_{nom\ neut}$ is$_{3sg}$
          "it is a crime that the consul has been killed"

      b *consul   occisus   aequus   est
          consul$_{nom\ masc}$ killed$_{nom\ masc}$ fair$_{nom\ masc}$ is$_{3sg}$
          "it is fair that the consul has been killed"

With the group of one-place predicates illustrated in (11a), the embedded predication has no semantic function other than being evaluated: its semantic function is, accordingly, in Functional Grammar marked as Zero (∅). In connection with this, factivity of the embedded predication is optional with many of these predicates. If they govern an embedded predication which is not factive, however, the latter will syntactically be expressed in different constructions (a single infinitive, for example, or an *ut*+subjunctive clause). Thus there will be a semantic opposition between the AUC-construction exemplified in (11a) and the construction exemplified in (12) which is not factive:

(12)   occidere consulem facinus   est
       to-kill   consul$_{acc}$ crime$_{nom}$ is$_{3sg}$
       "it is a crime to kill the consul"

Since the embedded predication in (12) has the same semantic function in relation to its predicate as the AUC in (11a), the conclusion must be drawn that at least for such predicates the semantic property of factivity must somehow be indicated separately in the underlying predicational structure (Section 10.5).

The AUC construction does not occur as a syntactic realization of embedded predications governed by predicates designating "mental cognition" such as *scire* "to know" and *intellegere* "to understand". The English equivalents of these predicates have been distinghished in Kiparsky and Kiparsky (1970, 348) and others as being "semantically" factive, but "syntactically" non-factive. In Latin they behave like "propositional" predicates as far as their syntactic behaviour is concerned (i.e. they behave as expositive and cognitive verbs and belong to the class of verbs *dicendi* and *sentiendi*).[14] The embedded predication governed by the latter two semantic classes of predicates designates the content of speech and thought respectively. In other words, with propositional predicates the semantic function of the embedded predication is neither that of Cause nor that of Phenomenon. How it should be labelled I shall leave open for the moment. It might be useful to distinguish a separate semantic function Content (Co) for such embedded predications. If we keep within the list of semantic functions recognized in Dik (1978a, 37–43), the only one available is that of (effected?) Goal. In either case, further argumentation is required for proving the value of the label.

The fact that predicates such as *scire* "to know" never syntactically behave as governing a factive complement despite their much discussed semantic factivity contrasts with the fact that there are in Latin, as well as in English and Hungarian, quite a number of predicates, both two-place and three-place, which may govern either a non-factive content clause, or a factive embedded predication:[15] instances are the predicates *admonere* "to admonish, remind", *memini* "to remember", *oblivisci* "to forget", and *nuntiare* "to inform". When governing factive embedded predications, some of them may be viewed as predicates with an Experiencer plus Phenomenon frame rather than as propositional predicates, such as *memini* "to remember"; others seem to resemble "causative" predicates rather than propositional predicates, when governing factive complements such as *admonere* "to remind". In other words, it may be claimed that such predicates have more than one frame, the arguments in the two frames carrying different semantic functions. Which semantic function we are dealing with determines whether an AUC-construction is possible. Realization of the embedded predication as an AUC always implies factivity, whereas other syntactic constructions are used for expressing the different types of content-clauses. Consider (13b–c):[16]

(13) a patris   occisi   me   admonuit
         father$_{gen}$ killed$_{gen}$ me$_{acc}$ reminded$_{3sg}$
         "he reminded me of the fact that my father had been killed"

    b   patrem   occisum esse admonuit
        father$_{acc}$ killed$_{acc}$ to-be reminded$_{3sg}$
       "he reminded me that my father had been killed"

    c   admonuit   me   ut   patrem   occiderem
        he-admonished me$_{acc}$ that father$_{acc}$ kill$_{1sg}$
       "he admonished me to kill my father"

In the case of predicates such as *admonere* it is obvious that factivity must be indicated somehow in the underlying predicational structure, since it conditions the AUC construction exemplified in (13a). The AUC is excluded in (13b, c). The same conclusion was drawn with respect to one-place predicates (11–12). Moreover since factivity is not an obligatory feature of Phenomenon and Cause arguments, it is not sufficient merely to distinguish the embedded predications involved by distinct semantic function labels.

    Before suggesting how the semantic condition of factivity could be accounted for within the framework of Functional Grammar, I shall consider whether the factor "factivity" which I claim to be a condition for triggering the optional rule of AUC formation in Latin is a sufficient condition. As I have shown elsewhere (Chapter 4), one of the conditions which may lead to variations in the way in which predications containing embedded predications may be syntactically realized may be pragmatic (de Groot, Chapter 3; Dik, Chapter 8; Gvozdanović, Chapter 6). The reason is that in such predications various essentially different pragmatic function arrangements are possible. This may result in a differentiation of these patterns on a syntactic level as well, e.g. by triggering special placement rules or other expression rules. Therefore I shall now investigate whether, in addition to the semantic condition of factivity, pragmatic function arrangement is of any significance in determining the possibility of application of the rule effecting AUC formation.

10.4.2 *Pragmatic function arrangement and AUC formation*

In Chapter 4 I demonstrated that within certain types of predications containing embedded predications several alternative pragmatic function arrangements are possible in principle. Which pragmatic arrangement a predication has may have certain consequences for the way in which it is expressed in Latin. Sentence Focus (for a definition of Focus, see Dik, 1978a, 149) may fall either on the embedded predication as a whole or on some other constituent of the main predication; it may, however, also fall upon an element *within* the embedded predication. I have shown that when Focus falls upon some element within the embedded predication, this embedded predication looses its "unity" from a pragmatic point of view. In Latin, such pragmatic function arrangement is a condition for a rule effecting a syntactic realization of the embedded predication in which the pragmatic "splitting up" of the embedded predication (a constituent which semantically forms an entity, being an argument of the governing predicate) is mirrored by a syntactic splitting-up: one of the constituents of the embedded predication receives a position and a syntactic function within the governing clause. The term used to describe this phenomenon was "pseudo-argument formation".[17]

In Latin, the two syntactic constructions which exhibit the particular pseudo-argument formation alluded to, are the so-called Nominativus cum Infinitivo (NcI)-construction (also known as the personal passive) on the one hand, and the construction consisting of a so-called proleptic accusative and a finite clause on the other.[18] The first construction frequently occurs with predicates designating the production of speech and thought, that is, with propositional predicates; the second occurs with the same semantic class of predicates as well as with some others, including predicates designating perception. The phenomenon is especially frequent with dependent question clauses, in which the pragmatic function arrangement is obviously such that an element from within the embedded predication carries Focus in the sentence as a whole. Most of these predicates (verbs of perception excluded) never govern "factive" predications,[19] and so they do not occur with the AUC-construction.

I shall now investigate whether any particular pragmatic function arrangement forms a condition in order for the rule of AUC formation to apply. Does the specific pragmatic function arrangement which conditions the application of the rule of pseudo-argument formation occur in the case of factive embedded predications as well? Is it, or any other pragmatic function arrangement, a condition which must be satisfied before AUC formation can apply?

Arguments which suggested the relevance of pragmatic function arrangement in the case of the syntactic constructions exhibiting pseudo-argument formation included: (i) the existence of certain restrictions on the relative order of the pseudo-argument in relation to its "proper" predicate; (ii) the impossibility of co-occurrence of the pseudo-argument construction with pronominal elements coreferent (anaphorically or preparatively) to the embedded predication as a whole; and (iii) the impossibility of a Theme+ predication arrangement of the embedded predication when the latter is realized in the construction reserved for embedded predications which are pragmatically "split up" (see 4.2.2.2). I shall therefore examine the behaviour of AUC-NPs with respect to the first two criteria (there is insufficient material for testing (iii)).

(i) With respect to the relative order of the predicate of the embedded predication and its Subj argument, there is no indication that there are any constraints upon the relative order of Head and Modifier within the AUC. Laughton (1964, 88) points out that "in the AUC . . . the position of the participle in relation to its noun is syntactically indifferent. No principles of varying emphasis can be detected". In other words, the predicate of the embedded predication in underlying structure can either precede its argument (the Head), as in (14a), or follow it (14b). Furthermore, the NP as a whole can either precede (14b) or follow (14a) its governing predicate,[20] as appears from a glance at some attested instances of the AUC given in (14a, b). In the examples that follow, the essential constituents of the AUC (the Head and its Modifier) are italicized; the morphological information and the literal paraphrase are omitted.

(14) a   . . . quorum benevolentiam nobis conciliarat per me quondam
          te socio *defensa res publica*
          ". . . whose favour had won for us the fact that the state had
          once been defended by me with you as an ally" (Cic. *Fam.*
          4, 13, 2)

      b   non me bonorum direptio, non . . ., non . . ., non *praeda*
          consulum ex meis fortunis crudelissime *capta* permovet
          "I am not moved by the plundering of my possessions, not
          by . . ., not by . . ., not by the fact that booty . . . has pitilessly
          been taken from my fortunes" (Cic. *Dom.* 146)

Thus, there is no evidence in favour of assuming that one of the elements within the embedded predication (whether the Head of the Modifier of the AUC-NP) must always have a special pragmatic status as Focus in the sentence as a whole, as opposed to what was found to be the case in sentences exhibiting pseudo-argument formation. Obligatory Focus status of Head or Modifier in the sentence as a whole would not be very plausible in view of this lack of constraints.

The other way round, various instances show that, in sentences containing an AUC, sentence Focus may quite well fall upon a constituent of the sentence which does not belong to the embedded predication, for example the attested sentence (15):

(15)   Quid ego istius decreta, quid rapinas, quid . . . *possessiones datas* proferam?
"Why should I mention his decisions, why his robbings, why the fact that possessions have been given away . . . ?" (Cic. *Phil.* 2, 62)

Sentences such as (15) show that AUC-Nds are not required to be pragmatically split up, but may quite well form a pragmatic unit as a whole, i.e. as a whole carry a pragmatic function. In (15), this pragmatic function may be said to be Topic, or part of the Topic (Bolkestein, Chapter 4, Section 4.2.2.2).[21] I conclude that in contrast with the condition determining pseudo-argument formation there is no requirement that sentence Focus must fall upon an element within the embedded predication.

The fact that factive embedded predications frequently as a whole carry a pragmatic function is implied by the observations made in Kiefer (1978, 171ff.). Kiefer, discussing the pragmatic status of factive embedded predications in Hungarian, does not distinguish between embedded predications which are split up pragmatically and those which are not. However, his examples from Hungarian include both factive predications which are Topic in the sentence as a whole and factive predications which carry Focus. In Hungarian the difference may be explicitated by means of a difference in the position of a pronominal element coreferential to the embedded predication in the main clause. Note that the presence of such a pronominal element is itself already an indication that the embedded predication as a whole carries a pragmatic function (cf. criterion (ii)).

(ii) As far as the second criterion is concerned—the phenomenon that when an embedded predication is pragmatically "split up" there may not be a coreferential pronoun anaphorically or preparatively referring to it—it is easily demonstrated that the Latin AUC, when compared to cases of pseudo-argument formation, exhibits a quite different behaviour in this respect. An AUC, for example, frequently occurs as one member of a series of expressions designating states of affairs; syntactically these expressions may mutually differ, e.g. be state of affairs nouns and finite clauses. State of affairs nouns do not admit of pragmatic splitting-up anyway. For attested instances see (14b) and (15) above and various other examples quoted in Laughton (1964, 90). Moreover, not seldom we find coreferential pronominal elements, both anaphoric and preparative, e.g. (16a) below. Furthermore, as pointed out in Laughton as well (1964, 90–91), an AUC may itself function as an apposition to a whole sentence. Such cases are all instances of factive embedded predications which form an entity not only from the semantic point of view but also from the pragmatic point of view. In such a case the rules effecting pseudo-argument formation cannot apply.

Examples (16b, c) indicate that the AUC as a whole may form an answer to a question. This implies that in Latin factive embedded predications realized as an AUC may not only carry Topic-function in the sentence but may carry Focus as well:[22]

(16) a nec aequitati quicquam tam infestum quam *convocati homines* "and nothing is as hostile to justice as the fact that people have been called to a meeting" (Cic. *Caec.* 33)

      b Quid aliud habet in se nisi quam *Cn. Carbomem spoliatum?* "what else does it imply apart from the fact that Cn.C. has been robbed" (Cic. *Ver.* 1, 11)

      c Quid vides? :: mulierculas video sedentis "What do you see? :: I see women sit . . ." (Pl. *Rud.* 168)

Sentences such as (16b, c) are evidence that factivity does not always imply being Topic. This supports the claim made in Kiefer (1978, 202) with respect to factive embedded predications in Hungarian. On the basis of the fact that factive predications may be Topic as well as Focus, Kiefer argues against the view that factivity could be explained purely in pragmatic terms. The latter opinion is found in various authors, including Kempson (1975, 81, 136). It may have been suggested by two phenomena which are not unconnected. First, cases of factive embedded predications which carry Focus seem to be statistically much less frequent than cases of factive embedded predications which are Topic or part of the Topic. Secondly— and this may be the cause of the statistical difference—factive embedded predications are often claimed to be "definite" or to have a Deep Structure similar to that attributed to definite NPs. The latter suggestion is found in Kiparsky and Kiparsky (1970, 356) and Kempson (1975, 135). Indeed I would agree with the observation that factive embedded predications are definite, as long as definiteness is defined as in Dik (1978a, 61) as presented as "identifiable for the Addressee". It should, however, be realized, that "identifiability" is not necessarily in one-to-one relation with being Topic, despite the fact that Topics often are definite. The difference between the two notions is stressed in Dik (1978a, 182) and also in Chafe (1976). Within Functional Grammar "definiteness" is explicitly recognized to be defined in pragmatic terms. It is, however, accorded quite a different status in the underlying predication than the pragmatic functions Topic and Focus: it is accounted for by means of a term-operator specifying the term involved as identifiable. If factive embedded predications are always definite, the examples (16b, c) prove that the difference in status between Topicness and definiteness is justified. I shall return to the question of how factivity may be represented in underlying structure in Section 10.5.

Since it has been demonstrated that factive embedded predications realized as an AUC are not required to be pragmatically split up but on the contrary may frequently carry as a whole either Topic or Focus function in the sentence, it might be supposed that for the rule of AUC formation to apply the opposite condition holds from that holding for pseudo-argument formation. It might be supposed, in other words, that "pragmatic unity" is the relevant condition. However, I have found some instances—not very frequent, according to Kühner-Stegmann (1912, I, 785)—in which an element within the AUC is the Focus of a question, e.g. (17a–b):

(17)   a   tu vero *quibus rebus gestis, quo hoste superato* . . . ausus est?
           "but you, after having fulfilled what feats, after having won over what enemy . . . have you dared?" (Cic. *Ver.* 2, 3, 185)

       b   Quis illic est *quem* huc *advenientem* conspicor?
           "Who is that man whom I see coming towards us?"
           (Pl. *Ep.* 435)

However, the status of both (17a) and (17b) is open to doubt. In (17b) we are on the one hand dealing with a cleft construction instead of a straight question; on the other hand, it may be disputed whether the Accusative cum Participio construction found with predicates designating direct perception, such as *conspicor* "to notice, observe" in (17b), is in fact an instance of the AUC, that is of an embedded predication, or that we are rather dealing with NPs of a different type, namely the type discussed in Section 10.1 and exemplified by (2). In the latter case the participle is a restrictor.[23] In the case of (17a) we are dealing firstly with an AUC which does not have the status of an argument in relation to the governing predicate but that of a satellite. Apart from that, the few instances of questioned "ablativus absolutus" as the construction is called, all seem to concern so-called rhetorical questions, in which the speaker is not interested in getting information concerning the identity of the questioned element. Thus, it is doubtful whether sentences such as (17a, b) offer sufficient evidence in favour of the claim that one of the constituents of the AUC (the Head of the NP, that is, the Subj of the embedded predication) may carry Focus in the sentence as a whole. This means that there is still some doubt concerning the conclusion that in the case of predications containing factive complements pragmatic function arrangement is irrelevant in determining when the rule of AUC-formation may apply.

Note that if pragmatic function arrangement does not form a condition for the application of AUC formation, this rule, conditioned by the semantic property of factivity, may be viewed as applying either *after* pragmatic function assignment or *before* it. As yet I have no arguments in favour of one solution or the other.

I shall now turn to the question of how to account for the relevant condition of factivity in the predication underlying the sentences containing factive embedded predications; in other words I shall consider how this condition could be represented in the predication assumed to underly (1a), or, to be more precise, how the predication given in (9) could be extended so as to contain the relevant information.

10.5   The representation of factivity in underlying predications

In the previous sections it has been demonstrated that there is a specific semantic condition which determines whether the rule of AUC-formation proposed in Section 10.3 may or may not apply to an embedded predication. To exclude application of the rule in the case of embedded predications to which it may not apply, this condition—which as we have seen is the condition that the embedded predication involved must be factive—must be represented in the underlying predication in some way or another. The need for incorporating a property such as factivity in the underlying structure of sentences has in fact already been recognized by Kiparsky and Kiparsky (1970, 365). Their own proposal, given in the same article, is to describe factive clauses in English as being governed in Deep Structure by a+definite NP *the fact that*; this NP may be deleted and in that case be absent from the surface structure. A different proposal is made in Kempson (1975, 125ff.) and I shall return to this below.

Within the framework of Functional Grammar three approaches are conceivable with respect to the way in which the property of factivity may be represented in a predication, and they are illustrated in (18)–(20):

(18) $(x_i: \text{fact}(x_i): [\text{occiderev}_{\text{pass}} (x_j)_{\text{Ag}} (\text{consul})_{\text{GoSubj}}] (x_i))$

(19)   a $(x_i: [\text{fact occiderev}_{\text{pass}} (x_j)_{\text{Ag}} (\text{consul})_{\text{GoSubj}}] (x_i))$

b $(x_i: [\text{f occiderev}_{\text{pass}} (x_j)_{\text{Ag}} (\text{consul})_{\text{GoSubj}}] (x_i))$

(20) $(\text{f } x_i: [\text{occiderev}_{\text{pass}} (x_j)_{\text{Ag}} (\text{consul})_{\text{GoSubj}}] (x_i))$

In the first alternative (18) factivity is treated as due to the presence of a predicate characterizing x_i. Since this predicate is the first, most leftward, predicate characterizing x_i, it would be expected to be expressed as the nominal Head of a nominal phrase (Dik (1978a, 59)).[24] This approach is perhaps implied in Dik (1978a, 16–17): an expression containing *the fact that* is there mentioned—in passing—as having a term-structure, similar to that of other Head plus (attributive) Modifier constructions, including that of relative clauses. It is also more or less equivalent to the proposal made in Kiparsky and Kiparsky (1970, 356), in which the embedded predication is also given a status comparable to that of a Modifier.[25] In Dik (1978a, 16–17), however, the description applies only to constructions containing the actual lexical item *fact* in English; there is no indication that it is meant to cover factive embedded predications not governed by such a lexical item as well. In Kiparsky and Kiparsky, on the other hand, constructions containing *the fact that* and factive embedded predications are analysed as having the same underlying structure.

In the second solution (19a, b), on the other hand, factivity is treated as internal to the predication specifying x_i, namely as an element affecting its predicate. In (19a) this element is viewed as forming a derived predicate through modification of the predicate (see Dik (1978a, 16) for a brief remark on predicate formation). In (19b) it is described as a predicate operator, here indicated by means of the symbol 'f'. According to this approach, its status is comparable to that attributed to predicate operators such as tense, modality, negation, etc. (on such predicate operators see Dik (1979b, 88)).

In the third alternative, given in (20), factivity is treated as due to the presence of a "term-operator" (provisionally symbolized by 'f'). The presence of such a term-operator indicates that the term involved has a specific status (on term-operators see Dik (1978a, 60–62; 1979b, 84–85)).

In all three solutions, the optional rule of AUC-formation, i.e. the rule which effects the selection of a syntactic category different from what might be expected for expressing the embedded predication, namely as an NP by means of participialization of the predicate of the embedded predication, can be described as being triggered by the presence of a predicate *fact* or an operator f somewhere within the internal structure of the term.

What arguments do we have in favour of choosing between these alternatives? The following observations may be relevant for evaluating the merits of the various solutions.

(i) Treating the embedded predication as a restrictor, or Modifier, in relation to a Headnoun *fact*, as in (18a), does not adequately represent the phenomenon that explicit presence of the embedded predication is required in the sentence.[26] In this respect, the relation between a lexical item *fact* in English, and the embedded predication governed by it is similar to that between a one-place predicate and its argument.

(ii) In the case of Latin a lexical item with the meaning 'fact' does not exist in the language. This means that in the case of both (18) and of (19a), in the underlying predication a predicate, resp. modification of a predicate, is present which does not correspond to an actual item in the language.[27] In Functional Grammar, however, there is a claim that there is a close relationship between the predicates which figure in underlying predications in a language (i.e. in the fund of predicates to be used for term-formation in that language) on the one hand, and the lexical items found in the language under consideration on the other (Dik, 1978a, 46–47). This means that although in some languages (such as English) "factivity" may conceivably be described as a predicate, in the case of Latin this is not a satisfactory assumption.[28]

(iii) Apart from these objections, it is not at all clear what possible class of intended referents the first, i.e. the most leftward part of (18a) designates.

(iv) With respect to the alternatives given in (19a, b) it is perhaps relevant to observe that describing factivity as a modification of the predicate, or as a predicate-operator, i.e. as affecting only the predicate within the embedded predication, implies that the way in which the semantic properties of the governing predicates (including the property of allowing or requiring factive embedded predications) on the one hand and the presence of elements within the embedded predication on the other, are related is quite complicated. It seems more natural and more in accordance with the general view of semantic selection restrictions to account for the property of factivity as having the term as a whole in its scope, and not just part of it. Intuitively, the rule-triggering effect of its presence seems to be more likely when the condition figures on a hierarchically higher level in the structure of the term, than when it is lower down.

On the basis of these considerations I conclude that at least for a language such as Latin, the solution given in (20) is the most attractive one. In this solution factivity is treated as having the status of a term-operator which has the function of specifying the status of all possible members of the intended class of referents designated by the predication. In Dik (1978a, 61–62) it is explicitly pointed out that within a Functional Grammar framework term-operators, as opposed to predicates, need not always have overt markers in the language: in some languages, certain term-operators may not have an actual linguistic representation, such as e.g. the operators distinguished for specifying "definiteness" and "indefiniteness" (they do not have one in Latin for example). It is even suggested that such operators may not all have cross-linguistic relevance. According to this analysis, there exists a relation between the semantic properties of a predicate on the one hand and the presence of certain term-operators in the internal structure of their arguments on the other. The existence of such a relation is not wholly without parallels: it may be claimed, for example, that certain predicates impose a constraint to the effect that their Subj arguments must —in one of their frames—be "more than one" (e.g. the predicates *to marry, to meet, to shake hands* in Engl.).

A solution which to a certain extent is comparable to solution (20) is given in Kempson (1975, 120, 134–135), although it is there couched in somewhat different terms. In Kempson, the phenomenon of factivity is treated as due to the presence of a particular term-operator as well, in combination with pragmatic factors such as the knowledge shared by the speaker and the hearer. Kempson claims that the operator involved is the same operator as the one which she distinguishes as relevant for describing both "definite" and "indefinite" noun phrases (Kempson, 1975, 113, 135). The definition of this operator (in Kempson symbolized by "Spec") is that it characterizes "the fact that a single fixed object is referred to by that noun phrase" (Kempson, 1975, 120). This qualification is considered to be sufficient for representing the relevant factors in the predication assumed to underly sentences containing factive embedded predications. A rather better formulation, as I have pointed out above (Section 10.4.2), is that factive embedded predications as their intended referent always have a (one) identifiable occurrence of the state of affairs designated. Whether this state of affairs has already been mentioned in the previous context and is known, or offers "new" information is irrelevant: as I have demonstrated in Section 10.4.2, factive embedded predications will often carry the pragmatic function Topic, but carrying Focus is not at all excluded.

The formulation that factive embedded predications are identifiable implies that in the underlying predication they may be specified as being so by means of the definiteness operator distinguished for that purpose in Functional Grammar. It might therefore be suggested—with a modification of Kempson—that there is no need for distinguishing a separate term-operator "f" for factivity at all and that it is sufficient to specify the embedded predications concerned by means of this definiteness operator. However, I am not at all certain that there may not exist other types of embedded predications, non-factive ones, for which it would be justified to claim definiteness as well. (Note that, in English, nouns which govern (propositional) embedded predications, such as *the idea that, the view that, the conviction that, the claim that*, as well as nouns governing other types of embedded predications, such as *the intention to, the wish to*, are usually definite. In Latin, parallel constructions, i.e. of a noun governing a predication, are less frequent; usually embedded predications appear without being governed by a noun specifying their type.)

Pending further research in the descriptive problems of embedded predications, I therefore maintain my proposal to distinguish a separate term-operator "f" which has the function of specifying embedded predications as being factive. Predicates which in one of their argument positions may have an embedded predication must in the lexicon be provided with information concerning whether or not they allow or require the presence of the operator in the structure of the term involved.

To summarize, I assume that embedded predications liable to the optional rule of AUC formation in Latin along the lines sketched in Section 10.3 must be specified in the underlying predication as being factive by means of a term-operator signifying that all members of the class of possible referents of the term are facts. As we have seen, there is some evidence that this condition is sufficient (10.4.2) and that there are no further constraints, for example as to pragmatic function arrangement over the underlying predication, which form a condition for the possibility of application of the expression rule involved.

10.6 Summary and conclusion

In this chapter I have shown that the Latin construction known as the "dominant participle" or "ab urbe condita" construction (AUC), although syntactically resembling a nominal phrase with internally a Head Modifier structure, cannot in fact be described as a nominal term with the internal structure of a nominal Head plus a participial restrictor. AUC-NPs must be described as having the underlying structure of an embedded predication. This predication as a whole forms the (predicational) predicate specifying the term. In this way observable differences in behaviour between other complex NPs and the construction under consideration, are accounted for by the internal differences in term-structure of the NPs involved.

I furthermore claim that for certain types of embedded predication in Latin, a special rule of AUC formation applies optionally. This rule selects a syntactic category for the embedded predication to be expressed in, namely that of a nominal phrase. This is effected by means of participialization of the predicate of that predication. The condition which determines that this rule may apply is semantic, namely the factor "factivity". No conditions of a pragmatic nature were found to exist. As far as pragmatic function arrangement is concerned, it appears that factive embedded predications statistically are often Topic in the sentence as a whole: this is not surprising in view of the definition of factivity as "implied by the speaker to be true" and of the fact that factive predications seem to be definite, in the sense of designating identifiable states of affairs. However, instances in which the factive predication as a whole carries Focus in the sentence occur as well. Thus factive embedded predications in general as a whole carry a pragmatic function in the sentence, and usually that of Topic. On the other hand, some attested instances seem to prove, that it is not impossible for a constituent *within* a factive predication (namely the Head-noun of the NP, i.e. the Subj argument of the predication) to carry Focus in the sentence.

The semantic condition of factivity is thus the only condition to be satisfied for optionally triggering the rule of AUC-formation. I argue that this condition must be accounted for in the predication underlying sentences containing the construction. Various alternatives are discussed for representing the notion of factivity in underlying predications within a Functional Grammar framework. On the basis of the absence of a nominal or an adjectival lexical item "fact" or a verbal one "be a fact" in Latin, preference is given to an approach in which factivity is treated as a "term-operator", provisionally symbolized by "f", which is especially relevant for terms with the internal structure of a predication. It is necessary, that the possibility for this operator to be present with certain predicates should be specified in the lexicon of the language, in the lexical entry for the individual predicates.

Notes

1 I use the term Object (Obj) in the traditional sense, for accusative constituents which may become Subject (Subj) in passivization: it is not clear whether a rule of Obj assignment as formulated in Dik (1978a, ch. 5) should be assumed to exist in Latin. (Cf. Chapter 4, note 27.)

2 The so-called ablativus absolutus (AA) construction is an example of the AUC as satellite.

3 I mention only Kühner-Stegmann (1912); for further bibliographical information see Bolkestein (1980b).

4 Symbols such as N, V, part and NP are categorial specifications; Ag and Go and Ø specify semantic functions. The indications "pass" and "act" may be added to predicates as instructions for expression rules; they are determined by Subj assignment.

5 The distinction between restrictive and non-restrictive Modifiers, although having consequences for the omittability of the Modifier, is not relevant with respect to the distinction under discussion here.

6 Cf. note 4. I distinguish the semantic functions Experiencer and Phenomenon, although these functions are not recognized in Dik (1978a, 41–43). See however Dik, Chapter 2, ex. (56)–(57).

7 On the level of NP-complementation, finite clauses and AcI-clauses are less frequent as equivalents to the AUC. Bolkestein (1980b) offers a discussion of a type of NP-complements which is in semantic opposition with the AUC.

8 Cf. note 6.

9 On case-marking see Dik (1978a, 158; 1979b, 86). See also note 1.

10 On the problem of the relative order of expression rules, cf. Dik, Chapter 1, Section 1.2; "nom" and "acc" in the following predications are instructions for the expression rule realizing the final sentence. Cf. also note 4.

11 Bolkestein (1980b) mentions certain conditions in which Latin uses not the AUC but a "non-factive" construction for expressing embedded predications which could be analysed as factive, and some conditions in which the AUC is found for embedded predications which are not factive, namely on NP level and in Prepositional phrases. This is impossible on "argument-level".

12 Cf. note 6. A survey of Hungarian predicates which may govern factive complements is given in Kiefer (1978).

13 AcI-clauses, on the other hand, are not restricted to one semantic type of embedded predication, cf. Bolkestein (1976a).

14 I shall not go into the question of how "factive" the verb *to know* really is. For some recent observations see Vendler (1980), Lyons (1977, 772, 794), Kiefer (1978, 183 ff.).

15 In the literature one finds labels such as "semi-factives", "half-factives" (see also Kiparsky and Kiparsky, 1970, 360). The same labels are occasionally used for other types of predicates. Vendler (1980) applies it to a class of "propositional" predicates which may govern dependent question clauses.

The two types of presupposition involved are treated by Vendler as the same. Kiefer (1978) offers many examples of Hungarian predicates, which are very similar in meaning to the Latin ones, and may also govern factive and non factive complements. See also Kempson (1975, 128).

16   On different types of Content-clauses see Bolkestein (1976a).

17   In Allwood (1976) the observation is made, that in Swedish the complex NP-constraint posited in TG is sometimes violated because of pragmatic reasons (in his terminology "referential units", i.e. semantic units, may be broken up by "topicalization").

18   In de Groot (Chapter 3) and many older grammars of Latin, this phenomenon is called "sentence-intertwining" or a comparable term. See also Bolkestein (Chapter 4).

19   With predicates designating perception, the so-called Accusativus cum Participio (AcP) construction is common when they refer to direct perception. Whether or not the AcP must be analysed as an instance of the AUC (i.e. as involving an embedded predication) has not been decisively proved as yet. In Bolkestein (1976b) I analyse the AcP as an instance of a nominal Object plus a participial restrictor, i.e. as having a structure such as (2); I am now of the opinion that we are actually dealing with an AUC.

20   This was argued to be impossible in the case of the "proleptic accusative" and very rare in the case of the NcI-construction (see Bolkestein, Chapter 4). An "ablativus absolutus" (cf. note 2) normally precedes the sentence as a whole (Kühner-Stegmann, 1912, I, 785). This is perhaps due to its identifiability.

21   See also Dik (1978a, 143–144) on the problem of how to determine Topic.

22   I have found instances of both normal sentence Focus and of "contrastive" Focus, e.g. in sequences such as *"non solum . . . sed etiam AUC* "not only . . . but AUC as well".

23   See note 19. The best proof would be an instance in which the Head-noun designates an entity which is not directly perceivable, whereas the NP as a whole designates a state of affairs which is perceivable, in which this entity is involved. I have not found such instances.

24   Theoretically, one could also conceive of a structure in which "fact" figures as a restrictor, the embedded predication being Head. However, such a structure does not have a possible interpretation, so I shall leave it out of account. Apart from this objection it suffers from the same general defect as the solution indicated in (18).

25   The treatment of various types of complex NPs in TG suffers from a lack of recognition of differences in the semantic relations between Head-nouns and their Modifiers or complements. No essential difference is made in the description.

26   In English the expression *be a fact* or *this fact, that fact* etc. may of course be used anaphorically, i.e. coreferential to a predication.

27   If (18) was valid for Latin, we would be dealing with an element which has to be obligatorily deleted: this is an impossible notion in a FG-framework.

232   *Predication and Expression in Functional Grammar*

References

ALLWOOD, J. S.
1976   The complex np constraint as a non-universal rule and some semantic factors influencing the acceptability of Swedish sentences which violate the cnpc. *In* J. Stillings (ed.). "U/MASS Occasional Papers in Linguistics, Vol II. Amherst.

BOLKESTEIN, A. M.
1976a The relation between form and meaning of Latin subordinate clauses governed by verba dicendi. *Mnemosyne* **39**, 156–175; 268–300.
1976b AcI- and *ut*-clauses with verba dicendi in Latin. Part I: AcI-clauses vs Object plus Complement-patterns. *Glotta* **54**, 263–291.
1979   Subject-to-Object raising in Latin? *Lingua* **48**, 15–34.
1980a The "ab urbe condita"-construction in Latin: a strange type of raising? *In* S. Daalder and M. Gerritsen (ed.). "Linguistics in the Netherlands 1980". Amsterdam, North-Holland, 80–92.
1980b De ab urbe condita constructie in het Latijn. *Lampas* **13**, 80–98.

CHAFE, W. L.
1976   Givenness, Contrastiveness, Definiteness, Subjects, Topics and Point of View. *In* Ch.N. Li (ed.), "Subject and Topic". London and New York, Academic Press, 25–56.

DIK, S. C.
1978a "Functional Grammar". North-Holland Linguistic Series 37. Amsterdam, North-Holland.
1979a Raising in a Functional Grammar. *Lingua* **47**, 119–140.
1979b Funktionele Morfologie. *In* T. Hoekstra and H. van der Hulst (ed.). "Morfologie in Nederland". GLOT-Special, Leiden, 72–100.
1980   "Studies in Functional Grammar". London and New York, Academic Press.

KEMPSON, R. M.
1975   "Presupposition and the delimitation of semantics". Cambridge, Cambridge University Press.

KIEFER, F.
1978   Factivity in Hungarian. *Studies in Language* **2**, 165–197.

KIPARSKY, P. and C. Kiparsky
1970   Fact. *In* D. D. Steinberg and L. A. Jakobovits (ed.). "Semantics". Cambridge, Cambridge University Press, 345–369.

KÜHNER, R. and C. Stegmann
1912   "Ausführliche Grammatik der Lateinischen Sprache, II: Satzlehre". Hannover, repr. Verlag Hahnsche Buchhandlung 1971, in two vols.

KWEE, Tjoe Liong
1981   "In search of an appropriate relative clause". *In* T. Hoekstra, H. van der Hulst and M. Moortgat (ed.). "Perspectives on Functional Grammar". Dordrecht, Foris.

LAUGHTON, E.
1964   "The participle in Cicero". Oxford, Oxford University Press.

LYONS, J.
  1977   "Semantics". Two vols. Cambridge, Cambridge University Press.
VENDLER, Z.
  1980   Telling the facts. *In* J. R. Searle, F. Kiefer and M. Bierwisch (ed.). "Speech Act Theory and Pragmatics". Dordrecht, Reidel, 273–290.

11 Relative Clause Formation in Ancient Greek

ALBERT RIJKSBARON

Department of Greek
University of Amsterdam

11.0 Introduction

In Dik (1978) relative clauses are only briefly discussed (cf. the author's remarks on p. 213). On p. 65 we find, in connection with

(1) the boy who studies in the library

the following proposal as to the underlying representation of this term:

(2) $(d1x_1: boy_N(x_1): [study_V (x_1)_{Ag}]_{Action} (d1y_1: library_N (y_1))_{Loc})$

·This should be read as: the definite singular x_1 such that x_1 is a boy such that x_1 studies in the definite singular y_1 such that y_1 is a library. As will be noticed, an operator that would yield the relative pronoun is lacking; as it stands, (2) could also be the underlying representation of

(3) the boy studying in the library

See also Dik (1978, 65). To arrive at (1) we need, then, the insertion of a relativization operator R. This can most easily be done by assigning R to the Agent variable x of the embedded predicate (Dik, 1979, 9):[1]

(4) $study_V (Rx_1)_{Ag}$

Of course, since (4) cannot be present in the underlying representation of (3), we would get different representations for (1) and (3); if (1) and (3) are semantically equivalent, this would be a disadvantage. On the other hand, as pointed out by Dik (1978, 66), there are strong arguments for inserting *studying* directly into the representation of (3), e.g. the fact that such a participle does not take all the values of the categories tense and aspect, whereas relative clauses do. It will also have been observed that we are concerned here only with restrictive relative clauses. Non-restrictive ones will have to get a different representation, in which e.g. "study$_V$ (Rx$_i$)$_{Ag}$" may be given a parenthesis-like status:

(5)   (d1x$_i$: boy$_N$(x$_i$) – study$_V$ (Rx$_i$)$_{Ag}$ (d1x$_j$: library$_N$ (x$_j$))$_{Loc}$ –)

(5) would then give us *the boy, who studies in the library*. An alternative way of differentiating these two types may be found in assigning different brackets to the terms involved, if, as Touratier (1980, 370ff.) argues, the relationship between antecedent (headnoun) and relative clause is not the same for the two types. In his opinion, when the definite article is present with the headnoun, for non-restrictive clauses the antecedent is formed by the group: Article+Noun, for restrictive ones solely by the Noun (see also Quirk *et al.* (1972, 155) on cataphoric *the*). An analysis into immediate constituents (Touratier, 1980, 371) would give us the following diagrams for restrictive (6) and non-restrictive (7) clauses:

(6)   NP

        Art   Nominal Member

                                  N   Rel Clause

        the   boy   who studies in the library

(7)   NP

                   NP   Rel Clause

        Art   N

        the   boy   who studies in the library

Reformulation within the framework of FG would yield the following underlying representations:

(6) = (8)   (d1x$_i$: (boy$_N$ (x$_i$): study$_V$ (Rx$_i$)$_{Ag}$ (d1x$_j$: library$_N$ (x$_j$))$_{Loc}$))

(7) = (9)   ((d1x_i: boy$_N$ (x_i)) (study$_V$ (Rx_i)$_{Ag}$ (d1x_j: library$_N$ (x_j))$_{Loc}$))

Both in (5) and (9) the relative clause does not have the status of a restrictor; one might call them, rather, adnominal satellites.

In connection with (3), it will be noticed, furthermore, that predicative participles will not be covered by an underlying representation like (2). One possibility to account for an expression such as (10):

(10)   The boy went away laughing

is by assigning to this expression the following representation:

(11)   go away$_V$ (d1x_i: boy (x_i))$_{Ag}$ laugh (x_i))$_{Circumstance}$

Observe that in (11) "laugh" has been given the status of a satellite. This is connected with the phenomenon that a participle like *laughing* in (10) shows much resemblance to a finite subordinate clause like *while he was laughing*; in fact, this clause would have the same underlying representation as *laughing* in (10). The eventual realization of "laugh" in (11) as a predicative participle or as a conjunctional clause will be effected by expression-rules.[2]

11.1   Relative clauses in Ancient Greek

In the remainder of this chapter I shall discuss a number of Ancient Greek relative clauses that present some problems in Functional Grammar (indeed in any linguistic theory), the main problem being whether we should give three types of relative clauses which differ at "surface" level one underlying representation.

11.1.1   The data

Consider the following sentences:

(12)   περιεσταύρωσαν αὐτοὺς τοῖς   δένδρεσιν   ἃ   ἔκοψαν
       periestaúrōsan autoùs toîs$_{dat}$ déndresin$_{dat}$ hà$_{acc}$ ékopsan
       "They fenced them about with the trees they had cut"

(13)   περιεσταύρωσαν αὐτοὺς τοῖς   δένδρεσιν   οἷς   ἔκοψαν
       periestaúrōsan autoùs toîs$_{dat}$ déndresin$_{dat}$ hoîs$_{dat}$ ékopsan

(14)   περιεσταύρωσαν αὐτοὺς οἷς   ἔκοψαν δένδρεσιν
       periestaúrōsan autoùs hoîs$_{dat}$ ékopsan déndresin$_{dat}$[3]

In (12) we find, apart from a Goal in the accusative caseform (*autoùs*), an instrumental Modifier, marked by the dative (*toîs déndresin*), which itself is modified by a relative clause (*hà ékopsan*). The relative pronoun (*hà*) is in the accusative caseform. It has the semantic function of Goal with the embedded predicate *ékopsan*. Sentence (13) exhibits the same structure. However, the relative pronoun (*hoîs*) is not marked by the accusative but appears in the caseform of its Headnoun (*toîs déndresin*); cf. the traditional term "attraction", or "assimilation". In (14), finally, we have a rather different construction, in that there is no Headnoun in the matrix-clause to which the "relative" pronoun *hoîs* might refer. It looks as if this noun has been "displaced" and turns up as a constituent of the embedded clause.

11.1.2   Conditions of attraction

I add a number of further observations, particularly concerning the conditions under which attraction applies. As is noted in the grammars, case-attraction of the relative pronoun occurs mainly—or, rather, can be seen most clearly—when the head noun is in the genitive or dative and when the relative pronoun "normally" would appear in the accusative. I take this caseform to be the formal sign, in FG terms, of the semantic function Goal.[4] Also, there has to be an Agent Subject and a verb in the active voice in the embedded clause: when the relative pronoun has the semantic function Goal but the syntactic function Subject and so in principle will appear in the nominative (the verb appearing in the passive voice), attraction does not apply. The following construction, then, does not occur, as far as I know:

(15) ?τοῖς δένδρεσιν   οἷς   ἐκόπη   (ὑπὸ τῶν πολιτῶν)
     toîs déndresin_dat hoîs_dat ekópē (aor indic pass) (hupò tôn politôn)
     ". . . with the trees that had been cut (by the citizens)"

It should be noticed, in this connection, that non-attracted passive relative clauses (restrictive ones, see below) are rare as well.[5] Cf.:

(15) a   τοῖς δένδρεσιν   ἃ   ἐκόπη (ὑπὸ τῶν πολιτῶν)
     toîs déndresin_dat hà_nom ekópē (hupò tôn politôn)

If the passive voice is "chosen", so to speak, for the expression of (restrictive) embedded predications, these preferably will be realized as *participles* (see also pp. 244f.):

(16)   τοῖς δένδρεσι τοῖς κοπεῖσιν   (ὑπὸ τῶν πολιτῶν)
toîs déndresi toîs kopeîsin (aor part pass) (hupò tôn politôn)
". . . with the trees the having-been-cut (by the citizens)"[6]

I should add that in principle there seem to be no factors that would preclude the formation of (15); it may just be that there was no need for this construction, given the availability of the participles. Matters are different with (13), since there is no *active* participial alternative for this construction (*"the they-having-cut trees"). From the above observations we may infer that the following tendency exists: if a noun is modified by a restrictive Modifier involving an embedded predication and if the noun functions as the Goal of the embedded predicate, this Modifier will be expressed either by a relative clause in the active voice (in which the relative pronoun is the overt expression of Goal)[7] or by a participle in the passive voice (in which case the functional relationship of the noun to the embedded predicate is not expressed overtly.[8] (See also 11.3.) The formulation given above implies that attraction is blocked not only with passive relative clauses but also when the relative pronoun functions as the AgSubj (PoSubj) rather than as the Goal of the embedded clause. In fact, the following expression is not well-formed, it would seem:

(17) *. . . τοῖς δένδρεσιν   οἷς   ἐνθαῦτα ἔκειτο
. . . toîs déndresin$_{dat}$ hoîs$_{dat}$ enthaûta ékeito
". . . the trees that were lying there"

Here, too, a participial clause will be preferred (*toîs . . . keiménois*). Attraction is also blocked—this, too, is implied by what is said above—in the following cases:

(*a*) When the embedded verb governs a "non-accusative":

(18) πολὺ ἐκήδετο τῶν   στρατιώτων   οἷς   ἐβοήθησεν
polù ekédeto tôn$_{gen}$ stratiótōn$_{gen}$ hoîs$_{dat}$ eboéthēsen
"he cared much for the soldiers that he had assisted"

The regular dative *hoîs*, triggered by *eboéthēsen*, may not be changed into an attracted *hôn* (gen).[9]

(*b*) When the headnoun is in the nominative:

(19) αὕτη ἐστιν ἡ χώρα   ἥν   ἐκτήσατο ὁ βασιλεύς
haútē estin hē khōra$_{nom}$ hēn$_{acc}$ ektēsato   ho basileús
"This is the country which the king has acquired"

The accusative *hḕn* may not be replaced by the nominative *hḗ*.[10] The explanation for the non-occurrence of attraction in cases like (19) may be that the presence of two nominative constituents, i.e. of two possible candidates for the subject-function, would lead to a serious functional confusion. It is not easy to see how the case of non-attraction in (18) may be accounted for. Apparently the accusative, being in many respects the most neutral oblique case, could be dispensed with in some cases as a formal functional sign, whereas the dative (and the genitive) could not. We might also infer that the dative constituents with verbs like *boēthéō*, while being arguments of that verb, apparently do not have the same functional status as accusative constituents with verbs governing the accusative, that is to say, are not Goal.

(*c*) Finally, attraction is also blocked when the relative pronoun is governed by an adposition, as in:

(20) πρὸς τῇ πόλει ἐφ' ἣν οἱ πολέμιοι ὡρμήθησαν
pròs têi$_{dat}$ pólei$_{dat}$ eph' hḕn$_{acc}$ hoi polémioi hōrmḗthēsan
"near the city to which the enemy had rushed"

It will have been observed that nothing has yet been said about constructions of type (14), i.e. with "displaced" Headnoun. This is deliberate; I do not believe that such constructions are the output of some operations on (12), via an intermediate stage (13). On the contrary, I shall argue below that such expressions are generated directly. *A fortiori*, then, it is impossible to indicate, for example, under which conditions (12) is "converted" into (14).[11]

A further important condition concerning attraction and so far only alluded to is that it only occurs with restrictive clauses. (Some implications of this condition will become apparent below, when comparison is made with noun–adjective/participle constructions.) Thus, in the following expressions the relative pronouns, οὓς (*hoùs*) and ὃν (*hòn*) respectively, may not be attracted:

(21) ποταμὸν . . . πλήρη δ' ἰχθύων μεγάλων καὶ πραέων, οὓς οἱ Σύροι θεοὺς ἐνόμιζον potamòn . . . plḗrē d' ikhthúōn$_{gen}$ megálōn$_{gen}$ kaì praéōn$_{gen}$, hoùs$_{acc}$ hoi Súroi theoùs enómizon "a river . . . full of big tame fishes, which the Syri considered as gods" (Xenoph. *Anab.* 1, 4, 9)

(22) καὶ τρίτον ἔτος τῷ πολέμῳ ἐτελεύτα τῷδε, ὃν Θουκυδίδης

ξυνέγραψεν καὶ τρίτον ἔτος τôι$_{dat}$ πολέμôι$_{dat}$ ἐτελεύτα τôιδε$_{dat}$, hὸν$_{acc}$ Thoukudídēs xunégrapsen "And thus ended the third year of this war, of which Thucydides wrote the history" (Thuc. 2, 103)[12]

As regards example (14), structures of this type (with "displaced" head-noun) also involve restrictive "relative" clauses; moreover, headnoun + "relative" clause always form a definite description (cf. again, below, on noun–adjective/participle constructions. For the term "definite description" see e.g. Lyons (1977, 179)). In the following discussion I will treat sentences of the type exemplified by examples (12)–(14) as semantically equivalent. This, I should add, is not quite established, but so far I have been unable to detect any substantial differences between them (see also 11.5). Of course, if they are semantically alike, there may still be pragmatic and/or stylistic differences. Since this point is connected with possible differences between the various noun–adjective/participle constructions— which, I shall argue below, are an important factor in the analysis of relative clauses—I shall postpone the discussion of these differences until after the discussion of noun–adjective/participle constructions.[13]

11.2   An analysis in FG terms

How, then, are we to handle clauses like those in (12)–(14) within the framework of Functional Grammar? I propose for them the following common underlying representation (the matrix-verb *periestaúrōsan* and its arguments are assumed to be already specified):

(23)   (dmx$_i$: déndron$_N$ (x$_i$): kóptein$_V$ (x$_j$)$_{AgSubj}$ (Rx$_i$)$_{Goal}$)$_{Instr}$

to be read as: the definite plural x$_i$ such that x$_i$ is a *déndron* such that *kóptein* (they ; = x$_j$, not further specified) x$_i$ (relativized), the whole functioning as an instrumental modifier with *periestaúrōsan*.

To arrive at the actual expressions (12)–(14) this representation is then subjected to a number of expression-rules (cf. Dik, 1978: 157ff.). Among these, I suggest, are the following:

(24)   dmx$_i$→Art m dat/(____)$_{Instr}$; Rx$_i$→RelPron m acc/(____)$_{Goal}$

(25)   dmx$_i$→Art m dat/(____)$_{Instr}$; Rx$_i$→ RelPron m dat/(____)$_{Goal}$)$_{Instr}$

(26)   dmx$_i$→RelPron m dat/(____(Rx$_i$)$_{Goal}$)$_{Instr}$; Rx$_i$→∅

Instr in rule (24) triggers the plural article in the dative case for the definiteness-operator (of course, plural and dative are also assigned to *déndron*, which holds for the other sentences, too). The second part triggers the (plural) relative pronoun in the accusative case for the term on which R operates, which is marked as Goal.

Rule (25) has the same effect, but for the assignment of the dative to the relative pronoun. Instrument, one might say, triggers the dative for every non-Agent Subject nominal available and thus predominates over Goal. By this morphological adjustment, the formal gap between headnoun and relative clause as to case-assignment—number and gender of the relative pronoun are already in accordance with the Headnoun—is bridged. The fact that the functional status of the relative pronoun is thereby obscured is apparently not disturbing; in fact as we have seen this status is automatically retrievable: only Goal-terms may undergo attraction (cf. p. 238). Expressed somewhat metaphorically, on encountering an Rx_i marked as Goal the grammar may interpret this label as a signal to apply directly to this term the label which marks the expression as a whole. Note, finally, that the second part of rules (24) and (25) may be combined:

$$Rx_i \rightarrow RelPron \begin{Bmatrix} acc \\ dat \end{Bmatrix} /((\underline{\quad})_{Goal})_{Instr}$$

These two rules would give us the following, still unordered, set, cf. (27) ({ , } symbolizes an unordered set; the verb, number and gender are assumed to be already specified):

(27)   {Art_{dat}, $déndron_{dat}$, Verb, $RelPron_{acc/dat}$}

The actual expression will then be arrived at by the following constituent-order rule (CO rule):

(28)   {Art, Noun, Verb, RelPron}$\rightarrow$Art Noun RelPron Verb

That is, RelPron goes to the P1 position, which is the favourite place of conjunctions, questionwords and relative pronouns (Dik, 1978, 178ff.). Application of the appropriate morphophonological rules gives us, finally, *toîs déndresin hà (hoîs) ékopsan*—as in (12)–(13). Alternatively, one could also assign to (27) the syntactic frame (29):

(29)   {d_{Art}, $Head_{Noun}$, $Modifier_{RelClause}$}

combined with a general expression rule for relative clauses: RelPron (= P1) Verb and a CO rule which takes care of directing the relative clause-Modifier to a position after the Head.[14]

By rule (26) finally, dm is realized as what formally is a plural relative pronoun in the dative when in the context a Goal Rx_i is present, whereupon Rx_i itself gets zero-realization, the result being:

(30)   {RelPron$_{dat}$, déndron$_{dat}$, Verb}

The correct result, *hoîs ékopsan déndresin* cf. (14), will be arrived at by the following CO rule:

(31)   {RelPron, Noun, Verb}→RelPron Verb Noun

Alternatively, we might assign the syntactic frame:

(32)   {d$_{RelPron}$, Head$_{Noun}$, Modifier$_{Verb}$}

to (30), which then will be subjected to a CO rule of the form

(33)   {d, Head, Mod}→d Mod Head

(Cf. also below, 11.3.)[15]

11.3   Parallels with noun–adjective/participle constructions

Although one might object that the above considerations, especially CO rules like (31) or (33), look rather *ad hoc* (note that CO rules of type (28) will be needed elsewhere in the grammar, e.g. for ensuring the correct position of questionwords), as has been already hinted at in the preceding pages, the analyses put forward above may be supported by a comparison with the rules governing the position of restrictive adjectives and participles.[16]

Consider the following NPs (which are supposed to function as Instrument):

(34)   τοῖς καλοῖς δένδρεσιν
        toîs kaloîs déndresin
        "with the beautiful trees"

(35)   τοῖς δένδρεσι τοῖς καλοῖς
        toîs déndresi toîs kaloîs
        "with the trees the beautiful" / "with the beautiful trees"

(36)   τοῖς κοπεῖσι δένδρεσιν
        toîs kopeîsi déndresin
        "with the having-been-cut trees" / "with the trees that had been cut"

(37) τοῖς δένδρεσι τοῖς κοπεῖσιν
      toîs déndresi toîs kopeîsin
      "with the trees the having-been-cut" / "with the trees that had
      been cut"

Again (cf. 11.1.2), I assume that there are no substantial semantic differences between (34) and (35), on the one hand, and (36) and (37), on the
other. As for the first pair, these NPs may be given the following underlying representation:

(38) (dmx$_1$: déndron$_N$ (x$_i$): kalós$_{Adj}$ (x$_i$))$_{Instr}$

As for (36) and (37), the direct introduction of participles in their underlying representation does not recommend itself, otherwise than for e.g.
studying in English (cf. 11.0), since these participles, while being adjectival,
may take all the values of tense/aspect and voice available in Greek. This
means that a predicate, in our case *kóptein*, should appear in the underlying
representation, accompanied by its arguments, in this case Agent and
Goal:

(39) (dmx$_1$: déndron$_N$ (x$_i$): kóptein$_V$ (x$_j$)$_{Ag}$ (x$_i$)$_{Go}$)$_{Instr}$

Of course, but for the presence of R, this representation is identical to the
one underlying relative clauses (cf. also p. 239); possible "surface" differences between the expressions derived from this representation are due, I
suggest, to the assignment or non-assignment of the syntactic function
Subject. In a generalized way this may be formulated as follows: For any
term having a representation of the form

(40) (dx$_1$: Noun(x$_i$): Verb(x$_j$)$_{Ag}$ (x$_i$)$_{Go}$)

  (i) If Subject is assigned to Ag, the second restrictor will be realized
      as a relative clause, in which the verb is in the active voice and the
      Goal-variable turns up as the relative pronoun (which may or may
      not be attracted; cf. (12–13)). Alternatively, we may get an expres-
      sion with Headnoun-"displacement" (cf. example (14));

  (ii) If Subject is assigned to the Goal-variable, this will again yield a
       relative clause; the verb has the passive voice, the Goal-variable is
       realized as a relative pronoun in the nominative (which may not be
       attracted, cf. (15)–(15a)); an Agent-constituent is optional;

(iii) If Subject is not assigned at all, neither to Ag nor to Go, the Verb is realized as a participle in the passive voice and the Goal-variable gets zero-realization. Again, an Agent-constituent may or may not be present, cf. (16).

If we now return to our actual examples (12)–(14), (15a), and (36)–(37), we may schematize their derivation as follows:

(41) $(\text{dmx}_i: \text{déndron}_N\ (x_i): \text{kópteín}_V\ (x_j)_{Ag}\ (x_i)_{Go})_{Instr}$

(41) $\begin{cases} \text{if AgSubj, then} & \begin{bmatrix} V\ Act \\ (Rx_i)_{Go} \end{bmatrix} \text{subjected to rules (24)–(26)} \\ \text{if GoSubj, then} & \begin{bmatrix} V\ Pass \\ (Rx_i)_{Go} \end{bmatrix} \text{subjected to rule (28)} \\ \text{if Subj is not assigned, then} & \begin{bmatrix} V\ Pass\ Part \\ (x_i)_{Go} \to \emptyset \end{bmatrix} \text{see below} \end{cases}$

(The optional Agent-constituents are not represented.)

The further derivation of the passive participle is taken care of by the rules which govern the formation of nominal constituents, i.e. it follows the same path as the derivation of adjectives. How then can we arrive at (34)–(35) and (36)–(37), respectively, from the representations (38) and (39)? First of all, dm will yield the article and a case-assignment rule will provide the correct case-markings, which gives us the following unordered set:

(42) $\{\text{Art}_{dat},\ \text{déndron}_{dat},\ \text{kalós}_{dat}\}$

(43) $\{\text{Art}_{dat},\ \text{déndron}_{dat},\ \text{kopeís}_{dat}\}$

(The rules concerning number and gender are omitted.) To arrive at the correct expressions we need some CO rules. One of these rules might run:

(44) $\{\text{Art, Noun, Adj/Part}\} \to \text{Art Adj/Part Noun}$

alternatively (cf. (29)):

(45) $\{\text{d, Head, Mod}\} \to \text{d Mod Head}$

which will lead to *toîs kaloîs déndresin/toîs kopeîsi déndresin*. The second rule is of the form:

(46) $\{\text{Art, Noun, Adj/Part}\} \to \text{Art Noun Art Adj/Part}$

or

(47)   {d, Head, Mod}→d Head d Mod

by which the definiteness operator is placed before the noun and at the
same time is "duplicated", the duplicate being placed between Noun
(Head) and Adj/Part (Mod).[17]

As already noted in passing (note 13), there exists still another, though
less frequent type, both with adjectives/participles and with relative
clauses. Consider:

(48)   δένδρεσι τοῖς καλοῖς déndresi$_{dat}$ toîs$_{dat}$ kaloîs$_{dat}$

(49)   δένδρεσι τοῖς κοπεῖσιν déndresi$_{dat}$ toîs$_{dat}$ kopeîsin$_{part\ pass\ dat}$

(50)   δένδρεσιν οἷς (ἃ) ἔκοψαν déndresin hoîs$_{dat}$ (hà)$_{acc}$ ékopsan

In these cases, then, a definite article premodifying the headnoun is lacking. Here too, of course, the question arises whether there are any semantic
differences between this type and the types already discussed. In 11.5.1
I shall argue that (48) in some of its uses is equivalent, semantically but
not pragmatically, to the structures Art Adj Noun and Art Noun Art Adj;
in this case, then, it may be derived from the same underlying representation as the latter two (cf. p. 244). (*Mutatis mutandis* the same holds for (49)
and (50)). The simplest way to derive (48) from (38), (49) from (39), and
(50) from (23) is by a rule involving zero-expression of Art and RelPron,
respectively. Specifically, the output of rules (46) and (28) will be subjected
to the following rules:

(51)   Art Noun Art Adj/Part→Noun Art Adj/Part

(52)   Art Noun RelPron Verb→Noun RelPron Verb

This zero-expression occurs only under the pragmatic condition that the
referent of the headnoun is fully identifiable, either by contextual knowledge or by knowledge of the world at large.[18]

11.4   Conclusions of Sections 11.1–3

There are a number of similarities between NPs involving relative clauses
and those involving participles and adjectives, both in their actual form
and their underlying representation and to some extent in the expression-
rules involved. Compare:

(23)   (dmx$_i$: déndron$_N$ (x$_i$): kóptein$_V$ (x$_j$)$_{AgSubj}$ (Rx$_i$)$_{Goal}$)$_{Instr}$ rel clause

(39)   (dmx$_1$: déndron$_N$ (x$_i$): kóptein$_V$ (x$_j$)$_{Ag}$ (x$_i$)$_{Goal}$)$_{Instr}$ part

(38)   (dmx$_i$: déndron$_N$ (x$_i$): kalós$_{Adj}$ (x$_i$))$_{Instr}$ adjective

(13)   τοῖς δένδρεσιν οἷς ἔκοψαν   rel clause
       toîs déndresin hoîs ékopsan

(37)   τοῖς δένδρεσι τοῖς κοπεῖσιν   part
       toîs déndresi toîs kopeîsin

(35)   τοῖς δένδρεσι τοῖς καλοῖς   adjective
       toîs déndresi toîs kaloîs

(14)   οἷς ἔκοψαν δένδρεσιν   "rel clause"
       hoîs ékopsan déndresin

(36)   τοῖς κοπεῖσι δένδρεσιν   part
       toîs kopeîsi déndresin

(34)   τοῖς καλοῖς δένδρεσιν   adjective
       toîs kaloîs déndresin

(31)   {RelPron, Noun, Verb}→RelPron Verb Noun

(44)   {Art, Noun, Adj/Part}→Art Adj/Part Noun

All this suggests that the two types of relative clause that differ from the functionally regular type as exemplified by (12), have to be viewed synchronically, and possibly also historically (cf. note 27), as being due to the influence of the noun–adjective and especially the noun–participle patterns. The semantic similarity between the adjectival/participial restrictors and the relative clause leads to a formal adjustment of the latter type to the former, causing the embedded predicate to become "deverbalized" or "adjectivalized"; one might also say that the relative pronoun is "articulized".[19] The language strives, so to speak, to produce similar realizations for similar underlying representations, the result being a neat parallelism between relative clause and participle/adjective. The type exemplified by sentence (14) is the most conspicuous proof of this tendency; it is of special importance, in this connection, that the embedded verb stands between "relative pronoun" and Headnoun, just as the participle/adjective stands between article and Headnoun: there is no *a priori* reason why this verb could not have been placed *after* the Headnoun.[20]

11.5 Semantic, pragmatic and stylistic (dis)similarities

After these proposals as to how we may account for the formation of Ancient Greek relative clauses within the framework of Functional Grammar, I shall now consider in some detail a fairly controversial question which so far has been only alluded to: are there any differences—semantic, pragmatic or stylistic—between the various noun–relative clause and noun–adjective/participle constructions? I shall first consider the three noun–adjective constructions (11.5.1); Art Adj Noun, Art Noun Art Adj and Noun Art Adj (what is said below also holds for participles; I shall not discuss them separately). I shall then make some observations on the various noun–relative clause patterns (11.5.2).

11.5.1 Noun–adjective constructions

Kühner and Gerth remark (1898–1909, 1613ff.), in connection with ὁ ἀγαθὸς ἀνήρ (ho agathòs anér) and ὁ ἀνὴρ ὁ ἀγαθός (ho anèr ho agathós) ("the good man"), that there are differences in emphasis. In their opinion the emphasis in the first type is on the adjective and in the second on the noun, which—by virtue of the article—is presented as something which is known or has been mentioned before. In the third type, ἀνὴρ ὁ ἀγαθός (anér ho agathós), the emphasis is again on the noun which, however, is not as yet known; it is only by the adjective that the noun is defined. In the latter two types a contrast with other nouns is involved. Gildersleeve (1900–1911, 280ff.), following Aristotle *Rhetor.* 1407b, 26–37, states that *ho agathòs anér* "is the most simple, natural, and straightforward, and is briefer (σύντομος) than the second, ὁ ἀνὴρ ὁ ἀγαθός, which is more deliberate, and somewhat more rhetorical, pompous (ὀγκώδης), passionate." As to the third type, Gildersleeve calls this the "self-corrective or slipshod use."

From these remarks, vague as they are, it is clear that (a) Kühner and Gerth see no substantial semantic differences between the first two types but the possibility of a semantic difference between these types and the third one is not excluded; (b) they view such differences as may exist in terms of emphasis (of focus, as we might say); (c) Gildersleeve considers the differences between the three types as wholly stylistic.

Turning to the actual usage of the three types we can indeed say that the first two types are semantically equivalent. One illustration: in book 3, 30–65 Herodotus refers to "the royal throne" both as τῷ θρόνῳ τῷ βασιληίῳ (tôi thrónōi tôi basilēíōi) and as τὸν βασιλήιον θρόνον (tòn basiléion thrónon). As to the differences in emphasis, this is a complicated matter. In principle, there is some truth in Kühner and Gerth's remarks, cf., on the one hand, examples of opposed adjectives like (53) and (54):

(53) οὐ τοίνυν τῆς ἐπιούσης ἡμέρας οἶμαι αὐτὸ ἥξειν ἀλλὰ τῆς ἑτέρας
ou toínun tês epioúsēs hēméras oîmai autò héxein allà tês hetéras
"Well, I think it will not come in today, but tomorrow"
(Plato, *Crito*, 44a)

(54) τὰ μὲν ἐμὰ πράγματα . . . τὰ δ' ὑμέτερα
tà mèn emà prágmata . . . tà d' humétera . . .
"my interests . . . and yours" (Lysias, 8, 7)

and, on the other, of opposed nouns like (55):

(55) φημὶ οὐ μόνον τῶν σωμάτων τῶν ἡμετέρων πατέρας εἶναι, ἀλλὰ καὶ
τῆς ἐλευθερίας τῆς τε ἡμετέρας καὶ ξυμπάντων τῶν ἐν τῇδε τῇ
ἠπείρῳ phēmi ou mónon tôn sōmátōn tôn hēmetérōn patéras eînai,
allà kaì tês eleutherías tês te hēmetéras kaì xumpántōn tôn en têide
têi ēpeírōi ". . . I say that (they) were the begetters not merely of our
bodies but of our freedom also, and the freedom of all dwellers in this
continent" (Plato, *Menex*. 240e)

(The English translations are taken from the Loeb series.) It is also worth mentioning, in this connection, that ἄλλος (állos "other"), which inherently implies contrast with other items of the same class, is placed almost exclusively between article and noun. However, this point should not be pressed. Opposed adjectives are not bound to appear between article and noun; more importantly, in contexts where no factors like contrast are involved at all, it is very difficult indeed to determine why one rather than the other position has been chosen (on the somewhat special position of the third type see below). Statistically the first type, Art Adj Noun, is generally the most common (cf. the figures as given for a number of authors in Gildersleeve (1900–1911, 280–281). Now, we might be inclined to infer from this that this is the most "natural" position, in Gildersleeve's words. However there lurk some dangers. There are, for instance, considerable variations among authors; e.g. in Andocides the second position prevails, and in Antiphon the ratio between the first and the second position is about 1 : 1. It makes little sense, then, for these authors, to say that the Art Adj Noun type is more "natural" than the type Art Noun Art Adj. Of course, they

still may be at variance with the norm, and this may have struck the hearer/
reader as something uncommon, but then we are no longer dealing with
pragmatics but with stylistics. All this is not to deny that the types *potentially* have different pragmatic possibilities.[21] The third type deserves some
further treatment. As I said above (p. 246), this type partly is semantically
equivalent to the other two. The omission of the article was argued to be
due to the fact that the referent of the noun-phrase, in the given context or
by general knowledge of the world, is fully identifiable. This holds, e.g.
for δέσποιναν τὴν ἐμήν (déspoinan tèn emén "my mistress") in Herodotus
1, 8, 3, γυναῖκα τὴν ἐμήν (gunaîka tèn emén "my wife") (Hdt. 1, 9, 1),
γῆν τὴν Περσίδα (gên tèn Persída "the Persian land") (Hdt. 7, 8, γ, 1), etc.
In these cases, then, the speaker, taking for granted that the hearer will be
able to identify the instended reference of the NP, feels free to dispense
with the definiteness-marker. Note that the omission of the article, while
occurring regularly, especially with possessive adjectives, is optional: the
article may be present, more or less redundantly.[22]

In other cases, however, this type gets a rather different interpretation,
viz. when it functions as, what may be called a "specific description"
Consider the following sentence:

(56) ἐγὼ δὲ σύνειμι μὲν θεοῖς, σύνειμι δὲ ἀνθρώποις τοῖς ἀγαθοῖς
      egò dè súneimi mèn theoîs, súneimi dè anthrōpois toîs agathoîs
      "I company with the gods, and I company with the good men"
                                                    (Xen. *Memorab.* 2, 1, 32)

Here, the speaker does not assume that the hearer is able to identify the
referents of *anthrópois toîs agathoís*; in fact neither the context nor general
knowledge will enable him to identify them. The speaker himself, however,
will have some specific persons in mind. Specificity, then, may be defined
as: reference is made to an entity, where identity is known to the speaker
but not necessarily to the hearer.[23] Whether we are dealing with a specific
description or with a definite description with omitted first article can only
be decided by taking into account context, situation and the semantic
characteristics of the NP as a whole. As to the latter, geographical adjectives
such as Περσίς (Persís "Persian") will not easily be used, in the Greek
world at least, in specific descriptions.

Which underlying representation are we to assign to specific descriptions? The most simple solution is, I think, to introduce a specificness-
operator into this representation, together with an appropriate CO rule as
to the place of the specific article; for (56) this gives us:

(57)   (smx$_i$: ánthrōpos (x$_i$): agathós (x$_i$))

and the CO rule:

(58)   {s, Noun, Adj}→Noun s Adj
the result being, when put into the dative,

anthrṓpois toîs agathoîs.[24] In this analysis, *toîs* has the form of, but is not identical to, the definite article.

In concluding this section we note that:

(a)   the three noun-adjective types are, on the whole, semantically equivalent; the third type, however, also has a semantically different interpretation;

(b)   there are potentially pragmatic differences between the types, e.g. as regards possibilities of contrast;

(c)   very often, however, these differences are non-operative, with the result that

(d)   such differences as may exist generally will belong to the domain of stylistics.

11.5.2   Noun–relative clause constructions

As to the NPs involving relative clauses, we note the following. Within the group Art Noun RelClause, the type with attracted relative pronoun ((*toîs*) *déndresin hoîs ékopsan*)[25] is statistically by far the most common: attraction is the rule, non-attraction the exception. For example, the figures for the works of Xenophon are (cf. Rehdantz' commentary on *Anab.* 1, 3, 17): attraction, 187 times; omission of attraction, 31 times (among them also a number of non-restrictive clauses, so the real numbers will be even lower). This holds for literary as well as non-literary texts, e.g. inscriptions; see Meisterhans (1900, 238): "Die Assimilation (= attraction, A.R.) ist für die klassische und nach-klassische Zeit durchaus die Regel." See also Mayser (1934, II, 3, 101) on the papyri and Blass-Debrunner-Rehkopf (1979, 243). This raises the question of what is the matter with those relative pronouns which, despite apparently satisfying the conditions discussed on pp. 238ff., are nevertheless not attracted. Bohlmann (1882, 8ff.) observes that attraction does not occur when the relative clause is "too long". This is a rather subjective notion, but there appears to be some truth in it. At least, we note that clauses which have their relative pronoun attracted show a strong tendency to consist of just a verb and an AgSubj and a Goal, without there being added temporal, causal etc. satellites. (This holds even more strongly for clauses with "displaced" headnoun.) This phenomenon, too, testifies to the "deverbalized" character of the embedded predicate.

Even so, there are indeed instances of "short" relative clauses not being attracted. The effect of this rather exceptional phenomenon may be that the relative clause, having a looser formal tie with its headnoun, stands more on its own and thus makes its contents more prominent (see also Bohlmann, 1882 27). In this way we might explain e.g.:

(59) ἐπισκήπτουσί τε ὑμῖν   πρὸς τῶν   ὅρκων   οὓς   οἱ
      episkḗptousí te humîn pròs tôn$_{gen}$ hórkōn$_{gen}$ hoùs$_{acc}$ hoi

      πατέρες ὤμοσαν
      patéres ṓmosan
      ". . . and they adjure you, by the oaths which your fathers swore"
                                                        (Thucyd. 2, 73, 3)

The relative pronoun having the non-attracted accusative (*hoùs*) emphasizes the importance of the contents of the relative clause.[26] One might think that by this non-attraction such a clause comes near to a non-restrictive clause (cf. 11.1.2), but in practice this makes little sense.

Turning to clauses with headnoun-"displacement" (*hoîs ékopsan déndresin*), it may first of all be asked in what respect they differ from the type with—attracted or non-attracted—relative clause. Assuming them to be semantically equivalent, comparison with the noun–adjective types would suggest that there are in principle pragmatic differences between the various types (cf. 11.5.1). It is, however, very difficult, even more so than with the noun–adjective constructions, to detect clear, explicit instances of such differences. As with their adjectival counterparts, such differences as may exist will mainly be a matter of stylistics, but the situation is not wholly similar: although with the adjectives the type Art Adj Noun is the most common, this is not the case with "RelPron" Verb Noun: the examples with a real relative clause are far more frequent. Thus, if the adjectival type has served as a model for the "RelPron" Verb Noun type, this has not led to the latter following the former as regards frequency. This, is perhaps, not too surprising; a pseudo-relative clause like *hoîs ékopsan déndresin*, having an "adjectival" finite verb, may have been felt as something special, at least by writers of *Kunstprosa*. Interestingly, in non-literary Greek the "RelPron" Verb Noun type is a far more common phenomenon (Mayser, 1934, II, 3, 98–104).

Appendix: the feasibility of a promotion analysis

According to some transformational linguists, headnoun+relative clause
constructions are the result of the promotion of the noun out of a relative
clause (e.g. Schachter, 1973). Following this approach, one might envisage
a similar analysis for Greek relative clauses. Thus, *hoîs ékopsan déndresin*
might be regarded as basic and *toîs déndresin hoîs* (or: *hà*) *ékopsan* as
derivative, being influenced by the parallel adjectival type *toîs déndresi toîs
kaloîs*. Theoretically, this is a feasible line of reasoning, but it will become
difficult to account for the "non-attracted" type *toîs déndresin hà ékopsan*
because there is no *a priori* reason why such a formally deviant type should
have been created. An adjectival parallel is, of course, lacking. Historically,
a promotion analysis is confronted with the problem that, in Homer, clauses
of the type "RelPron" Verb Noun are exceptional,[27] whereas real relative
clauses (all without attraction) abound.

Acknowledgements

This paper is an expanded and revised version of Rijksbaron (1980). I am
indebted to the co-authors of this volume, especially Simon Dik, and also to
C. J. Ruijgh and Elseline Vester for their criticism and suggestions.

Notes

1   Since Ag implies Action, I omit the latter label. I also omit the square
brackets around the predicate and its arguments, since these are of little
relevance here. The variables will be noted as term-variables, x_i etc. (Dik,
1978, 56).
2   Otherwise than with attributive *studying* above, the direct introduction of
laughing into the underlying representation of (10) does not recommend
itself, for in this case the participle may take other tense/aspect values
(*having laughed*).
3   The examples are based on Thucyd. 2, 75, 1.
4   Cf. Kühner and Gerth (1898–1909, 2406 ff.). "Accusative" includes
"accusative of content" or "cognate object." Of course, when both the main
verb and the embedded verb govern an accusative, the relative pronoun in
principle may have got its form from either verb. Note that English has a
more or less comparable phenomenon in the (optional) zero-realization of
the relative pronoun when it has object function.
5   This observation is based upon Herodotus and the material provided by
Bohlmann (1882). For an example of a passive relative clause see Herodot.
4, 20, 1. With passive participles, just as with other passive forms, an overt

     agent-constituent is often lacking, usually because the agent is known contextually or because he is unknown.

6 In other words, the operator R, in the underlying representation of a relative clause, normally will trigger the active voice for the embedded verb. Cf. also Section 11.3.

7 Or covert, viz. when attraction has applied. Cf. Section 11.2.

8 There is one, pragmatically conditioned, exception to this rule. When such a restrictive modifier falls under the scope of a focusing element (e.g. a demonstrative pronoun), the passive participle is blocked: only finite verb-clauses are allowed. We find, then, e.g. ταύτην τὴν πόλιν ἥ νῦν X καλεῖται (taútēn tèn pólin hè nûn X kaleîtai "that city which nowadays is called X"). Cf. Herodotus 4, 14, 3; 4, 45, 5; 4, 160, 1 etc.

9 Attraction of a genitive or dative is not blocked, however, in autonomous relative clauses, i.e. clauses that have no headnoun, and are themselves nounlike (cf. Ruijgh 1971: 310 ff.). Cf. e.g. παρ' ὧν μὲν βοηθεῖς οὐκ ἀπολήψει χάριν (par' hôn mèn boētheîs ouk apolépsei khárin, liter. "from whom you are helping you will receive no thanks", Aeschin. 2, 117), where we have *hôn* (genitive), triggered by *pará*, instead of *hoîs* (dative), which would be the regular case with *boēthêin* "to help". I strongly doubt, however, whether we really have attraction here; in any case, *par' hôn* cannot be a reduced form of *parà toútōn hôn*, since this is not allowed. In my opinion, *(par') hôn boētheîs* is, rather, formed directly as the genitive-form of *hoîs boētheîs*, just as *par' hôn horaîs* ("from whom you see") would be the genitive of *hoùs horaîs*. As in many other languages (e.g. Dutch and English), autonomous relative clauses would seem to form a category *sui generis*, rather than being shortened variants of constructions with a headnoun. But I cannot pursue this matter further, here. Cf. also Lagas (1942: 23), Gonda (1954–55: 21), Monteil (1963: 150 ff.) and Ruijgh (1971: 335, on *eis hó* ("until"), *ex hoû* ("since")).

10 Insertion of the headnoun in the case-form required by the embedded verb, is not excluded: αὕτη ἐστιν ἣν ἐκτήσατο χώραν (haútē estin hèn ektēsato khóran "this is the country he has acquired").

11 This is not to say that the conditions on such constructions may not be similar. I do not think, for instance, that such clauses easily will have a passive verb; here, too, a passive participle will be preferred. Further investigations are needed to clarify this point.

12 That we are dealing with restrictive clauses has been noticed by, for example, Stahl (1907, 523) and Smyth (1956, 567); Bohlmann (1882, 7) has something similar. Touratier (1980) contains a full discussion of the notion "restrictiveness" (notably pp. 241–361). Despite its having a number of attractive points, he doubts the usefulness of a logically based extensional analysis; instead he advocates an intensional approach (p. 360). Since this matter is not directly relevant to the present subject, I refrain from reviewing more fully Touratier's interesting views. Note that zero-realization of the English relative pronoun (cf. note 4) is also confined to restrictive clauses.

13   Matters are further complicated by the existence of yet another type, viz. δένδρεσιν οἷς ἔκοψαν (déndresin hoîs ékopsan). I shall discuss this type together with comparable noun–adjective/participle constructions in Section 11.3.

14   The status of Heads and Modifiers is not worked out in detail in FG; for some remarks see Dik (1978, 59–60; 63 ff.). Notably, it is not clear at which stage their assignment should occur and what purpose it serves. As a general rule Dik proposes (p. 59): "the first restrictor (viz. of the possible values of the x_1 to the left, A.R.) will become the Head of the term phrase." By this rule *déndron* would, indeed, become Head.

15   Of course, (33) should be "instructed" to apply only to Mods that are labelled as "non-RelClause"; otherwise, (29) would also be affected. If the analysis is correct, we may expect that an article premodifying such a clause will not readily occur. In fact I know of only one example: Plato *Cratyl.* 435a: τῇ ᾗ φῇς σὺ σκληρότητι (têi hêi phêis sù sklērótēti "the harshness you are talking about"). The article may function as a focus-marker, cf. also the presence of the emphatic subject *sù* in the embedded clause. Given the rareness of this construction, there may also be another factor involved: the phrase may itself be an example of "harshness".

16   How we may distinguish these from non-restrictive adjectives and par-ciples is another matter and falls outside the scope of this chapter.

17   This occurs in other languages, too, e.g. Arabic (Benveniste 1966, 213) and Hebrew. According to Seiler (1960, 133) the second article in (35) and (37) merely has a *Gelenkfunktion* which might suggest that it is semantically empty. This, however, is not the case; for whereas it may not be as "real" a definite article as the first one, it distinguishes this type from yet another type, Art Noun Adj/Part, in which Adj/Part is used predicatively, e.g. *toîs déndresi kaloîs*. For the different interpretational possibilities of this type see Kühner and Gerth (1898–1909, 1614).

18   To my knowledge only Mayser (1934, II, 2, 57) has drawn attention to this use of the type Noun Art Adj. Note that the second article cannot be omitted; this would yield an indefinite description.

19   Suggestions to this effect also occur in the traditional grammars, e.g. Kühner and Gerth (1898–1909, 2406); Smyth (1956, 567). See also Benveniste (1966, 217) on some "article-like" cases of *hós* in Homer. Willemen (1969, 23 ff.) explicitly draws attention to the parallelism between article and relative pronoun. In the Ionic dialect of Herodotus this parallelism is even more conspicuous; there, the oblique case-forms, as well as the nomin/acc neuter, singular and plural, of the relative pronoun *hós* are formally indis-tinguishable from those of the definite article *ho*. As C. J. Ruijgh observes, the difference may even be confined to nom sg masc *hòs* : *ho*, because the accentual variation nom plur masc *hoì* (rel) : *hoi* (art), nom sg fem *hè* (rel) : *hē* (art) and nom plur fem *haì* (rel) : *hai* (art) may well be a spell-ing convention. Notice that in the ancient grammatical tradition the term ἄρθρον (whence Lat. *articulus*) comprised both the article and the relative

pronoun. This may reflect a feeling that they had similar functions. (Note that clauses (14) and NPs (34) may be premodified by a demonstrative pronoun, Hdt. 6, 13, 1.) I add, finally, that the "articulized" relative pronoun keeps some features at least of a "real" relative pronoun. It may e.g. be modified by -*per*; articles may not.

20   There are some real and apparent exceptions to this rule. As to the latter, in combinations like οὗ χρόνου (hoû khrónou "which time" (gen)) mentioned by Mayser (1934: II, 3, 98) *hoû* functions as a relative *adjective* rather than as a kind of article. Moreover, this NP functions as a conjunction-like (relative) modifier of Time (cf. Engl. "during which time"), as a set group, that is; this means, of course, that the verb of the clause introduced by *hoû khrónou* does not function as a restrictor of this NP (otherwise than with examples like (14)). For possible classical examples of adjectival *hós* see Hdt. 2, 90, 1; 3, 99, 2; but cf. also note 27. For a real exception see Herodot. 7, 151; here, it is *pròs Xérxēn* which is "adjectivalized", not the embedded verb. This may give prominence to *pròs Xérxēn*. It is also possible that we are dealing with a contamination of two constructions: (a) *hē pròs Xérxēn philíē* "the friendship towards Xerxes"), and (b) *tḕn xunekerásanto philíēn (pròs Xérxēn)* "the friendship they had compounded (with X.)". Cf. also Thucyd. 7, 54, which perhaps may be explained in the same way.

21   Cf. also Brunel (1964, 58 ff.). I mention one further point. When no contrast is involved, the different positions may correspond with differences as to topic: with the word order Art Adj Noun, the adjective may have topic function, with the order Art N Art Adj, the noun. However, this will be difficult to prove; a writer has, after all, a considerable freedom as to which constituent should be selected for topic function. The remarks in the text also apply to the papyri, cf. Mayser (1934, II, 2, 52 ff.). Dover (1960, 5) warns against drawing rash conclusions from statistical data. Bolinger (1952) provides an illuminating discussion of some difficulties encountered in studying word-order phenomena in a modern language.

22   Sometimes the manuscripts hesitate between a reading with, and a reading without the first article: Herodot. 1, 116, 2; 4, 115, 2; Thucyd. 2, 71, 4.

23   Hawkins (1978, 204 ff.) discusses specificity in a similar way. Cf. also Lyons (1977, 188 ff.). He uses the term "specific though unidentified". This is not correct, I think; the *speaker* may have a fully identified referent in mind. I am aware that much more may be said—and in fact has been said—about definite, specific and indefinite descriptions, notably concerning the referential or non-referential potential of these descriptions. In my opinion, the discussion often suffers from over-concentration on problems of referentiality; these problems would seem to be connected not so much with the nature of the NP involved as with the characteristics of the clause or sentence as a whole.

24   It is also possible that constructions of the type Noun Art Adj always involve specific descriptions and that they are used as equivalent to definite descriptions under the appropriate contextual conditions (cf. pp. 246, 250).

25   The dual semantic possibilities of the type Noun Art Adj (cf. p. 250) also

exist for the type Noun RelPron Verb. For a definite description with omitted first article see Herodot. 4, 78, 3; 7, 164, 2; for a specific description, Herodot. 1, 45, 3. Contrary to what I stated in Rijksbaron (1980), an attracted relative clause may also occur in an indefinite description, Thucyd. 4, 36, 1. The relative pronoun is *not* a definite (or specific) article after all.

26   In this connection it is somewhat embarrassing that Thucyd. 2, 75, 1, on which examples (12)–(14) were based, has *há* and not *hoîs*, which seems fully acceptable. I think it would be rather far-fetched to say that this serves to highlight the importance of the relative clause. There may just be a group where no palpable differences exist between attraction and non-attraction. For the elusiveness of such distinctions cf. also the remarks of Quirk *et al.* (1972, 870) on the stylistic factors connected with the various relative pronouns of English.

27   There is, in fact, only one example (*Il.* 4, 44). According to Chantraine (1948–53, 2165) the type Art Adj Noun is a "novel" construction in Homer, so perhaps there was no fixed model for the type "RelPron" Verb Noun. The cases mentioned by Chantraine (p. 2, 238) are not real examples of "noun-displacement", since these have relative adjectives (*hóssos* etc.); their structure, too, differs from that of examples like (14), the word-order being RelAdj Noun Verb (rather than RelAdj Verb Noun). More problematic are some instances of this deviant word-order with *hós*, e.g. *Il.* 4, 306: *hòs dé k' anēr* (noun) *hikētai* (verb) . . . "the man who reaches . . ." (lit. "who man reaches . . ."). Possibly, *hós* functions as a variant of the relative adjective *hoîos* (cf. also K-G 2, 400). Finally, there may be another factor involved. There would seem to be a tendency for clauses which exhibit the order "RelPron" Noun Verb to precede the main clause rather than to follow it, as with clauses having the order "RelPron" Verb Noun (cf. (14)). Furthermore, the Headnoun of the "relative clause" may have different functions in the main clause (Agent, as in *Il.* 4, 306; Locative, as (probably) in *Il.* 19, 167; Goal, as in Hdt. 3, 99, 2). As such, then, the "relative clause ' is functionally indeterminate; this points to the "relative clause", and especially its Headnoun, having Theme-position. This may well be responsible for the fronting of the Headnoun. For a number of characteristics of Themes cf. Dik (1978, 142 ff.).

References

BENVENISTE, E.
  1966   La phrase relative. *In* "Problèmes de Linguistique Générale". Paris, Gallimard, 208–222.
BLASS, F., A. Debrunner and F. Rehkopf
  1979[15]   "Grammatik des neutestamentlichen Griechisch". Göttingen.
BOHLMANN, C.
  1882   *De attractionis usu et progressu, qualis fuerit in enuntiationibus relativis apud Herodotum, Antiphontem, Thucydidem, Andocidem, Lysiam.* Bratislava (thesis).

BOLINGER, D. L.
1952   Linear modification. *PMLA* **67**, 1117–1145.
BRUNEL, J.
1964   "La construction de l'adjectif dans les groupes nominaux du grec". Paris.
CHANTRAINE, P.
1948–53   "Grammaire homérique". Paris (Vol. 2: Syntaxe).
DIK, S. C.
1978   "Functional Grammar". Amsterdam, North-Holland.
1979   "Seventeen Sentences: basic principles and application of Functional Grammar". Publication of the Institute for General Linguistics, University of Amsterdam, 22 (*Also in* Edith A. Moravcsik and Jessica Wirth (ed.). "Current Approaches to Syntax". New York (Syntax and Semantics 13)).
DOVER, K. J.
1960   "Greek word order". Cambridge, Cambridge University Press.
GILDERSLEEVE, B. L.
1900–11   "Syntax of classical Greek". New York, Groningen Bouma (repr. 1980).
GONDA, J.
1954–55   "The original character of the Indo-European relative pronoun io-". *Lingua* **4**, 1–41.
HAWKINS, J. A.
1978   "Definiteness and indefiniteness". London, Croom Helm.
KÜHNER, R. and B. Gerth
1898–1909   "Ausführliche Grammatik der griechischen Sprache", 2. Teil: *Satzlehre*. 2 Bände. Hanover, Hansche (repr. 1976).
LAGAS, R. J. A.
1942   "Syntactische perseveratie- en anticipatieverschijnselen". Amsterdam.
LYONS, J.
1977   "Semantics". 2 vols. Cambridge, Cambridge University Press.
MAYSER, E.
1934   "Grammatik der griechischen Papyri aus der Ptolemäerzeit". 2. Teil: *Satzlehre*. 3 Bände. Berlin, Walter de Gruyter.
MEISTERHANS, K.
1900   "Grammatik der attischen Inschriften". Berlin, Weidmannsche (3rd edition, revised by E. Schwyzer).
MONTEIL, P.
1963   "La phrase relative en grec ancien". Paris, Klincksieck.
QUIRK, R., S. Greenbaum, G. Leech and J. Svartvik
1972   "A grammar of contemporary English". London, Longmans.
RIJKSBARON, A.
1980   Ancient Greek relative clauses and Functional Grammar. *In* S. Daalder and M. Gerritsen (ed.). "Linguistics in the Netherlands 1980". Amsterdam, North-Holland, 121–126.

RUIJGH, C. J.
  1971   "Autour de 'τε épique'. Etudes sur la syntaxe grecque". Amsterdam,
       Hakkert.
SCHACHTER, P.
  1973   Focus and relativization. *Language* **49**, 19–47.
SEILER, H. J.
  1960   "Relativsatz, Attribut und Apposition". Wiesbaden, Horrassowitz.
SMYTH, H. W.
  1956   "Greek grammar". Cambridge (Mass.) (revised by G. M. Messing).
STAHL, J. M.
  1907   "Kritisch-historische Syntax des griechischen Verbums der klassischen
       Zeit". Heidelberg.
TOURATIER, Chr.
  1980   "La relative. Essai de théorie syntaxique". Paris.
WILLEMEN, C.
  1969   "Het Attische ὅς-syntagma en de daarmee in verband staande Japanse
       constructies". Ghent (unpubl.).

Author Index

Allwood, J. S., 122, 231

Bally, Ch., 145
Bennett, C. E., 109f
Benveniste, E., 255
Blass, F., 251
Bohlmann, C., 251f
Bolinger, D. L., 256
Bolkestein, A. M., 70, 76, 79, 90f, 101, 105, 109, 110, 206, 212, 214, 230, 231
Brito, A. M., 165f
Browne, W. E., 126
Brunel, J., 256

Chafe, W. L., 222
Chantraine, P., 257
Chomsky, N., 38, 191f, 201
Collier, R., 140
Corbeau, L., 151

Debrunner, A., 251
Dik, S. C., 41f, 53f, 64, 66f, 70, 76, 80, 84, 86, 91, 104, 106, 109, 128, 133, 145, 147, 149f, 159f, 162, 186f, 192, 202, 210f, 217f, 222, 225f, 230, 235, 253, 255, 257
Dover, K. J., 256
Duarte, I. S., 165f

Ebeling, C. L., 126
Eskénazi, A., 145f, 151

Gerth, B., 248f, 253, 255, 257
Gildersleeve, B. L., 248f
Gonda, J., 254
Grevisse, M., 144, 151
Groot, C. de, 60f
Gvozdanović, J., 139, 145

Halliday, M. A. K., 126
't Hart, J., 140
Hawkins, J. A., 256
Horváth, J., 45

Ivić, M., 132f
Ivić, P., 126, 140

Kakouriotis, A., 35f
Kempson, R. M., 215, 222, 224, 227, 231
Kiefer, F., 215, 221, 222, 230, 231
Kiparsky, C. & P., 110, 212, 215, 222, 224, 225, 230
Kirk, W. H., 110
Kiss, K. É., 45, 62
Kruyt, T., 127
Kühner, R., 65f, 72f, 81, 86, 91, 103, 108f, 223, 230f, 248f, 253, 255, 257
Kwee, T. L., 39, 207

Lagas, R. J. A., 254
Lasnik, H., 201
Laughton, E., 220f
Lehiste, I., 126, 140
Lyons, J., 126, 230, 241, 256

Martin, R., 145f, 151
Mayser, E., 251f, 255f
Meisterhans, K., 251
Milner, J., 201
Moliner, M., 196
Monteil, P., 254

Nooteboom, S., 127f

Perlmutter, D. H., 165f
Pieltain, P., 144f, 161

Quicoli, A. C., 178, 184
Quirk, R. *et al.*, 236, 257

Rehkopf, F., 251
Rivero, M. L., 191
Ross, J. R., 158
Ruwet, N., 146f, 155, 158, 161, 163
Ruijgh, C. J., 254f
Rijksbaron, A., 253

Sandfeld, Chr., 137
Schachter, P., 23, 253
Scherer, A., 110
Séchehaye, A., 145, 161
Seiler, H. J., 255
Smyth, H. W., 254f
Spitzer, L., 145

Stahl, J. M., 254
Stegmann, C., 65f, 72f, 81, 86, 91, 103, 108f, 223, 230f
Szantyr, A., 65f, 76, 86, 91, 103, 108f

Terken, J., 127
Thesaurus Linguae Latinae, 65, 69
Tomić, M. O., 126
Touratier, Chr., 236, 254

Vendler, Z., 230f

Willemen, C., 255

Zolnai, Gy., 41

Subject Index

Absolute form, 115
Ab urbe condita construction, 31, 206f
Accent, 125, 129, 131f, 138f
Accusativus cum infinitivo, 29f, 79f, 90, 105
Agreement, 14, 28, 52f, 60, 144f, 180, 211f
Anaphora, *see* Pronoun
Ancient Greek, 235f
Argument, 6
Attraction, 108, 195, 237f

Case, 28, *see also* Semantic function
  assignment, 28
  marking, 43f, 57f, 87, 89, 212
Cause, 215, 217f
Comment, *see* Focus
Constituent order, 11f, 16, 80f, 87, 89, 94, 102f, 118f, 148f, 165f, 219f, 241f, 245f
  free, 44, 83, 109
Content, 217

Deep structure, 2
Definiteness, 52f, 166, 222f, 228
Dislocation, *see* Displacement
Displacement, 23f, 47f, 72f, 133, 137, 145, 161, 175f, 191
  plus morphological adjustment, *see* Pseudo-argument
Dominant participle, *see* Ab urbe condita construction
Dutch, 113f

English, 9f, 20f, 31, 37, 235f
Equi NP, 84
Experiencer, 38, 215, 217, 230
Expression rule, 11f, 35, 57f, 91, 211, 230, 241f, 245f
  order of, 60, 180, 212f
Extraction, 67, *see also* Theme

Extraposition, *see* Displacement

Factivity, 110, 215f
Filtering devices, 4
Focus, 10, 44f, 128f, 146, 154, 218f, 223f, 229
  contrastive, 88, 96f, 99, 110, 129, 231
  on embedded predication, 46f, 96f, 110, 218f
  position of, 45f
  within embedded predication, 46f, 96f, 218f
Frame of reference, *see* Informational status
French, 143f
Function, *see* Semantic function, Syntactic function, Pragmatic function
Functional pattern, 14, 44, 118, 171
Functional sentence perspective, *see* Pragmatic function assignment

Goal, 13, 55, 217

Hungarian, 41f

Impersonal constructions, 143f, 186f
Informational status, 126f, 131f, 135, 138
Intertwining, 41f, 74f, 108, 199f, 231, *see also* Prolepsis
Intonation, 125f, 129, 134, 139

Latin, 29f, 63f, 205f
Lexical items, 4
LIPOC (Language-independent preferred order of constituents), 15f, 47, 79, 104f, 147f, 152, 154, 156, 159, 186

Modal verbs, 92, 100f
Modern Greek, 35f
Modifier, 22, *see also* Noun phrase
Morphological adjustment, 27f, 52f, 247

Nominalization, 213
Nominativus cum infinitivo, 90f, 219, 231
Non-finite expression, 28f, 64, 84, 90f, 212
Noun–adjective/participle construction, *see* Noun phrase, complex
Noun phrase, complex, 207f, 223f, 231, 243f, 246, 248f, 255

Object, 132f, 145, 161
  assignment, 8f, 43, 54, 84, 109, 149, 230
  definite, 52f
  indefinite, 52f
  position, 14, 62, 84

P1 position, 15, 24f, 45, 65f, 94, 118, 165f
Passive, 42, 152f, 155f, *see also* Subject assignment
Personal passive, *see* Nominativus cum infinitivo
Phenomenon, 208, 215f, 230
Placement rule, 11f, 14, 45, 171, 200
Portuguese, 165f
Pragmatic function, 3f, 12, 125, 128f, 134f
  assignment, 10f, 44f, 96f, 104, 107, 126, 218f, 229
Predicate, 4
  adjectival, 6
  nominal, 6
  verbal, 6
Predicate formation (rule), 32, 157, 159f, 209f, 225
Predicate-frame, 6, 28, 31f, 37f, 55f, 76, 83, 154f, 176f, 186f, 193f
Predicate operator, 4, 225
Predication, 4
  complex, 19f, 41f, 63f, 113f, 125f, 205f

Prolepsis, 74f, 91, *see also* Intertwining
Pronominalization, 145, 158, 160
Pronoun,
  anaphorical, 46f, 66f, 72, 81f, 94f, 102, 106, 111, 198, 219
  impersonal, 144f, 150, 153
  relative, 237f, 251f
Pseudo-argument (formation), 28, 51f, 63f, 74f, 147, 154f, 189, 219, 221

Quantifier floating, 167f
Question word, 23f

Raising, 29, 63, 175f, *see also* Pseudo-argument
Recipient, 13
Relative clause, 22, 235f
  autonomous, 254
  promotion analysis, 253
Relative pronoun, 237f
  attraction of, 237f, 251f

Satellites, 6, 49, 57, 137, 230
Selection restriction, 38, 57f, 78, 147, 155f, 160, 207
Semantic constraints, *see* Selection restriction
Semantic function, 3, 6, 12
Semantic function hierarchy (SFH), 9, 43
Séquence, 144f
Spanish, 185f
Specificness, 250f
State of affairs, 32f, 43
Structure-changing operations, 4
Subject, 125, 133, 144f, 165f
  assignment, 42, 144f, 181f, 244f
  definite, 166f
  indefinite, 166f
  position, 14, 165f
Surface structure, 2
Syntactic category, 213
Syntactic function, 3, 12
  assignment, 8f, 34f, 42f, 53f, 76, 83f, 110, 210f, 230
  exceptional assignment, *see* Raising

Tail, 128f, 131, 138
Tensed-S constraint, 38
Term, 4
  anaphorical, 21
  complex, 22f
Term operator, 7, 223, 225, 227f, 235
Theme, 48f, 128f, 134f, 192
  embedded, 70f, 85, 95, 118f
Theme,Predication organization, 24f,
  65f, 73, 82f, 113f, 170, 220
Topic, 10, 44f, 86, 89, 96f, 128, 149f,
  165f

  on embedded predication, 46f, 96f,
    110, 150f, 218f
  position of, 45f, 150f, 187
  within embedded predication, 46f,
    96, 178f, 218f

Verb, semantic classes, 75, 90, 214f,
  223, 231, *see also* predicate

Word order, *see* Constituent order

Selective Index of Predicates

Admonish, Lat. *(adhortari)*, 81, 84
Appear, Fr. *(paraître)*, 154
Be, Hung. *(van)*, 49, 51
  difficult, Fr. *((être) difficile)*, 155f
  easy, Sp. *(facil)*, 193f
  possible, Sp. *(poder)*, 186f
  preferable, Sp. *(preferible)*, 193f
  regrettable, Fr. *((être) regrettable)*, 148f, 153f, 202
Believe, Eng., 2, 20f, 64, 76, 91
  Hung. *(hisz)*, 48f
  Serbo-Cr. *(vjerovati)*, 136
Cause, Lat. *(facere)*, 75, 80, 87
Complain, Hung. *(panaszkodik)*, 58
Expect, Eng., 29, 37f
Know, Lat. *(scire)*, 73, 75, 77f, 81f, 83, 217, 230
Like, Hung. *(szeret)*, 53
May be, Fr. *(pouvoir)*, 157f
Must, Fr. *(devoir)*, 157f
  Fr. *(falloir)*, 154
  Lat. *(debere)*, 92
Please, Hung. *(örül)*, 58
Remind, Lat. *(admonēre)*, 218
Say, Hung. *(mond)*, 50f
  Lat. *(dicere)*, 71, 81, 90f
See, Eng., 26, 31f
  Lat. *(vidēre)*, 73, 78, 83, 223, 231
  Serbo-Cr. *(vidjeti)*, 137
Seem, Fr. *(sembler)*, 146f, 153f, 202
  Port. *(parecer)*, 176f
  Sp. *(parecer)*, 186f
Think, Serbo-Cr. *(misliti)*, 133f
Threaten, Fr. *(menacer)*, 157
Turn out, Sp. *(resultar)*, 186
Understand, Lat. *(intellegere)*, 217
Want, Hung. *(akar)*, 52f
  Serbo-Cr. *(htjeti)*, 36f
  M. Greek *(θέlο)*, 36f
  Lat. *(velle)*, 75, 78f, 87, 90